☆ DO ELECTIONS MATTER?

☆ DO ☆
ELECTIONS
MATTER?

Benjamin Ginsberg and Alan Stone, Editors

Third Edition

M.E. Sharpe
Armonk, New York
London, England

Library of Congress Cataloging-in-Publication Data

Ginsberg, Benjamin.
Do elections matter? / edited by Benjamin Ginsberg and Alan Stone.—3rd ed.
p.   cm.
Includes bibliographical references and index.
ISBN 1-56324-445-4 (alk. paper).—ISBN 1-56324-446-2 (pbk. : alk. paper)
1. Elections.
2. Voting.
3. Political parties.
4. Public policy (Law)
I. Ginsberg, Benjamin.
II. Stone, Alan, 1941–   .
III. Title.
JF1001.D6   1996
324.973—dc20
95-26785
Do
CIP

Printed in the United States of America

The paper used in this publication meets the minimum requirements of
American National Standard for Information Sciences—
Permanence of Paper for Printed Library Materials,
ANSI Z 39.48-1984.

BM (c)   10   9   8   7   6   5   4   3   2   1
BM (p)   10   9   8   7   6   5   4   3   2   1

For the late Anna and Herman Ginsberg,
and for Roberta Stone

Contents

About the Editors and Contributors

Timothy A. Byrnes is associate professor of political science at Colgate University.

Chris Cookson is a doctoral candidate at the University of Houston.

Gregory Flemming is a doctoral candidate at the University of Wisconsin-Madison.

John Frendreis is professor of political science at Loyola University of Chicago.

Thomas Ferguson is Professor of Political Science at the University of Massachusetts, Boston.

Benjamin Ginsberg is the David Bernstein Professor of Political Science at the Johns Hopkins University.

Alan R. Gitelson is professor of political science at Loyola University of Chicago.

John C. Green is professor of political science and director of the Ray Bliss Institute at the University of Akron.

James L. Guth is professor of political science at Furman University.

Richard Joslyn is professor of political science at Temple University.

Lyman A. Kellstedt is professor of political science at Wheaton College.

Kathleen Knight is associate professor of Political Science at the University of Houston.

Anne Layzell is a doctoral candidate at Loyola University of Chicago.

Ross Lence is associate professor of political science at the University of Houston.

Carolyn V. Lewis is assistant professor of political science at Western Michigan University.

Bruce I. Oppenheimer is professor of political science at Vanderbilt University.

Corwin E. Smidt is professor of political science at Calvin College.

Alan Stone is professor of political science at the University of Houston.

Daniel Wirls is associate professor of politics at the University of California, Santa Cruz.

Kenneth Woodside is associate professor of political science at the University of Guelph in Ontario.

Tables and Figures

Tables

Figures

Preface to
the Third Edition

The agenda for contemporary electoral research in the United States was set by the great voting studies of the 1950s, in particular the Campbell, Converse, Miller, and Stokes study *The American Voter* and Berelson, Lazersfeld, and McPhee's *Voting*. These two volumes, and the literally thousands of articles and books that followed in their wake, were mainly concerned with how voters made their decisions. The authors of *The American Voter* sought to account for variation in whether a given individual voter is going to vote and which candidate he will choose. Similarly, the authors of *Voting* aimed to determine how people come to vote as they do. Both groups acknowledged that their primary focus on *how* voters decided rested on the assumption that *what* voters decided was important. In the three decades since the publication of these seminal works, election analysts have continued to show considerably more interest in the behavior of voters than in the effects, implications, and significance of elections. At the same time, scholars concerned with political institutions and public policies have focused primarily on questions of process or the evaluation of particular policies or institutions. Few studies have bridged the gap, yet the problem is important and challenging.

What are the linkages between voting, parties, and elections, on the one hand, and policy outputs, whether in the form of legislation, administrative action, or judicial decisions, on the other? It is when one joins these topics that one is essentially asking: Do elections matter? Clearly, one cannot answer the question with a simple yes or no, but posing it in this way allows us to consider many topics of great concern—the growth of the administrative state, the increasing activism of the judiciary, and the seemingly unmanageable problem of the federal budget (which contains many items, such as pensions, about which elected officials can do little).

The essays in this third edition address these issues. Most were commissioned specifically for this edition and did not appear in the first (1986) or second (1991) editions of the book. In the first section, the authors examine the implications of the 1994 congressional elections. For the first time in more than fifty years, Republicans won control of both houses of Congress and from this new political base moved to bring about major changes in American policy and institutions. Understanding how and why this election came to matter is important both for social scientists and citizens.

The second section of the volume is a more general analysis of the ways in which elections can affect policy in the United States. The 1994 election also plays a prominent role in this section, but the authors mainly focus on more general questions about the conditions under which elections are and are not likely to be important in the American political process.

The third section of the volume focuses on the growing role of ideology in American elections. Only a few years ago, it was conventional to characterize American electoral politics as a choice between tweedledum and tweedledee. Today, there appear to be sharp differences between the two parties and among political candidates in many races. This growing ideological divergence, in turn, has profound implications for how much elections "matter."

What unites all of the essays in this third edition is the same view that informed the first two editions. The underlying question "do elections matter?" continues to be a vitally important one. It is our hope that this third edition will make as valuable and instructive a contribution to readers' thinking about politics as the first two did.

☆ DO ☆
ELECTIONS
MATTER?

1

HOW DID THE 1994 ELECTION MATTER?

The 1994 election results took most observers of the United States by surprise. For political scientists, regardless of their particular ideologies or policy preferences, the election was a blessing because it ignited intense debate on a variety of issues. The essays in this book examine many of the issues, but they do not definitively answer the questions. Rather, we hope that the issues are refined and sharpened beyond the extent to which the citizen and student is exposed in his or her newspaper or by his or her pontificating broadcaster. Political science, in this respect, mirrors politics but is superior to it because the discussions are, at their best, carried out at a higher level. We have made every effort to assure that the discussions in this book are at a decent level.

A specific election result, on the one hand, may have little to tell us about past or future elections or the probable public policies they portend. That is, an election may be a unique event. On the other hand, a particular election may portend the beginning or continuation of a trend in elections or policies. The 1994 election was clearly associated with a collection of policies that Speaker of the House of Representatives Newt Gingrich developed and most Republican Party candidates accepted. It is hard to recall when the candidates of a major party have been as united about a package of policies as they were about the "Contract with America" that Gingrich designed. It is also clear that most Republican candidates at the national level in 1994 publicized their endorsement of the "Contract with America" and that the

Democrats, especially President Bill Clinton, ridiculed and attacked the document. It was not uncommon for Democratic pundits to view the "Contract with America" as a Republican strategic blunder.

And then it happened. The Republican victory was extraordinary, even for a mid-presidential term election in which dissatisfactions are usually focused on the president's party. The Republican victory occurred not just at the national level but at the state and local ones as well. The Democrats lost a greater percentage of their open House seats than any party has done in a congressional election since 1790. Defection upon defection has occurred in Democratic ranks, and so on. But does this extraordinary election signal a long-term shift, or is it indicative of temporary disaffection? The question will remain definitively unanswered, regardless of the 1996 results. Yes, there is widespread voter dissatisfaction. On the one hand, certainly the collapse and public distrust of the centerpiece of Clinton's program—health care reform—as well as unease concerning the president's character and abilities did not help the Democratic cause. But, on the other hand, there is little evidence that the public accepted, or even understood, the details of the "Contract with America."

We are left, then, with more questions than answers. The essays in this book reflect the divisions of opinion within the scholarly community. The issues are approached in a variety of ways, including comparatively, historically, and analytically. At the end of the book, the reader may be left with many questions, but we trust that these will be at a higher level than before undertaking this journey.

1.1

The 1994 National Elections
A Debacle for the Democrats

Benjamin Ginsberg

After two years of legislative struggle, the Clinton administration suffered a stunning defeat in the November 1994 national election. For the first time since 1946, Republicans won simultaneous control of both houses of Congress. This put the GOP in a position to block President Clinton's legislative efforts and to promote its own policy agenda.

In Senate races, the Republicans realized a net gain of eight seats to achieve a 52–48 majority. Immediately after the election, Senator Richard Shelby of Alabama, a conservative Democrat who frequently voted with the Republicans, announced that he was formally joining the GOP. This gave the Republicans fifty-three votes in the upper chamber. In House races, the Republicans gained an astonishing fifty-two seats to win a 230 to 204 majority (one seat is held by an independent). Subsequent party switches gave the Republicans a 55–45 edge in the Senate and a 232–202 House majority by mid-1995. While the Republicans had controlled the Senate as recently as 1986, the House of Representatives had been a Democratic bastion since 1954.

Republicans also posted a net gain of eleven governorships and won control of fifteen additional chambers in state legislatures. A number of the Democratic Party's leading figures were defeated. These included Governor Mario Cuomo of New York, former House Ways and Means Committee chair Dan Rostenkowski of Illinois, House Judiciary Committee chair Jack Brooks of Texas, three-term Senator Jim Sasser of Tennessee and, most shocking of all, House Speaker Thomas Foley of Washington. Foley was the first sitting Speaker to be defeated for reelection to his own congressional seat since 1860. All told, thirty-four incumbent Democratic representatives, three incumbent Democratic senators, and four incumbent Democratic governors were defeated. On the Republican side, not one of the ten incumbent senators, fifteen incumbent governors, or 155 incumbent House members seeking reelection was defeated. The South, which had voted Republican in presidential elections for twenty years, now seemed to have turned to the GOP at the congressional level as well. Republicans posted gains among nearly all groups in the populace, with white, male voters, in particular, switching to the GOP. The nation's electoral map had been substantially altered (Figure 1). Interest in the hard-fought race had even produced a slight increase in voter turnout, albeit to a still abysmal 39 percent.

In the wake of their electoral triumph, Republicans moved to name Robert Dole of Kansas to the post of Senate majority leader and Representative Newt Gingrich of Georgia to the House speakership. Only two years earlier, Gingrich had been widely viewed as a Republican "firebrand" whose vitriolic attacks on the House leadership were usually dismissed by the media as dangerous and irresponsible. Other Republicans who would move to leadership positions included archconservative Strom Thurmond of South Carolina, who replaced Sam Nunn of Georgia as chairperson of the Senate Armed Services Committee, and outspoken Clinton critic Alphonse D'Amato of New York, who would now head the Senate Banking Committee. At the same time, Representative Floyd Spence, a conservative South Carolinian, replaced Ron Dellums of California, an avowed pacifist, as chairperson of the House Armed Services Committee.

The 1994 election seemed to represent a nationwide repudiation of the Democratic Party. Why did this occur? Why, after two years, had the Clinton administration's bright beginnings and promises of "change" ended with an electoral disaster? What would the election mean for the Democratic and Republican Parties and for the nation?

Origins of Republican Success

The roots of the 1994 Democratic debacle can be traced back to the events of the late 1960s that helped to reshape both major U.S. political parties. From the 1930s through the mid-1960s, the Democratic Party was the nation's dominant political force. The Democrats were led by a coalition of southern white politicians and northern urban machine bosses and labor leaders. The party drew its votes primarily from large cities, from the South, and from minorities, unionized workers, Jews, and Catholics.

Though occasionally winning presidential elections and, less often, control of Congress, the Republicans had been the nation's minority party since Franklin Roosevelt's victory and the beginnings of the New Deal in

Figure 1. **1994 Races for the Senate**

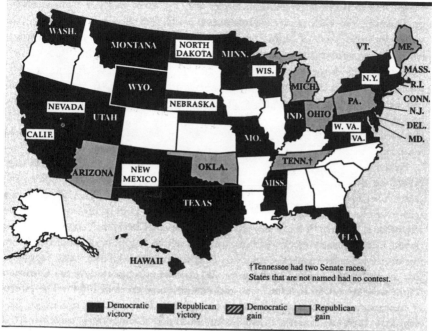

†Tennessee had two Senate races.
States that are not named had no contest.

| Democratic victory | Republican victory | Democratic gain | Republican gain |

1933. The Republicans were led by northeastern and midwestern Protestants whose roots were in the business community. The GOP drew its support primarily from middle- and upper-middle class suburban voters in the northeast, from rural areas, and from the small towns and cities of the midwest.

Civil Rights, the Vietnam War, and National Party Politics

In the 1960s, two powerful tidal waves brought about the reconstruction of both national party coalitions. These were the anti–Vietnam War movement and the Civil Rights movement. The anti–Vietnam War movement galvanized liberal activists in the Democratic Party. These activists attacked and, during the late 1960s, destroyed much of the power of the machine bosses and labor leaders who had been so prominent in Democratic Party affairs. Liberal activists proceeded to organize a congeries of "public interest" groups to fight on behalf of such liberal goals as consumer and environmental regulation; an end to the arms race; expanded rights and opportunities for women, gays, and the physically handicapped; and gun control. These groups struggled for the election of liberal congressional and presidential candidates, as well as for legislation designed to achieve their aims. During the 1970s, liberal forces in Congress were successful in enacting significant pieces of legislation in many of these areas.

For its part, the Civil Rights movement attacked and sharply curtailed the power of the southern white politicians who had been the third leg of the Democratic Party's leadership troika. In addition, the Civil Rights movement brought about the enfranchisement of millions of African American voters in the South, nearly all of whom could be counted upon to support the Democrats. These developments dramatically changed the character of the Democratic Party.

The New Democratic Party

The new prominence and energy of liberal activists in the Democratic Party after the late 1960s added greatly to the Democratic advantage in local and congressional elections. Democrats already possessed an edge in this arena because of incumbency effects. Democrats had usually controlled Congress and a majority of state and local offices since the New Deal. Incumbents have many electoral advantages and, more often than not, are able to secure reelection. Particularly important, of course, is the ability of incumbents to bring home "pork" in the form of federal projects and spending in their districts. In general, the more senior the incumbents, the more pork they can provide for their constituents. Thus, incumbency worked to perpetuate Democratic power by giving voters a reason to cast their ballots for the Democratic candidate regardless of issues and ideology.

Democrats, however, were far more successful than Republicans in congressional and local races even in contests to fill open seats where they did not possess the advantage of incumbency. Until recent years, at least, these races tended to be fought on the basis of local rather than national issues. Victory in these elections, moreover, depended upon the capacity of candidates to organize armies of volunteers to hand out leaflets, call likely voters, post handbills, and engage in the day-to-day efforts needed to mobilize constituent support.

Their armies of liberal activists gave Democratic candidates the equivalent of an infantry force on the ground that the Republicans could seldom match. Therefore, even when incumbent Democrats died or retired, they were usually replaced by other Democrats. In this way, Democratic control of Congress was perpetuated. Moreover, because the Democratic activists who were so important in congressional races were liberals who tended to favor like-minded Democratic candidates, the prominence of somewhat left-of-center forces within the Democratic congressional delegation increased markedly after the 1960s.

Republican Advantage

The same liberal activism, however, that helped propel the Democrats to victory in congressional elections often proved to be a hindrance in the presidential electoral arena. Particularly after the 1968 Democratic presidential election and the party's adoption of new nominating rules based upon the recommendations of the McGovern-Fraser Commission, liberal activists came to play a decisive role in the selection of Democratic presidential candidates. Though Democratic liberals were not always able to name the candidate of their choosing, they were in a position to block the nomination of candidates they opposed.

The result was that the Democratic nominating process often produced candidates who were seen as too liberal by much of the general electorate. This perception contributed to defeat after defeat for Democratic presidential candidates. For example, in 1972, Democratic candidate George McGovern suffered an electoral drubbing at the hands of Richard Nixon after proposing to decrease the tax burden of lower-income voters at the expense of middle- and upper-income voters. Similarly, in 1984, Democratic candidate Walter Mondale was routed by Ronald Reagan after pledging to increase taxes and social spending if elected.

The Democratic Party's difficulties in presidential elections were compounded by the aftermath of the Civil Rights movement. The national Democratic Party had helped to bring about the enfranchisement of millions of black voters in the South. To secure the loyalty of these voters as well as to cement the loyalty of black voters in the North, the national Democratic leadership supported a variety of civil rights and social programs designed to serve the needs of African Americans.

Unfortunately, however, the association of the national Democratic Party with civil rights and the aspirations of blacks had the effect of alienating millions of white Democrats, including southerners and blue-collar northerners, who felt that black gains came at their expense. Alienated white voters defected to George Wallace's third-party candidacy in the 1968 presidential contest. Subsequently, many began voting for Republican presidential candidates.

Efforts by Democratic presidential candidates to rebuild their party's support among southern whites and blue-collar Northerners were hampered by the harsh racial arithmetic of U.S. politics. In the wake of the Voting Rights Act, the Democratic Party depended upon African Americans for more than 20 percent of its votes in national presidential elections. At the same time, the Democrats relied upon whites who, for one reason or another, were unfriendly to blacks for a more or less equal portion of their strength in presidential races. This meant that efforts by Democratic candidates to bolster their support among blacks by focusing on civil rights and social programs tended to lose as much support among whites as was gained among blacks. Conversely, Democratic candidates, who avoided overt efforts to court black support in order to avoid losing white backing, were hurt by declines in black voter turnout. For example, in 1984, Walter Mondale assiduously courted black support and, for his trouble, was abandoned by southern white Democrats. In 1988, Michael Dukakis carefully avoided too close an association with blacks and was punished by a steep decline in black-voter turnout.

Thus, liberal activism and civil rights combined to weaken the Democratic Party in national presidential elections. From 1968 onward, the Republicans moved with alacrity to take advantage of this weakness. Republican presidential candidates developed a number of issues and symbols designed to make the point that the Democrats were too liberal and too eager to appease blacks at the expense of white voters. Beginning in 1968, Republicans emphasized a "southern strategy," consisting of opposition to school busing to achieve racial integration and resistance to affirmative action programs.

At the same time, Republicans devised a number of issues and positions designed to distinguish their candidates from what they declared to be the excessive liberalism of the Democrats. These included support for school prayer and opposition to abortion, advocacy of sharp cuts in corporate taxes and the tax rates of middle- and upper-income voters, a watering down of consumer and environmental regulatory programs, efforts to reduce crime and increase public safety, and increased spending on national defense. During the Reagan and Bush presidencies, taxes were cut, defense spending increased, federal regulatory efforts reduced, support for civil rights programs curtailed, and at least token efforts were made on behalf of restricting abortion and reintroducing prayer in the public schools.

These Republican appeals and programs were quite successful in presidential elections. Southern and some northern blue-collar voters were drawn to the Republicans' positions on issues of race. Socially conservative and religious voters were energized and mobilized in large numbers by the Republicans' strong opposition to abortion and support for school prayer. Large numbers of middle- and upper-middle-class voters were drawn to Republicanism by tax cuts. The business community responded positively to Republican efforts to reduce the government's regulatory efforts as well as to the prospect of continuing high levels of defense spending. These issues and programs carried the Republicans to triumph in five of six presidential contests between 1968 and 1992. The South and West, in particular, became Republican strongholds in presidential elections and led some analysts to assert that the Republicans had a virtual "lock" on the electoral college.

The issues that allowed the Republicans to achieve such an impressive record of success at the presidential level during this period still did not bring the GOP victory in the congressional electoral arena or in state and local races. Presidential races are mainly media campaigns in which opposing forces compete to win the attention and favor of the electorate through television spot advertisements, media events, and favorable press coverage. This form of politics emphasizes the use of issues and symbols.

Congressional and local races, by contrast, were typically fought "on the ground" by armies of volunteers. The national media could devote little attention to any individual local race, while local media tended to focus upon local issues and personalities. As a result, national issues, for the most part, had little effect upon the outcomes of local races.

Frequently, Democratic members of Congress, making vigorous use of the federal pork barrel, won handily in districts that were carried by the Republican presidential candidate. Presidential and congressional elections seemed to exist in different political universes. Voters who supported a Richard Nixon or a Ronald Reagan at the presidential level seemed still to love their Democratic congressional representatives. Senatorial elections have some of the characteristics of both national and local races. Both the media and activists can be important. Therefore, though Republicans had less success in capturing the Senate than the White House, they had a better record in Senate races than in contests for the House.

Divided Government

For thirty years, the typical pattern of U.S. politics was Republican control of the White House and Democratic control of Congress, especially of the House of Representatives. This pattern seemed to have become such a permanent feature of the U.S. political landscape that each political party began to seek to fortify its own institutional redoubt, while undermining its opponent's political bastion. Thus, Democrats sought to strengthen Congress while weakening the presidency. Republicans, for their part, endeavored to expand presidential powers while limiting those of Congress.

For this reason, Democratic congresses enacted such pieces of legislation as the War Powers Act, the Budget and Impoundment Control Act, and the Arms Export Control Act, which sought to place limits upon the use of presidential power at home and abroad. In a similar vein, the Ethics in Government Act provided Democratic congresses with a mechanism for initiating formal investigations and even the prosecution of executive branch officials—usually Republican appointees. The so-called Iran-Contra investigations, for example, led to a number of indictments of high-ranking Republicans.

For their part, Republicans sought to weaken Congress through the enactment of sharp cuts in the domestic spending programs upon which congressional Democrats rely to build constituency support. Republicans also supported a policy of successful *faits accomplis* in foreign affairs such as the Reagan administration's invasion of Grenada and bombing of Libya. Favorable popular reaction to these presidential initiatives was seen as undermining the War Powers Act and untying the hands of the White House in foreign and military affairs.

Breaking the Deadlock

While engaging in these sorts of institutional struggles, each party also sought to devise strategies that might allow it to expand its power by capturing its opponent's political base. Moderate and conservative Democrats argued that the party would win presidential elections if it nominated an ideologically centrist candidate who ran on issues that would appeal to the middle-class voters who had rejected more liberal Democratic nominees. Moderate Democrats organized the Democratic Leadership Council (DLC), which sought to develop new issues and advance the political fortunes of Democratic moderates. Many Democrats also advocated a Democratic version of the GOP's "southern strategy." This was the notion that a moderate southerner would be the party's ideal presidential candidate. Such an individual might not only attract middle-class voters in the North but might also lead southern whites, who had defected to the Republicans at the presidential level, to return to their Democratic roots.

While Democrats pondered ways in which they might capture the presidency, some Republicans considered strategies that might allow them to storm the seemingly impregnable Democratic fortress on Capitol Hill. In the 1970s and 1980s, the Republican National Committee (RNC) embarked upon an effort to recruit attractive Republican candidates for congressional and local races. The RNC also sought to create a national fund-raising apparatus to replace, or at least augment, the historically decentralized fiscal efforts that characterized both U.S. political parties. The RNC was able to create a nationwide direct mail fund-raising machine that allowed it to raise millions of dollars in small contributions. These funds could then be allocated to those local races where they might do the most good.

At the same time, Republicans began to reach out to antiabortion forces and religious conservatives. These groups represented important voting blocs. Even more important, however, if the religious fervor of these groups could be converted into political activism, these forces could become a source of Republican volunteers and activists in the same way that the fervor of anti–Vietnam War forces fueled Democratic activism for years to come. In other words, religious conservatives potentially could give the Republicans the infantry armies needed to compete effectively in local and congressional races.

Finally, Republican strategists sought ways to "nationalize" congressional and local races. For thirty years, Republican issues such as taxes, defense, and abortion had brought the GOP victory in presidential contests. Yet, these issues appeared not to have much impact upon the subpresidential level. Local Democratic candidates usually sought to avoid identification with national issues and ideologies, calculating that they could only be hurt by them. The question for Republicans was how to tie popular local Democrats to the national party's often unpopular issues and ideological stances.

Carter and Clinton: Democratic Presidential Success

The Democratic southern/moderate strategy produced two presidential victories. The first was the election of Jimmy Carter in 1976. The second was, of course, the election of Bill Clinton in 1992. Carter seemed to be the ideal Democratic candidate. He was a white southerner with a good civil rights record. His political views seemed to be centrist in character. Carter's victory over incumbent Republican Gerald Ford led some Democrats to hope that their party's presidential problems were over.

Unfortunately, however, the moderate bent that allowed Carter to win the presidential election proved a handicap in office. Carter's middle-of-the-road programs and policies alienated liberal congressional Democrats who quickly attacked his presidency. Liberals were so offended by what they saw as Carter's conservative leanings that they supported a fierce challenge to his renomination in 1980 and gave him only lukewarm support against Reagan in the general election. Liberal Democrats, it would seem, supported the idea of a centrist campaign. They did not, however, go so far as to support a centrist administration. The Democratic Party's liberal wing had what appeared to be incompatible goals. Liberal forces wanted a centrist campaign that would win the election, followed by a liberal administration to govern the nation. In 1992, a solution to this dilemma seemed to be at hand.

The Clinton Presidency

Bill Clinton, the party's 1992 standard-bearer, had been a founder of the DLC and ran as a "New Democrat." Rather than focus on the party's traditional liberal message of social programs and civil rights, Clinton pledged deficit reduction, both a tax cut and improved health care services for middle-class voters, and a "reinvention of government," to achieve economy and efficiency in the delivery of governmental services. Both Clinton and his running mate, Al Gore, were white southerners, which reassured white southern voters that the Democrats had not abandoned them.

As to African Americans, New Democrat Clinton had little to say about civil rights and, indeed, went out of his way to distance himself from blacks. Clinton refused to pay much attention to black leader Reverend Jesse Jackson and, at one point in the campaign, went out of his way to attack an antiwhite rap song performed by a black singer, Sister Souljah. In these ways, the Democratic nominee was signaling to disaffected white voters that he did not intend to cater to blacks. Clinton and the "New Democrats" calculated that after twelve years of Reagan and Bush caps on domestic spending and lack of enforcement of civil rights laws, black politicians and voters would have no choice but to work hard for the success of the Democratic ticket.

The Clinton centrist strategy helped to bring about an electoral victory in 1992. Once in office, however, Clinton moved to avoid Carter's fate by shifting to a more liberal stance. As many commentators observed, Clinton "ran right but governed left." Some critics, like Representative Newt Gingrich, charged that Clinton was only showing his true, "Great Society, counterculture, McGovernick" colors. Clinton's shift, however, can be better understood as a matter of political calculus than personal predilection. Personally, Clinton seemed willing to do whatever worked. The reality of his position was that he could not govern without the support of the powerful liberal wing of the Democratic Party in Congress.

To be sure, the extent of Clinton's shift to the Left should not be overstated. A number of the new president's policies were decidedly centrist and even won the support of the business community and broad segments of the Republican Party. For example, in the realm of economic policy, the president allied himself with congressional Republicans to secure the passage of the North American Free Trade Agreement (NAFTA), which promised to create new opportunities for U.S. firms in the world economy. At the same time, the president's 1992 and 1993 budgets aimed to bring about some reduction in the nation's huge budget deficit. This limited the opportunity for any new social programs. In 1994, barriers to interstate banking were relaxed with the expectation that this would encourage competition in the banking and financial services industries. Clinton moved to take the issue of public safety away from the Republicans by introducing his own anticrime legislation. With the president's backing, Congress also approved a new loan program for college students—an initiative popular with middle-class voters. Clinton also worked to "reinvent" government, which meant cutting the size of the government's workforce. This, too, was a measure designed to appeal to middle-class taxpayers.

Despite these ideologically middle-of-the-road programs, a number of Clinton's other initiatives seemed calculated to please Democratic liberals. Soon after his election, Clinton dropped calls for a middle-class tax cut and, instead, called for tax increases on more affluent Americans. These were adopted in 1993. Clinton enraged social conservatives and the religious Right by supporting efforts to end discrimination against gays in the military.

The president also became embroiled in an ideologically charged area when he supported gun control efforts. Clinton endeavored to expand federal social spending under the rubric of "social investment." When this effort was defeated, the president added social programs to his omnibus crime control bill under the rubric of "crime prevention." The president made race and gender diversity a major criterion for federal appointments. He also provided ammunition for his conservative critics by nominating prominent left-of-center Democrats like Lani Gaunier and Roberta Achtenberg to high positions in his administration. Gaunier's name had to be withdrawn from consideration for the position of head of the Justice Department's civil rights division after a bitter political battle.

Most important, the White House crafted a health care reform proposal under the direction of First Lady Hillary Rodham Clinton, which at least appeared to set the stage for the creation of vast new bureaucracies and a federal takeover of the nation's health care system. Liberal Democrats, who generally favored a Canadian-style system totally operated by the government, saw the president's proposal as not going far enough in the direction of government management of health care. Conservatives and even moderates, however, came to fear that Clinton's initiative would increase the cost and reduce the quality and availability of health care services to middle- and upper-middle class Americans.

Clinton Under Siege

Though Clinton was clearly no "McGovernick," he had shifted to the Left enough to be vulnerable to attack. When it came, the assault on Clinton and his policies was ferocious. Interestingly enough, the first salvo fired at the White House came not from the Right but from the liberal national news media. The national media, especially the elite press such as the *New York Times* and the *Washington Post,* and the major television networks tend to be liberal and Democratic in their political orientation. As a result, the elite news media treated candidate Clinton sympathetically in 1992. Republican attacks on Clinton's checkered personal background were dismissed as efforts to divert attention from the "real issues" of national policy. Ancient and unverified rumors of George Bush's marital infidelities were dredged up in an effort to establish a measure of moral equivalence between the two candidates. In general, the elite press hailed Clinton's victory as a triumph for virtue over the fraudulent policies and unscrupulous politics of the Reagan and Bush years. Journalists expected great things from Clinton.

Despite this positive beginning, Clinton's relationship with the press soured quickly. The core of the problem was that the press and the White House had fundamentally different interpretations of the 1992 election. The press believed, with some justification, that Clinton's victory was due in no small measure to its support for the Democratic candidate. Journalists were well aware that their willingness to provide Clinton with favorable coverage and to give scant attention to the various questions raised about his private morality helped put Clinton in the White House.

Clinton and his staff, for their part, had a somewhat different view of the election. The Clintonites believed that they had won entirely through their own efforts. The president and his aides frequently boasted of Clinton's ability to reach the American people directly and without media help, through televised town meetings and appearances on television talk shows. The administration made its lack of respect for the media clear when the president declined to hold televised press conferences and the administration declared large portions of the White House press area off limits to journalists. This White House position posed a direct threat to the power and status of the national media. Since the 1960s, the media had exercised enormous influence in the U.S. political process and had attacked and destroyed those politicians who dared to challenge them. Spiro Agnew and Gary Hart were notable examples.

In the wake of the hubris demonstrated by the administration's peculiar adversarial posture toward the press, the national media quickly modified its coverage of the new president. Through the 1993 "Hairgate" and "Travelgate" incidents, Clinton was depicted as an arrogant and boorish individual who had no concern for ordinary Americans waiting at an airport and who was willing to fire loyal, longtime White House employees to give their jobs to his own relatives and associates. A number of journalists who previously supported the president declared that their attitude toward the White House had soured because of what they saw as the Clinton administration's repeated efforts to deceive the press and the public. One White House correspondent, Ruth Marcus of the *Washington Post,* averred that "repeated falsehoods and half-truths have corroded the relationship between this White House and the reporters who cover it."

The administration moved to improve its media coverage by hiring David Gergen, a successful Republican "spinmeister" and media relations expert. Gergen sought to soothe the ruffled feathers of the press by scheduling more press conferences and organizing small social events where Clinton met with and courted journalists. Clinton even began to hold a series of small off-the-record gatherings with important journalists, including correspondents for the major news networks, in an effort to create a more positive image for the embattled president. According to some journalists who attended the gatherings, Clinton sought to flatter them by asking their advice on administration initiatives. Clinton's efforts appeared to produce several sympathetic news stories. Some journalists, however, apparently were annoyed even by the president's attempts to be nice to them. One responded to Clinton's request for advice by declaring that, "advising presidents was not his province." Eventually, however, Gergen's strategy paid off and, by mid-1994, the press had begun to moderate its attacks upon Clinton. A number of journalists, indeed, began to ask whether they and their colleagues had not been too harsh in their criticisms. By this time, however, the damage had already been done. Clinton had been publicly depicted as boorish, arrogant, and unfeeling—hardly qualities likely to endear him to the electorate.

While liberal national journalists began to feel sorry for Clinton and tone down their attacks, another set of reporters and commentators were just beginning to take aim at the president. Over the past several years, a conservative media complex has begun to emerge in the United States in opposition to the liberal media. This complex includes two major newspapers, the *Wall Street Journal* and the *Washington Times,* several magazines such as the *American Spectator,* and a number of conservative radio and television talk programs.

Conservative religious leaders like the Reverend Jerry Falwell and Pat Robertson, head of the Christian Coalition, have used their television programs to attack the president's programs and to mount biting personal attacks on both Clinton and his wife, Hillary. For example, a videotape promoted by Falwell accuses Clinton of arranging for the murder of an Arkansas investigator who allegedly had evidence of the president's sexual misconduct. Other conservative groups not associated with the religious Right have also launched sharp assaults against the president. Nationally syndicated talk-show host, Rush Limbaugh, is a constant critic of the administration. Floyd Brown, head of a group called Citizens United, with forty employees and a $3 million annual budget, attacks Clinton on a daily radio show and faxes anti-Clinton news bulletins to more than twelve hundred journalists and talk show hosts. One of Brown's bulletins asserted that Deputy White House Counsel Vincent Foster had not shot himself in a Virginia park as reported by the police but had actually died in a White House "safe house." This allegation was then aired by Rush Limbaugh on his national radio program.

The emergence of this complex has meant that liberal policies and politicians are virtually certain to come under attack even when the liberal media is sympathetic to them. For example, charges that President Clinton and his wife were involved in financial improprieties as partners in the Whitewater Development Company, as well as allegations that, while governor, Clinton had sexually harassed an Arkansas state employee, Paula Jones, were first investigated and publicized by the conservative press. Only after these stories had received a good deal of coverage in the *Washington Times* and *American Spectator* did the mainstream liberal media begin to highlight them. Of course, once the stories broke, major television networks devoted substantial investigative resources and time to them. In due course, the liberal media probably gave the Whitewater and Jones charges as much play as the conservative media, often with as little regard for hard evidence.

Media attacks against Clinton gave congressional Republicans more than enough reason to demand hearings and the appointment of a special counsel to investigate the president's conduct, as well as that of his associates. Senate hearings in 1994 led to the forced resignation of Deputy Treasury Secretary Roger Altman, who was accused of having used his office to hinder the Whitewater probe.

Attacks by the media and by Clinton's Republican opponents were extremely effective. Substantial segments of the public came to see the president as an individual lacking scruples and moral standards. The success of this attack helps to explain why Clinton's standing in public opinion polls sagged in 1994 despite the strong performance of the U.S. economy in that same year. Usually, presidential popularity and the nation's economic performance are closely linked. Clinton had become an object of such opprobrium to many Americans that they were unwilling to credit him with any positive developments.

The Republican Congressional Campaign

At the same time that Republicans attacked the president, they launched a major effort to win control of the Congress. This effort had three elements.

The first, spearheaded by Representative Newt Gingrich, actually began during the late 1980s and involved an attempt to discredit the Democratic Party's congressional leadership. In 1989, Gingrich initiated a series of charges of financial improprieties that led to the resignation of Democratic House Speaker Jim Wright and the Democratic House Whip Tony Coelho. In 1991, Gingrich and his allies launched another series of attacks upon the operation of the House bank and post office that revealed that some House members were misusing these institutions for personal financial gain. Though some Republicans were affected by the ensuing scandals, most of the onus fell on the Democratic leadership of the House, which was ultimately responsible for the operations of the chamber.

The banking and post office exposés helped to undermine public confidence in the Congress and its leadership. The problem was exacerbated when evidence was revealed suggesting that Representative Dan Rostenkowski, the powerful Democratic chair of the House Ways and Means Committee, had been among those using his access to the House post office for personal advantage. Rostenkowski was indicted on federal criminal charges and forced to step down from leadership of the committee. By 1994, Gingrich, who had in the meantime become Republican Whip and was in line to become Republican leader after the 1994 election, had succeeded in depicting Democratic congressional leaders as a venal group out of touch with the needs of ordinary citizens. Such a leadership, and the Congress it led, might be electorally vulnerable.

The second element in the Republican effort to win control of Congress was the full-scale mobilization of the religious and social conservatives whom Republicans had been courting for a number of years. As Republican strategists had long hoped, by 1994 these groups were organized in a "Christian Coalition" that provided committed activists and volunteers for Republican congressional and local campaigns throughout the nation, particularly in the South.

At last, the Republicans had an infantry force to match the liberal activists mobilized by their Democratic foes. If anything, the fervor of the Republican infantry exceeded that of the Democrats. To be sure, Republicans like Virginia senatorial candidate Oliver North, who were seen by voters as too closely associated with the Christian Right, often were unsuccessful. However, Christian Coalition activists played a role in many races where Republican candidates were not overly identified with them. One postelection study suggested that more than 60 percent of the candidates supported by the Christian Right were successful in state, local, and congressional races in 1994. The efforts of conservative Republican activists to bring voters to the polls is one major reason that turnout among Republicans exceeded that of the Democrats for the first time in twenty-five years in a midterm election. This was especially marked in the South where the Christian Coalition was most active.

Finally, by 1994, Republicans had been presented with a way to nationalize congressional and local races. During the 1990s, hundreds of local radio and television stations had launched "talk programs" that featured political and social topics. These programs are inexpensive to produce and popular with large groups of viewers and listeners. While these programs are locally produced and reach only a local audience, their commentary tends to focus on national issues. Their effect is to bring national political issues and ideologies into the local community or congressional district. Often, the hosts of these programs seek to link local politicians to national stories. Talk radio and talk television programs, for example, played an important role in informing audiences about the role of their own representatives in the House banking and post office scandals. These programs inform audiences of the positions taken by their representatives on national political issues.

While many of the hosts of these programs are politically conservative, not all take right-wing positions. During the 1992 presidential campaign, Clinton was supported by many talk show hosts. By bringing national issues into local races, however, these programs make it more difficult for congressional and local Democratic candidates to insulate themselves from the issues and ideologies that, for thirty years, have damaged the Democratic Party's chances at the presidential level. This new media format made it less likely that a congressional district would vote Republican at the presidential level and, yet, keep its Democratic congressional representative in office. This phenomenon boded ill for Democrats, especially in the South. A Cable News Network (CNN) survey indicated that 64 percent of those voters who regularly listened to talk radio programs supported GOP candidates in the 1994 congressional elections.

Republican Victory and Its Aftermath

The end result of all these factors was the Democratic debacle of November 1994. For the first time in nearly a half-century, the Republicans would control both houses of Congress. Yet what would this mean? What would the Republicans do with their new-found power? U.S. history suggests that little can be inferred from election results. What matters is what victors do with their power once they have acquired it. Franklin Roosevelt made the Democrats the nation's majority party for fifty years not because he won the 1932 election but, rather, because of the programs he crafted after coming to power. Whether the 1994 election turns out to be significant is a function of what the Republicans do, once in power.

Some clues about GOP plans began to emerge even before the election. Republican leader Newt Gingrich had persuaded nearly all Republican congressional candidates in September 1994 to sign a "Contract with America." The contract, which Republicans pledged to attempt to implement if they won control of Congress, called for a variety of tax cuts as well as such popular political reforms as term limits and a balanced budget amendment. The contract was part of the GOP's effort to nationalize the election as well as a first step by the Republican leadership to impose party discipline on their new troops. New Republican members of Congress who failed to follow the leadership's dictates could be accused of breaking their pledge to the American people.

At the same time that he was compelling Republicans to sign a contract, Gingrich told a group of lobbyists that after Republicans took control of Congress, the GOP would launch legislative investigations to look into wrongdoing in the executive branch. Just as Democratic congresses had used their power to investigate Republican presidents, so a Republican Congress would use its power to investigate the conduct of the Clinton presidency.

With Newt Gingrich's elevation to the post of Speaker of the House in the aftermath of the GOP's electoral victory, the shape of the Republican plan is clear. Under Gingrich's leadership, Republicans will promote an agenda of tax cuts for middle- and upper-income voters. This will presumably require cuts in social spending to avoid exacerbating the budget deficit. To this end, Gingrich has already called for a basic rethinking of federal welfare and poverty programs.

At the same time, through legislative investigations, Republicans plan to keep the White House off balance and unable to develop its own legislative and policy initiatives. Executive institutions confronted by hostile investigations are typically unable to function effectively. There can be little doubt that the Senate Banking Committee, now chaired by New York Senator Alphonse D'Amato, and its House counterpart, now chaired by Iowa Representative Jim Leach, will take long and hard looks at the Whitewater imbroglio.

Thus, the results of the 1994 election indicate that President Clinton is likely to have a difficult two years before the next presidential election. Quite possibly, he will face serious challenges for the 1996 Democratic presidential nomination after leading the party to defeat in 1994. It seems certain that his legislative agenda will face serious opposition in a Congress controlled by the Republicans.

Of course, Republicans will have their own problems. There is ample potential for friction between Gingrich and Senate Majority Leader Robert

Dole, who orchestrated the defeat of Clinton's health care initiative. Republicans may split over their party's 1996 presidential nomination. In the Senate, Dole and Senator Phil Gramm of Texas are known to aspire to the presidency. More important, the policies favored by social conservatives, such as restrictions on abortion, are generally opposed by the economic conservatives who form the traditional backbone of the GOP coalition. Members of the latter group often view the social conservatives as a noisy and dangerous rabble who, at best, are a necessary evil if the GOP is to prevail in the electoral arena.

Nevertheless, the results of the 1994 congressional election offer the Republicans their best chance in a generation to become the nation's permanent majority party. If they are able to implement a program of tax and spending cuts favorable to the interests of middle-class voters, they may complete the work begun by Ronald Reagan and tie the middle-class electorate firmly to the GOP. At the same time, if social and religious conservatives can be satisfied with symbolic victories that do not require rank-and-file suburban Republicans actually to swallow school prayer and restrictions on abortion, the 1994 election may become a major turning point in U.S. political history.

1.2

The Question of Presidential Character

Chris Cookson, Ross Lence, and Alan Stone

Throughout history, leaders of countries have frequently been corrupt and vicious ideologues. The American framers were aware of this even before Adolf Hitler, Joseph Stalin, Fidel Castro, and other monsters rose to power. These twentieth-century tyrants had nothing on the likes of Genghis Khan, Charles II, and George III. A strong argument can be made that the United States of America was born from the very rejection of tyranny. Nowhere is this rejection more forcefully articulated than in the litany of charges and accusations leveled against George III in the American Declaration of Independence. The character of the leader of a country is obviously important. In this essay we will explore the consequences of the chief executive's character, looking first at the framers' views and then examining Richard Nixon and Bill Clinton, the two recent U.S. presidents whose characters have been most sharply questioned. The American framers, like many contemporary thinkers, held a dim view of human nature and strongly believed that power tended to corrupt.

The Framers' Vision

Once upon a time, not too long ago, every school child knew the story of Benjamin Franklin and the rising sun. On Monday, September 17, 1787, while members of the Federal Convention were busy signing the document that today we know as the Constitution of the United States of America, Franklin looked toward the President's chair and happily observed that he now had confidence that the sun painted on the back of that chair was in fact a rising, rather than a setting, sun.

What is often overlooked in repeating this story is the fact that the chair that Franklin referred to was no ordinary chair. It was occupied by the man who would be the new nation's first president—a man who would be the first and last to secure the unanimous assent of the electoral college. No man in the newly freed states was more respected, more admired, and, dare we say it, more loved, than George Washington. Drawn from his retirement, Washington, with his already legendary reputation and personal integrity, contributed much to the legitimacy conferred upon the Constitutional Convention.

We do not relate these matters merely to reinforce the apotheosis of the founding period but to emphasize the fact that in no part of the U.S. Constitution was the matter of character more important to the framers than in Article II where provision is made for the executive office and officer. Note that we maintain a distinction between the office and the officer. In considering the executive power with regard to both form and function, we are immediately confronted with problems of terminology. Many people use the terms *president* and *presidency* interchangeably, but to do so is to invite confusion and to obscure important distinctions. One prominent scholar clarified this matter by drawing precisely a distinction between the president and the presidency, between the officer and the office. The powers of the presidency are the powers of the office as set forth by Constitution and statute. These are formal powers established by and under law. They are the powers of the office available to any and all who take the position.

The power of the president, however, does not refer to the formal powers of the office itself but, rather, to the power available and employable in the exercise of that office. Power is distilled into a simple and usable definition of a president's "personal influence of an effective sort on governmental action."[1] Since the powers of the president of the United States involve personal influence, they cannot be severed from an assessment of his character and integrity.

These presumptions notwithstanding, it must also be noted that the Constitution itself makes no mention of character per se. The framers most assuredly did recognize the potential for deficiencies of character. There are provisions for the expulsion of members of Congress; the impeachment of judges who do not meet the test of "good behavior"; and the removal from office of the executive on charges of impeachment, and conviction thereof, for "treason, bribery, or other high crimes and misdemeanours." The particulars of those violations, however, were left for time and circumstance to discover.

But character is not the only matter left unattended by the Constitution. The U.S. Constitution is often noted for its brevity, and perhaps nowhere is the discontinuity between the paucity of words and the exercise of power more evident than in Article II, where that document takes up the question of the executive power of the United States. In only thirteen paragraphs we find all that the original Constitution had to say regarding the president and the presidency. Of these original thirteen, only one was substantially modified by the framers themselves, namely, the provisions relating to the actual operation of the electoral college. This was a consequence of the election of 1800, which necessitated thirty-two ballots in the House of Representatives to elect Thomas Jefferson over his running mate, Aaron Burr.

Following the adoption of the Twelfth Amendment in 1804, designed to provide for separate ballots for the president and vice-president, no other corrections to the framers' work on the executive and executive power were deemed necessary until the New Deal, beginning in 1933. Then, in the span of a mere three decades, no fewer than three additional amendments were thought necessary to clarify the office of the president, including the Twentieth Amendment (adopted in 1933), fixing additional conditions for the election of both the president and vice-president; the Twenty-second Amendment (adopted in 1951), which altered the term of the president; and the Twenty-fifth Amendment (adopted in 1967), to provide for presidential succession—an amendment whose convoluted nature makes us rejoice that no occasion has ever presented itself in which the amendment has been invoked.

It might be asked: Why has it been found necessary in modern times to correct the work of the framers on the matter of the executive power? And, in particular, how do changes such as the alteration of the presidential term affect the other presumptions and convictions of the founding era on the nature of man and government? Part of an answer to such inquiries, of course, is that the brevity of the Constitution has in one sense been the real source of its strength. The Constitution's silence regarding a host of matters has enabled the document to adjust to the exigencies of modern times: to be a "living constitution." Thus, we have witnessed not only the enormous growth of presidential powers but the extraordinary growth of the legislative and judicial branches as well.

In the immediate case of the president, all that the Constitution tells us about the executive powers is to be found in the four sentences of Article II, Section 2. The president, we are told, is the commander in chief; he holds the power to make treaties with the advice and consent of the Senate, to appoint officers of the government, and to appoint and receive ambassadors. All else remained for experience to determine.

In this context, it seems axiomatic in modern times to say that the powers of the presidency have developed as a function of the character and capacities of the men who have occupied the Oval Office. From Washington to

Clinton, each individual has brought to the office his unique view of the role of the president in the American polity, and each has left a mark upon the office, albeit with varying degrees of success. While there is no doubt that the modern president exercises many powers never envisioned by the members of the Constitutional Convention, there is considerably less agreement about the impact of those new powers upon republican government. What is certain, however, is that the often-cited notion of a "living constitution"—with its concomitant praise for flexibility and change—was insufficient to provide for the deficiencies or weaknesses of the framers' model for the executive power. Widespread concern that a president could entrench himself in power led to the Twenty-second Amendment, limiting the president to two terms of office. This was in response to Franklin D. Roosevelt's tradition-breaking four elections as president.

Still, it cannot be the increased institutional power alone that accounts for the contemporary concern for presidential power. As presidents from Andrew Jackson to the present have claimed, the president is the single officer of the national government who may be presumed to represent the majority of the American people as a united people. The president has become, in short, a symbol of American values, goals, and commitments. And it is for this reason that Americans are increasingly interested in the moral character of the president.

It might be useful to remind ourselves at this point what the Founding Fathers precisely thought about this matter of character and the executive. Obviously, the greatest source of the framers' view is to be found in the debates over the drafting and ratification of the U.S. Constitution,[2] especially in the work of the Federal Convention itself and the eloquent defense of the Constitution by Alexander Hamilton, John Jay, and James Madison in *The Federalist*.[3] Of equal importance to our inquiry into the founders' intentions concerning the executive power, however, is the implementation of the new regime itself during its formative years, from 1789–1800.

The Constitutional Convention of 1787 took upon itself the daunting task of creating a new government for the fledgling republic of the United States. While the convention met in secret, the indomitable James Madison painstakingly kept notes of the topics considered, the debates among and between the delegates, and the votes on the disposition of the various matters on the agenda. That collection, included in the Max Farrand volumes that collected documentary material on the founding, allows for a window into the thoughts and intentions of the delegates.

Among the basic presumptions and convictions upon which the framers' conception of government was founded was the notion that "In Republican government the legislative authority, necessarily, predominates."[4] Not unexpectedly, therefore, the most exhaustive consideration during that summer was the organization of the government, in general, and the legislative branch, in particular. Virtually every matter in the proposed constitution took its point of departure from the conclusions arrived at concerning the legislative power. Only after the initial discussion of the legislative authority had been concluded did the Convention turn, at the beginning of June, to the matter of the executive power. Before settling the matter of whether there should be a single or a plural executive in the proposed government, the delegates to the Convention cast their votes to provide for an executive elected by the national legislature for a term of seven years and without eligibility for a second term.

In mid-July, the Convention revisited the matter of presidential terms and now found itself badly divided. While there was general agreement that the length of the presidential term was critical in ensuring that "unfit characters" would not be elected, there was little agreement over the particulars. Luther Martin argued for a term of eleven years; Elbridge Gerry suggested fifteen years; Rufus King, twenty years; and William Davie, eight years. In spite of all the debate on this matter, on July 26 the Convention reasserted its preference for a seven-year term, a term which remained fixed until the committee report of September 4 called for the four-year term that eventually became part of the final document.

A second mechanism to ensure accountability in the executive officer, without sacrificing the energy and power thought necessary for the office, was the matter of executive salary. Perhaps the most insightful speech on this subject was delivered by James Wilson on behalf of Benjamin Franklin whose advanced age made it necessary to have his thoughts ordered by the written form. To quote Franklin:

> Sir, there are two passions which have a powerful influence on the affairs of men. These are ambition and avarice; the love of power and the love of money. Separately, each of these has great force in prompting men to action but when united in view of the same object, they have in many minds the most violent effects. Place before the eyes of such men a post of *honor,* that shall be at the same time a place of *profit,* and they will move heaven and earth to obtain it. . . .

> And of what kind are the men that will strive for this profitable pre-eminence, through all the bustle of cabal, the heat of contention, the infinite mutual abuse of parties, tearing to pieces the best of characters? It will not be the wise and moderate, the lovers of peace and good order, the men fittest for the trust. It will be the bold and the violent, the men of strong passions and indefatigable activity in their selfish pursuits. These will thrust themselves into your government and be your rulers.[5]

But this discussion of the procedural mechanisms of presidential terms and salary alone did not dissuade the critics of the dangers of executive power. While institutional arrangements could help mitigate the dangers of governmental injury, usurpation, and tyranny by supplying the "defect of better motive," they alone were insufficient. Provisions for impeachment of the executive officer are also necessary, argued Madison, "for defending the community against the incapacity, negligence, or perfidy of the chief magistrate."[6] While legislative bodies were also subject to corruption of their members, Madison was particularly concerned about the president. "In the case of the executive magistracy, which was to be administered by a single man, loss of capacity, or corruption, was more within the compass of probable events, and either of them might be fatal to the republic."[7]

Through his contributions to the *Federalist Papers*—the joint project of Hamilton, Jay, and Madison under the pseudonym of Publius to secure New York's ratification of the proposed constitution—Madison noted in his first essay that men are "much more disposed to vex and oppress one another, than to co-operate for their common good."[8] In language reminiscent of the English philosopher Thomas Hobbes, one is introduced to the passions of competition, diffidence, and glory, for as Madison made clear: "The latent causes of faction are . . . sown in the nature of man."[9]

And the same passions and weaknesses that mark individual men can be traced to the whole course of human events, private as well as public. In one of his single most eloquent passages in the *Federalist Papers,* Madison observed:

> It may be a reflection on human nature, that such devices should be necessary to controul the abuses of government. But what is government itself but the greatest of all reflections on human nature? If men were angels, no government would be necessary. If angels were to govern men, neither external nor internal controuls on government would be necessary. In framing a government which is to be administered by men over men, the great difficulty lies in this: You must first enable the government to controul the governed; and in the next place, oblige it to controul itself. A dependence on the people is no doubt the primary controul on the government; but experience has taught mankind the necessity of auxiliary precautions.[10]

But whatever Madison's fears were of the abuse of power in human affairs, no such fears seemed to motivate his coauthor, Hamilton. In his opening remarks on the business of the Convention, Hamilton could not conceal his clear preference for a hereditary executive.[11] This is the same Hamilton who was the sole author of the last twenty-one essays of the *Federalist Papers,* including all of those related to the executive and judicial powers of the new government. Beginning with the assumption that "a feeble executive implies a feeble execution of the government,"[12] Hamilton argued that the executive power of the new good government must be marked by unity, duration in office, an adequate provision for support, and competent powers. Time and again Hamilton praised the role of the executive in calming the passions of the people and in turning back the irregular operations of the legislature. Except for a single reference to the need for due responsibility in the executive officer, including censure and perhaps even punishment,[13] Hamilton seemed to have abandoned all of the admonishments and concerns of the *Federalist Papers* about the dangers of avarice, ambition, and greed, which had so often characterized rulers of government. Error, for Hamilton, seemed to be the exclusive domain of the people or their representatives.

Part of the reason that Hamilton could speak with such enthusiasm for the executive, of course, was that the historical experience of the United States of America under the Articles of Confederation had confirmed the need for a strong executive power to offset the centrifugal forces of the union. A second factor, no less important to our discussion, was the fact that there seemed to be a consensus throughout the states that George Washington, a man of noted integrity and universal respect, would be the first president. Many presumed that he would serve for life, as a republican replacement for the British monarchy—a presumption vehemently denounced by Washington himself.[14]

While it may have been useful for the immediate purposes of Hamilton and others to presume Washington's election, it should be noted that no such presumption motivated Washington himself. Repeatedly, in his correspondence, Washington spoke with apprehension of that impending day when he would be forced to decide whether to return to public life. In his letter to Benjamin Lincoln on October 26, 1788, for example, Washington revealed the reluctance he felt when called to the presidency:

> Motives of delicacy have prevented me hitherto from conversing or writing on this subject [Washington's candidacy in the electoral college], whenever I could avoid it with decency. I may, however, with great sincerity and I believe without offending against modesty or propriety say to *you,* that I most heartily wish the choice to which you allude may not fall upon me: and that, if it should, I must reserve to myself the right of making up my final decision, at the last moment.... [I]f from any inducement I shall be persuaded ultimately to accept, it will not be (so far as I know my own heart) from any of a private or personal nature. Every personal consideration conspires to rivet me (if I may use the expression) to retirement. At my time of life, and under my circumstances, nothing in this world can ever draw me from it, unless it be a *conviction* that the partiality of my Countrymen had made my services absolutely necessary, joined to a *fear* that my refusal might induce a belief that I

preferred the conservation of my own reputation and private ease, to the good of my Country. After all, if I should conceive myself in a manner constrained to accept, I call Heaven to witness, that this very act would be the greatest sacrifice to my personal feelings and wishes that ever I have been called upon to make.[15]

Sentiments such as these establish George Washington as a unique figure in presidential politics, if for no other reason than the reservation he felt about accepting the office. No such moderation and self-effacing character seemed to have marked his successors. Rancor in presidential elections has been the order of the day from the election of John Adams to that of William Jefferson Clinton. However the framers might talk of seeking men for president whose "character [is] proclaimed by fame throughout the empire,"[16] no institutional arrangements per se could guarantee such an outcome. Whatever the ingenious nature of the electoral college, all seemed lost with the rise of political parties—a phenomenon whose omission in the thought of the framers is most perplexing, given the British experience with factions. Whatever the intentions of the framers, it is clear that today the electoral college plays virtually no role in securing men of integrity and character for president but is, at best, a quaint institutional formality, denounced by many as aristocratic, archaic, arcane, and anachronistic.

Still, even the most cursory examination of the presidency in modern times suggests that it would be wise to reexamine in greater detail the framers' thoughts concerning the character of the executive office both in elections and in governing the nation.

The Modern Era

The twentieth century has confirmed the American framers' worst fears about the dangers of extended government and the attraction that political power has to malevolent and deceitful characters. Political scientist R. J. Rummel has conservatively estimated that the state has killed almost 170 million people in the twentieth century—and the century is not over yet![17] To the major tyrants—Stalin and Hitler—we can add hundreds of minor ones who have contributed to this astounding death toll of the twentieth century. The one rationalization for the strong state had been that it would deliver economic goods and social benefits better than private markets. But even this excuse is gone as the economies of statist regimes in the former Soviet Union and its Eastern European satellites collapsed while, in the capitalist West, public enterprises proved to be woeful performers compared to private ones. George Orwell's fable, *Animal Farm,* correctly described the evolution of the political and economic systems of regimes with strong states. David Horowitz succinctly reinforced the fundamental fear that the American framers had about political leaders who seek to expand the powers of the state—usually with the noble motive of helping the people: "I had believed in the left because of the good it had promised; I had learned to judge it by the evil it had done."[18] Not all political leaders are malevolent, of course, but as the framers felt, you must always guard against the worst possibility.

The American framers recognized not only the dangers of government, but also that it is a magnet for people who like to control others. "Enlightened statesmen will not always be at the helm," Madison asserted with characteristic understatement in the *Federalist,* no. 10. In that paper he also recognized the power of demagogues, relying on envy or hatred of the more fortunate, to sway the masses. The scheme the framers constructed was intended to guard against political leaders who would appeal to the less fortunate "for an abolition of debts, for an equal division of property or for any other improper or wicked project. . . ."[19]

Sincerity or a commitment to use government for "good" ends are clearly not the issue, for there is no question that evil results can as readily follow from good intentions as they can from malicious or deceitful ones. Even Hitler felt that he was using government for "good" ends. The human capacity for rationalization is virtually instinctive. As Madison observed, "As long as the connection subsists between his reason and his self-love, his opinions and his passions will have a reciprocal influence on each other. . . ."[20] Obviously, too, insincerity and the use of one's position for self-aggrandizement are equally to be feared. The American framers were far from sanguine that the institutional arrangements they advanced would ultimately guard against the kind of political leadership that they feared. Certainly, a free press and free elections, insofar as they can reject a political leader who is revealed to have an inappropriate character, are crucial supplements to the institutional arrangements. But some presidents fail not only for their programs but for their characters. In a nutshell, the public and the members of the legislative branch come to distrust them.

In the post–World War II era, two presidents have failed because of the character issue. Initially, it is important to specify what the character problem is in the late twentieth-century context. Certainly, few Americans expect their political leaders to be saints. Transgressions are permissible, but there is a line that can be crossed beyond which the transgressions render a person untrustworthy or unfit to hold office. An occasional lie, for example, is sometimes acceptable, but a congenital disregard for the truth is always unacceptable. In the latter case, the invisible line has been breached. Again, the circumstances of the transgression make a vital difference. Abuse of office is simply not tolerable. For example, there is little doubt that President John Kennedy had many extramarital affairs, but these were entirely private matters and did not involve government employees. In every other way, he led an exemplary life and served his nation with distinction during World War II and in a legislative capacity prior to becoming president. In brief, one could, of course, disagree with President Kennedy's position on issues, but no one could doubt the high quality of his character.

Richard Nixon, too, served his country in both military and political roles. On more than one occasion, however, his behavior raised significant character issues. But he was always able to weather the storm until the Watergate episode that led to his downfall—a criminal break-in at the Democratic National Committee Headquarters in the Watergate complex on June 17, 1972.[21] In January 1973 the seven burglars were either convicted or pled guilty. But President Nixon became personally involved on June 25 when John Dean, the president's counsel, asserted that the president, his staff, and others had conspired to cover up the facts about the break-in.[22] From that point until Nixon resigned on August 9, 1974, the president was unable to govern effectively. Participation in a conspiracy to cover up a burglary had undermined public and elite confidence in the president's character. The result was that Nixon was unable to promote plans for an ambitious domestic program. More importantly, foreign rivals correctly sensed that they were able to take advantage of the disruption that followed from the exposure of Nixon's character. The Vietnamese communists disregarded their solemn promises made in the Vietnam peace agreements that were signed in January 1973; by late April 1975 the communists completed their takeover of Vietnam. In the Middle East, Arab oil-producing nations imposed a total ban on petroleum exports to the United States from October 1973 to mid-March 1974. Congress, reasonably wary of Nixon's leadership, could do nothing to unify U.S. foreign policy. Indeed, many have argued that Congress abetted the disarray in order to bring Nixon down more quickly.[23]

While the presidencies of Gerald Ford, Jimmy Carter, Ronald Reagan, and George Bush all had their scandals and bad appointments, in none of these administrations did scandal undermine the president's legitimacy. Each of these presidents had their enemies. Adverse accusations about honesty and competence were leveled at each of them, but proof of disreputable character was largely lacking. Moreover, each had served in the military. Carter and Reagan had effectively governed large states; Ford had spent twenty-five years in the House of Representatives; and Bush headed a number of executive branch agencies, most importantly, the Central Intelligence Agency (CIA). Their records and experience must be borne in mind when we focus on Bush's successor—Bill Clinton—who catapulted to the presidency after serving as attorney general and then governor of a small state largely concealed from the national limelight. Arkansas and its governor's relative obscurity would initially work to Clinton's advantage, since little was known nationally about his character or his record. But later, as more became known about Clinton, the obscurity would work to his detriment.

Before discussing Clinton's character and its impact on his governance and legitimacy and the 1994 elections, some preliminary observations are necessary. First, we must remember that the critical point is not whether Clinton could be convicted of any charge using the canons of proof that are required in a court of law; however, if mounting evidence begins to shake public confidence, then the public comes to distrust the president's character. Although far from the proof required in a criminal proceeding (that is, beyond a reasonable doubt), the standard is still more rigorous than idle gossip. The reason is, of course, that most people want to believe that the president selected by the electoral system is fit to serve in that position. But as evidence aggregates to shake that belief, the public begins to question his character. Further erosion leads to withdrawal of support because he is deemed unfit to hold office. And this process can occur without the president having been convicted or even charged with a crime; he is supposed to be, to use the current cliché, a role model.

What is the role of the press in this process? One would have to be extraordinarily naïve to believe that contemporary journalists simply report facts. Rather, facts are filtered through ideological and conceptual predispositions that most journalists make no effort to conceal. For example, Clinton was aided immeasurably in the 1992 election campaign by the press's near uniform characterization of economic conditions during the campaign as a "recession." The term was employed incessantly to describe economic conditions allegedly prevailing during the latter part of the Bush presidency, which contributed to the view that the administration was not managing the economy successfully. Economists define a recession as the contractionary phase of the business cycle; it is measured by declines in two consecutive quarters. Yet, during 1991–1992, gross domestic product grew 2.6 percent in constant (1987) dollars, and in 1992–1993 it grew 3.0 percent.[24] Since the economy was the paramount issue in the campaign and deflected attention from the issues that had arisen about Clinton's character, it is difficult to measure how much the media's constant incantation that the U.S. economy was in a "recession" aided Clinton.

This does not suggest that the journalists in the leading print and television media engaged in an overt conspiracy to aid Clinton. Rather, the most influential media figures largely wear the same ideological blinders, and their views tend to be on the left side of the political spectrum. For example, the main survey of journalists working for the elite media (*New York Times, Washington Post, Wall Street Journal, Newsweek, U.S. News and World Report,* ABC, CBS, NBC, and PBS) discovered that their support of Democratic candidates in presidential elections has never been less than 80 percent. These journalists believe that the United States is a racist and unfair society; it misuses resources and is responsible for Third World poverty.[25] Notwithstanding this general ideological bias, there were responsible journalists, including some affiliated with the previously named institutions, who were willing to look closely at the Clinton record. And despite the media's liberal predisposition, its initial trust in Clinton soon evaporated so that the president began to claim that the media was treating him unfairly.[26]

The reason was character. Clinton virtually invited the media to evaluate his wife's character as well; on more than one occasion he proclaimed that voters were getting two for the price of one. His appointment of Hillary Rodham Clinton to head the important health care task force in January 1993 basically compelled the media to take the president at his word and evaluate both persons together. Unfortunately for the administration, Ruth Marcus, one of the fairest and most respected national political reporters, did just that. She concluded that, "The Clinton White House often seems to be following a pattern of knowing or reckless disregard for the truth. Apparently putting its short-term political interests ahead of accuracy, it regularly fails to provide trustworthy information—whether out of inability, unwillingness, or both. Examples of this inclination range from trivial to significant, but they are legion."[27] Marcus puts her finger on the difference between the Nixon and Clinton character issues. Nixon was involved in a single major miscarriage of justice. If the Watergate break-in had never occurred, Nixon would have finished his term in office. Clinton, on the other hand, is accused of engaging in numerous shady activities and of being unable to tell the truth, the whole truth and nothing but the truth. He is accused of seeking political and personal advantage to the complete exclusion of any other values. Such a person will not accord the office of the presidency the dignity that it deserves since in his mind he is more important than the institution. It does not follow that the president lacks an ideological base but, rather, that it will be subordinated to his career.[28]

From the foregoing, we can understand many of the president's actions. In a 1994 interview on MTV, the juvenile rock network, Clinton dignified a seventeen-year-old's question about the kind of undershorts he wears with an answer; it is almost unthinkable that any of Clinton's predecessors would have been asked such a question, never mind answering it. The decline in political dignity since the country's founding is marked by Clinton's response to this question, on the one hand, and by George Washington's refusal to allow even members of the Federal Convention to address him by his first name, on the other. More importantly, it is rare that President Clinton will pass up any opportunity for political advantage no matter how harmful the consequences will be. In a bitter 1993 race for mayor of New York City between a white Republican and an incumbent black Democrat, the President, eager to benefit politically from a Democratic victory, sanctimoniously asserted that, "Too many of us are still unwilling to vote for people who are different than we are."[29] Not only could this remark intensify distrust between the races, but it was patently untrue. Black mayors have been supported by whites in many places, including Los Angeles, Seattle, and New York, where Mayor David Dinkins was already serving. Again, in the aftermath of the 1995 tragic bombing of a federal building in Oklahoma City, Clinton, in a Minneapolis speech, charged his critics with inciting the vicious attack. Even his supporters were shocked at Clinton's apparent disregard for the difference between legitimate criticism and unlawful violence.[30]

The first event that raised the issue of President Clinton's character concerned his response to the military draft. It is important here to understand precisely what the character issue is on this topic. It is *not* whether the Vietnam War was right or wrong. It is *not* whether someone of draft age should or should not have served in the military. Honorable people stood on both sides of these issues and acted accordingly. Courage was present in those who participated in the Vietnam War and those who opposed it. The issue with respect to Clinton was whether he was deceitful both at the time he was subject to the military draft and, again later, when he ran for the presidency. The evidence compiled by Clinton's biographers as well as by reporters investigating the so-called draft issue *uniformly* points to the same factual conclusions. It is clear that the late Raymond Clinton, the president's influential uncle, and the office of Senator J. William Fulbright interceded with the draft board of Hot Springs, Arkansas, to pass over the president's file.

In February 1969, the president, studying then at Oxford University in England, was presented with a notice to report for an armed forces physical examination in London, which he passed. Returning to the United States, he faced the prospect of induction on July 28, 1969. He had already been using influence to avoid induction, but the only possible route to evade serving his country was to enroll in the Army Reserve Officers' Training Corps (ROTC) program at the University of Arkansas. Clinton traveled to the university to meet with Colonel Eugene J. Holmes, who headed the Army ROTC program there. Clinton told Holmes that he intended to enroll in the University of Arkansas Law School and would participate in the

ROTC program. Because of his commitment to enter the program in the spring of 1970, Clinton was reclassified on August 7, 1969, as 1-D, the status for reserve members or students taking military training. The reclassification saved Clinton from the draft for several months. But, in the new draft lottery, Clinton received a high draft number (311), which in effect guaranteed that he would not be drafted. Since he no longer had to fear the draft, Clinton sent a letter dated December 3—two days after the lottery—to Colonel Holmes, announcing that he would not enter the ROTC program at the University of Arkansas.[31] Clinton, in fact, entered the far more prestigious Yale Law School in 1970.

The issue, to reiterate, is not Clinton's position on the Vietnam War, but both Clinton's attempt to use influence to circumvent the legal obligations that others of his generation faced and his manipulative behavior, especially with respect to Colonel Holmes. In September 1992, Colonel Holmes wrote: "Even more significant was his lack of veracity in purposefully defrauding the military by deceiving me, both in concealing his anti-military activities overseas and his counterfeit intentions for later military service. These actions cause me to question both his patriotism and his integrity."[32] While the episode might be viewed in the context of Clinton's youth, his frequent shifting statements during the 1992 election campaign cannot. Twenty-three years later, Clinton changed his story about the episode from the initial claim that he had not received a draft notice to a variety of other stories, as the press continually uncovered information about the episode.[33]

One final point needs to be made about Clinton's character and the Vietnam War. To cast aspersions on Clinton's patriotism, as Colonel Holmes did, appears too strong, although it is understandable from a man who served his country heroically and endured years of imprisonment by the Japanese during World War II. But there is a character thread that runs through those years to the present. Every foreign policy stance Clinton takes is subservient to *his* self-interest. Harry Truman's courageous move in providing aid to enable Greece and Turkey to withstand the Soviet threat, his heroic and rapid defense of South Korea in the face of North Korea's invasion, Dwight Eisenhower's and Kennedy's aid to Vietnam, Kennedy's forcing the Soviet Union to back down in the Cuban missile crisis, and Carter's defiant stand in favor of human rights in foreign policy—all of which involved great risks—cannot be envisioned in Clinton's behavior. Instead, we have a president who has returned Cuban, Chinese, and Vietnamese refugees who risked their lives to escape from their respective tyrannical governments, and who has been largely detached about the inhumanity perpetrated by Russia against the Chechens.[34]

The unifying motivation is not lack of patriotism, as Colonel Holmes suggested, but self-interest measured in terms of political ambition to the exclusion of principle or concern about the appropriate role of the United States in world affairs. This overarching characterization would also explain President Clinton's immediate response to the 1995 publication of Robert McNamara's book, arguing that the U.S. participation in the Vietnam War was wrong and giving his apology for his role in that war as secretary of defense in the Kennedy and Johnson administrations.[35] One might think that, since becoming commander in chief, Clinton might not want to remind the public about the episodes that we have examined. Instead, almost immediately after the publication of *In Retrospect,* Clinton praised McNamara for "a lot of courage," asserting that, "Those who opposed the war believed the things that McNamara now says are true." The liberal journal of opinion, *The New Republic,* barely containing its anger, stated: "It was the job of the president to recognize the pain of the wounded and pain of the veterans and the pain of the families of the dead . . . but the president felt only his own pain. You'd think that the war in Vietnam owed its importance in American history to its impact on the career of William Jefferson Clinton."[36] One might add that, consistent with his foreign policy in general, Clinton also disregarded the postwar impact on the people of Vietnam: more than one million boat people, economic misery, and horrifying political repression, including the "reeducation" of vast numbers of people in concentration camps.

If the draft and foreign policy were the only areas that have given many people doubts about the quality of Clinton's character, the issue might be less bothersome. But there is so much else. Many of the other topics, however, involve conjecture or accusations that may or may not be true. Other topics, such as Clinton's Arkansas financial dealings, await further exploration as we are writing this. But even the little that is known about some of the topics raise serious character issues. If only a small number of the accusations are true or partially true, there is ample support for the perception that Clinton's character is deeply flawed. Even matters that are trivial have tended to support the view that the president's character is suspect. The president's admission that he smoked marijuana, immediately followed by the assertion that he did not inhale, has come to symbolize his lack of candor. Or consider a kind of episode in which most U.S. presidents would not have become involved—the firing of members of the White House travel office. Originally claiming that the firings took place because of mismanagement, it later turned out that the charge was false and that Hillary Clinton wanted to get "our people" in that office.[37]

Again, a president's sexual escapades should ordinarily be off-limits to the press—unless they involve consorting with foreign spies. While the latter has occurred in Europe, no one has ever suggested that it took place in the United States; Marilyn Monroe, with whom President Kennedy enjoyed a relationship, was clearly not a Soviet agent. But President Clinton, while Arkansas governor, has been charged with mixing politics with what should have been entirely his own affairs. Gennifer Flowers (with whom Clinton is alleged to have had an affair) taped conversations with then Governor Clinton, and those conversations clearly show a political intimacy that went beyond a mere sexual liaison. For example, discussing the 1992 Florida Primary, Clinton asserted, "We're leading in the polls in Florida . . . without Cuomo in there, but Cuomo's at 87 percent name recognition, and I have 54 percent. . . . Boy, he is so aggressive." In response to Flowers's remark that "I wouldn't be surprised if he didn't have some mafioso major connection," Clinton responded, "Well, he acts like one."[38] The intimacy might be acceptable, but it was discovered that Governor Clinton had rejected a job promotion for one Charlotte Perry in favor of Flowers.[39]

Once again, in the episode known as "Troopergate," two Arkansas state troopers have alleged, *without evidentiary support,* that Clinton enlisted their aid in obtaining sexual favors from women. Nevertheless, a *Los Angeles Times* investigation indicated that the troopers were veteran state employees and had signed affidavits in support of their allegations. Moreover, it is obvious that only troopers held in high regard would have been assigned the important task of aiding the governor. Finally, the investigation revealed that Clinton had made numerous phone calls to one of the women the troopers had named, including eleven phone calls on July 16, 1989.[40]

Stories about the sexual peccadillos of other presidents would have made little impact, because they would have stood out as small debits to be balanced against extraordinary credits. But, in Clinton's case, many feel that sleazy behavior is the rule and not the exception. For this reason, the burden of overcoming the negative implications about Clinton, as event piles upon event, is a formidable one. And in many of these events—obviously not the draft or the sexual ones—his wife is perceived to be a co-conspirator. Consider the allegations concerning her commodity trading in which an investment of approximately $1,000 in one of the riskiest markets was transformed into $100,000 in 1978–1979. During and after the 1992 campaign, Mrs. Clinton sought to explain her increase in wealth during that period as due to a gift from her parents. But when the Clintons' 1978 and 1979 tax returns were made public, the extraordinary profits that she made as a novice in commodity speculation—profits that would be the envy of professional commodity speculators—were also made public. As the press became attentive to the issue, Ruth Marcus summarized the official response: "The White House first refused to reveal the size of her initial investment, then—after a news report said she put no money down—disclosed that she started with $1,000. It initially said she managed to parlay that minimal investment by studying the market, reading the *Wall Street Journal* and consulting with her friend Jim Blair. When that explanation was greeted with skepticism, the story changed again—Hillary Clinton relied almost entirely on the advice of Blair, who executed most of the trades."[41]

Blair, counsel for Tyson Foods, had been exceptionally successful in the cattle futures market, and placing one's trading decisions in cattle futures in his hands was probably a very sound judgment. Nevertheless, there is no question that Mrs. Clinton was accorded privileges not usually granted to traders in that high-risk market. The investigation of *Washington Post* reporter David Maraniss showed that, "She seemed to get a break even on her first day in the market, when records show that she ordered ten cattle future contracts with her $1,000 when that normally requires a $12,000 investment."[42] And the breaks not accorded to other customers continued. Suspicions fall far short of proof, but the suspicions about these trading contracts continue when we realize that, unlike stock market transactions in which one can lose only the amount on one's investment, it is possible to lose much more in the futures game as it is played and that, therefore, Mrs. Clinton could have lost far more than the $1,000 she initially ventured. Yet the Clintons had few assets at the time; therefore, many observers have concluded that the trade would have been extraordinarily reckless—unless someone else promised to pick up the losses. The episode, then, once again raises strong suspicions about the Clintons' characters—suspicions reinforced by the failure of the White House to be forthcoming when the story broke, the shifts in Mrs. Clinton's explanation for the remarkable success achieved, her special treatment, and the administration's attempts to hinder an investigation of the trades by the Commodity Futures Trading Commission, the federal regulator with jurisdiction over such matters.[43]

There are many other such situations that we will not discuss, including the circumstances of the suicide of Vincent Foster, Mrs. Clinton's legal partner and the deputy White House counsel. But one event that calls for some mention concerns the episodes collectively known as "Whitewater." Investigations are still in progress as this is being written, and no evidence of the Clintons' having engaged in legally culpable wrongdoing has yet been developed. Accordingly, we will say little about these episodes. Nevertheless, the charges leveled against them are serious ones and have reinforced public suspicion about Bill Clinton's character. The facts and charges are extraordinarily complex, but reporter Terry Eastland has remarkably summarized them:

> In 1978, the Clintons joined with James and Susan McDougal in a real estate venture on the White River. Mrs. Clinton and her Rose Firm represented McDougal's Madison Guaranty S&L, which failed in 1989 at a cost to taxpayers of $47 million. Though the Clintons and the McDougals were 50–50 partners, the Clintons . . . invested only half as much as the McDougals. Federal authorities are investigating whether moneys were diverted from Madison to Whitewater and Clinton's gubernatorial campaign.
>
> Mrs. Clinton received a $2,000 monthly retainer for representing McDougal's savings and loan before the state securities commissioner, who was appointed by her husband. Both McDougal and the commissioner say the state did not give Madison preferential treatment.[44]

It is impossible to determine with precision the impact that the cumulative doubts about Clinton's character—and there are many more episodes that space precludes us from examining—had on the extraordinary Republican victory in the 1994 election. Democratic candidates tended to distance themselves from Clinton during the campaign even as they agreed with his policy positions, leading us to conclude plausibly that character did play a role in the results. And while Clinton had legislative successes, the centerpiece of his legislative program was a plan to restructure completely the U.S. health care industry. The plan was developed under the leadership of Hillary Clinton and Ira Magaziner, a close associate famous for advancing the cause of cold fusion as the ultimate energy source (now widely considered as a nonstarter).

Almost immediately upon the launching of the health care plan, doubts developed about the administration's claims. Phony cost projections, anxiety about new restrictions on patients' rights to choose physicians, fear of the adverse effects on pharmaceutical research, the regimentation of medical providers and, most importantly, trepidation about a decline in the overall quality of U.S. medicine greeted the plan. Although the Democrats controlled both houses of Congress, Clinton could not even get a modified version of his grand plan to be considered by Congress. Public distrust in the president's plan to transform a major component of the U.S. economy unquestionably played a major role in its decisive defeat.[45]

While Clinton claimed that distortions about the plan caused its failure, Democratic Senator Patrick Moynihan said, "The American people got it clear enough." Columnist George Will added, "Clinton's health care deception, the centerpiece of his presidency, flowed from his 1992 campaign, itself a long deception."[46] When the 1994 election returns came in, the nation showed its continued concern about character by depriving a president, whose probity they questioned, of the leadership role that most presidents have been accorded.

Modern chief executives will always be confronted by conflicts and problems that did not exist when they began office. In light of this, it is understandable that voters attempt to evaluate the character of candidates so that when these unexpected events occur the executive will deal with them effectively. The voters' concern with questions of presidential character is certainly a valid one. In this respect, elections certainly do matter.

Notes

1. Richard E. Neustadt, *Presidential Power and the Modern Presidents* (New York: Macmillan, 1990), p. ix.

2. Max Farrand, ed., *The Records of the Federal Convention of 1787* (4 vols.) (New Haven: Yale University Press, 1966), hereafter referred to as *Records.*

3. The best edition of which is George Carey and James McClellan, eds., *The Federalist* (Dubuque, Iowa: Kendall/Hunt 1990). All page citations refer to this edition.

4. *The Federalist,* no. 51, p. 267.

5. *Records,* vol. 1, p. 82.

6. *Records,* vol. 2, p. 65.

7. Ibid., p. 66.

8. *The Federalist,* no. 10, p. 44.

9. Ibid.

10. Ibid., no. 51, p. 267.

11. *Records,* vol. 1, p. 289.

12. *The Federalist,* no. 60, p. 312.

13. Ibid., no. 70, p. 365.

14. W. B. Allen, ed., *George Washington: A Collection* (Indianapolis, Ind.: Liberty Classics, 1988), pp. 203–204.

15. Ibid, pp. 424–425.

16. *Records,* vol. 2, p. 53.

17. See R. J. Rummel, *Death by Government* (New Brunswick, N.J.: Transaction Publishers, 1995).

18. David Horowitz, "Why I Am No Longer a Leftist," in Peter Collier and David Horowitz, *Second Thoughts* (New York: Madison Books, 1989), p. 57.

19. *The Federalist,* no. 10, p. 48.

20. Ibid., p. 44.

21. The best work on Richard Nixon remains Stephen E. Ambrose, *Nixon* (New York: Simon and Schuster, 1987). See also Joan Hoff-Wilson, *Nixon Reconsidered* (New York: Basic Books, 1994).

22. The facts are told in the book written by the two *Washington Post* reporters who discovered and pursued the story: Carl Bernstein and Bob Woodward, *All the President's Men* (New York: Simon and Schuster, 1974).

23. Interestingly, Nixon provided the best statement of this position. See Richard Nixon, *No More Vietnams* (New York: Simon and Schuster Touchstone, 1990), pp. 278–326.

24. U.S. Bureau of the Census, *Statistical Abstract of the United States: 1994* (Washington, D.C.: Government Printing Office, 1994), p. 448. On press coverage during the campaign, see Fred Barnes, "The Media on Clinton: How Tough," *Forbes Media Critic* (winter 1995): 38, 39.

25. See Robert S. Lichter, Stanley Rothman, and Linda S. Lichter, *The Media Elite* (Bethesda, Md.: Adler and Adler, 1986).

26. Barnes, "Media on Clinton," pp. 40, 41.

27. Ruth Marcus, "The White House Isn't Telling Us the Truth," *Washington Post,* August 21, 1994, C9.

28. This view does not depend on the psychological theory that Bill Clinton's character was shaped by his stepfather's alcoholism and violence, as advanced in Paul Fick, *Dysfunctional President* (New York: Birch Lane Press, 1995), pp. 198–209.

29. "Carded," *New Republic,* November 1, 1993, 7.

30. Mark R. Levin, "A President Long on Blame . . . Short on Decency," *Washington Times National Weekly Edition,* May 1–7, 1995, 33.

31. David Maraniss, *First in His Class* (New York: Simon and Schuster, 1995), pp. 190–205; Meredith L. Oakley, *On the Make* (Washington, D.C.: Regnery, 1995), pp. 77–82; William C. Rempel, "GOP Official Was Lobbied over Clinton Draft Notice," *Los Angeles Times,* September 26, 1992, A1; Michael Putzel, "Draft Questions Continue to Swirl Around Candidates," *Boston Globe,* September 21, 1992, 1; Ralph Frammolino, "ROTC Officer Unaware of Draft Notice," *Los Angeles Times,* April 6, 1992, A15; Ralph Frammolino, "Clinton Joined ROTC After He Got Draft Notice," *Los Angeles Times,* April 5, 1992, A1.

32. Quoted from an affidavit prepared by Colonel Holmes, which is reprinted in Floyd G. Brown, *Slick Willie* (Annapolis, Md.: Annapolis-Washington Book Publishers, 1992), p. 138.

33. Curtis Wilkie, "Clinton's Latest Credibility Challenge," *Boston Globe,* September 5, 1992, 6, and Jeffrey H. Birnbaum, "Lingering Debate over Clinton's Draft Record," *Wall Street Journal,* September 10, 1992, A16.

34. See, among numerous sources, Charles Krauthammer, "Clinton's Foreign Policy Is Disgraceful," *Houston Chronicle,* April 22, 1994, 32A; Grover J. Rees, "Clinton's Iron Curtain," *Wall Street Journal,* September 14, 1994, A22; Zbigniew Brzezinski, "America Is Moscow's Accomplice in Chechnya," *Houston Chronicle,* January 11, 1995, 11C; Armando Valladares, "Castro Outfoxes Clinton—and Guantanamo's Detainees Pay," *Wall Street Journal,* January 27, 1995, A11; A. M. Rosenthal, "In Irons to Cuba," *New York Times,* May 5, 1995, A15; Charles Krauthammer, "Clinton Prefers Golfing to Foreign Policy," *Houston Chronicle,* May 18, 1995, 18A; Tom Carter, "Cuba Policy Changed in Secret," *Washington Times National Weekly Edition,* May 22–28, 1995, 12; and Philip Shenon, "GOP Bill Would Pay for Vietnamese to Resettle in U.S.," *New York Times,* May 21, 1995, Y3.

35. Robert S. McNamara and Brian Van De Mark, *In Retrospect,* New York: Random House, 1995). For a trenchant critique of the book, see W. W. Rostow, "The Case for the War," *Times Literary Supplement,* June 9, 1995, 3–5.

36. "Notebook," *New Republic,* May 8, 1995, 8.

37. Marcus, "The White House," p. C9.

38. Reprinted in Brown, *Slick Willie,* p. 149.

39. L. Brent Bozell III, "Annoy the Media, Elect Bush," *Wall Street Journal,* November 2, 1992, A14.

40. See Mark Jurkowitz, "Why Was Troopergate Sleaze in *The Spectator* but News in *The Post?*" *BPI Entertainment News Wire,* February 17, 1995; Robert Shogan, "Ex-Arkansas State Worker Says Clinton Harassed Her," *Los Angeles Times,* February 12, 1994, A21; and William C. Rempel and Douglas Frantz, "Troopers Say Clinton Sought Silence on Personal Affairs," *Los Angeles Times,* December 21, 1993, A1.

41. Marcus, "The White House," p. C9.

42. Maraniss, *First in His Class,* p. 372.

43. See Michael Schroeder, "The Watchdog Who Barked at Hillary," *Business Week,* March 27, 1995, 44, and the articles and editorials collected from the *Wall Street*

Journal in Robert L. Bartley, ed., *Whitewater* (New York: Dow Jones, 1994), pp. 276–279, 311–339, and 359–360.

44. Terry Eastland, "Why the Press Quiet on Whitewater in 1992," *Forbes Media Critic* (summer 1994): 27, 29. See also Bartley, *Whitewater,* pp. 276–360, passim; Peter J. Boyer, "The Bridges of Madison Guaranty," *New Yorker,* January 17, 1994, 32–38; and L. J. Davis, "The Name of Rose," *New Republic,* April 4, 1994, 14–23.

45. Among the enormous amount of literature on the health care issue, excellent short analyses include Kevin Phillips, "The Traumatic Birth of Health Reform," *Los Angeles Times,* July 24, 1994, M1; Ruth Shalit, "Bitter Pills: The End of Drug Research," *New Republic,* December 13, 1993, 19; Daniel J. Mitchell, "The President's Costly Budget Buster," *Wall Street Journal,* December 23, 1993; and Joseph Bast, "Dead on Arrival—Clinton Health Plan," *Wall Street Journal,* June 10, 1993, A12.

46. George Will, "Clinton's Deceptions Didn't Fool Voters," *Houston Chronicle,* November 17, 1994, 18B.

1.3

The Decline and Ascent of Political Parties in Canada

The Collapse of the Conservatives and the Rise of Reform

Kenneth Woodside

In the autumn of 1993 two long established Canadian national political parties suffered severe electoral defeats in the general election. In spectacular fashion, the governing Progressive Conservative Party (hereafter called the Conservatives) saw its support fall from a majority of 157 seats in the 295-seat House of Commons to a mere 2 seats. For its part, the New Democratic Party (NDP), Canada's long-established social democratic party, saw its representation drop from 44 to 9 seats. The collapse of these two parties was so complete that they no longer qualified for official party status in the new House of Commons. Filling the electoral space created by these developments were the Reform Party, which went from 1 to 52 seats, and the Bloc Quebecois, which went from 8 to 54 seats. The Official Opposition during the previous government, the Liberals, now formed a new majority government with 177 seats. My purpose in this paper is to attempt to explain the fate of the Conservative Party and to speculate on whether or not the party is likely to enjoy a return to more successful times in the future. My discussion of the various potential futures that face the Conservative Party will require that I assess the likely permanence of the Reform Party's success since the two parties largely share the same constituency. I will also attempt to draw out the relevance of these developments in Canada for party politics in the United States. Comparative analysis is a crucial approach in the development of knowledge and the broad similarities between Canadian and U.S. politics and society, despite significant institutional and demographic differences, can make the Canadian experience seem highly relevant to an understanding of the U.S. experience. However, the institutional differences in the governmental systems of the two countries may produce different outcomes despite the many other similarities.

The decline and collapse of existing major national parties is not a common phenomenon and is usually associated with periods of extensive turmoil. In the United States, for instance, one of the first national political parties, the Federalists, in the era of George Washington, Alexander Hamilton, and John Adams, slowly faded away in the first two decades of the nineteenth century as its founding goals became less important in the new country. The spiritual successor of the Federalists, the Whigs, also saw its demise after the Compromise of 1850. This decline came as a result of the worsening and deepening of sectional divisions over slavery and the upheaval and strain in established political coalitions that these divisions created.[1] In Italy, the demise of the Action Party in the 1940s and especially the more recent collapse of the Christian Democrat Party, which had been part of the governing coalition in Italy throughout the postwar period, are further examples of the potential for party decline.[2] In the case of the Christian Democrats, the numerous allegations of extensive and long-standing corruption on the part of Christian Democrat deputies and party leaders as well as other centrist politicians ensured that the party would be seriously discredited. Another celebrated case of party decline is that of the British Liberal Party, which, having formed the government on a number of occasions in the late nineteenth and early twentieth centuries, was reduced to third-party status during the 1920s and has been unable in subsequent years to reverse this decline.[3]

The idea that political parties can be fundamentally transformed and even disappear seems in tune with political circumstances in the 1990s. Incumbents and incumbent governments are everywhere and in all countries threatened with defeat by a pervasive sense of dissatisfaction with and alienation from incumbent politicians. The range of potential outcomes becomes ever wider as possibilities, which were once regarded as remote, become tenable. In the former Soviet Union the Communist Party, which provided the glue that held the USSR together, has been reduced to a fringe party and the government that it controlled for over seventy years has ceased to exist. The states of Eastern Europe have been fundamentally transformed along with their party systems, and the ruling communist government in China has espoused capitalist solutions to economic growth for selected parts of the country. The Chinese Communist Party has itself gone into business, behaving in much the same way as a large business corporation. Political institutions are everywhere in turmoil and the fortunes of political parties are subject to rapid transformation.

There are a number of theoretical explanations that can be brought to bear on the situation in an effort to explain what happened to the Conservative and Reform Parties. In the next section we will describe these explanations. Following this description, we will consider the relevance of these explanations toward an understanding of the events of the 1993 election and the fate of the two parties. In the final section, we will consider the relevance of the Canadian cases to the U.S. party system.

Explanations for the Decline of Political Parties

This analysis will focus on three types of explanations for a party's electoral decline. The first type involves broad cultural and structural factors.[4] The argument would be that major events that aroused deep cultural and structural tensions brought about the demise of the Conservatives. These factors could include debates over constitutional change, such as the allocation of power to different levels of government, and sectional or regional divisions among various parts of the country. Regional divisions have the potential to become particularly virulent when they are reinforced by ethnic or racial differences. Cultural and structural factors can also surface in intense policy debates that touch on quasi-constitutional issues. These issues involve fundamental characteristics of the polity; any proposed changes would ostensibly draw keen interest and arouse considerable conflict. As fundamental issues, they are likely to have an impact on many groups in the society, an impact that may be difficult to assess. As a result, these issues can easily be overwhelmed by the politics of fear, with many threatening outcomes given a high probability of occurring. If a political party is seen to be on the unpopular side of too many of these types of issues, the party's electoral success may be seriously affected.

The second type of explanation focuses on the role of political institutions. These institutions deal with the type of electoral system, the nature of the institutions that exercise executive and legislative power, and whether governmental legal powers are shared by different levels of government, as in a federal system, or are concentrated in a single government, as in a unitary system. An electoral system can influence the fortunes of a party in the way that it aggregates the votes and translates the vote totals into seat totals. Canada has an electoral system that is often referred to as a plurality, or "first past the post" system.[5] The country is now divided into 295 roughly equal constituencies, and voters in each constituency get to vote for one of the candidates running for office in the constituency. Each of the major national political parties is likely to have a candidate running in each of the constituencies; the candidate who wins the most votes in the constituency also wins the seat and the right to represent that constituency in the House of Commons, the elected part of Canada's Parliament. Since there are commonly more than two parties running candidates in each constituency election, the winning candidate often receives less than a majority of the votes cast. Therefore, it is both possible and likely that a party winning a majority of the seats will have less than a majority of the vote if there are more than two parties contesting the election.

The Canadian system tends to underrepresent parties that may have substantial support across the country—say, 20 to 25 percent—but not concentrated enough to win many constituencies. It also tends to overrepresent political parties that have their support concentrated in a particular part of the country, allowing them to win constituency elections in that region without receiving many votes in other parts of the country. As a result, a party with its support distributed more or less evenly across the country could receive more votes nationally than a regionally based party but win many fewer seats. Clearly, the way in which the electoral system translates votes into seats can have an impact on a party's future prospects. The major alternative to the plurality system is a system based on proportional representation, or PR. A PR system will give each party a share of the seats that roughly compares with its share of the popular vote. This type of electoral system has less independent influence on the results of an election. Canada, however, does not use this system, although there have been periodic calls for its implementation.

Executive and legislative powers in Canada are exercised through a parliamentary system. The members of Parliament (MPs) elected in each of the 295 constituencies act as the legislators, passing the laws of the land. The party that can maintain the support of the majority of these MPs forms the government and exercises the executive powers that are based on the laws passed by the legislators. One of the distinctive features of the parliamentary system, as compared to the presidential-congressional system of the United States, is that responsibility for action or inaction is more easily attributed to the government, which is normally controlled by one party and that party is controlled by the prime minister. While Congress and the presidency may thwart each other, it is relatively more difficult to ascribe guilt for action or inaction to one or the other as institutions. Individual legislators and their party may be able to escape bearing responsibility for their behavior. In Canada, the action or inaction is clearly the responsibility of the government and voters can more obviously hold the governing party to account.

A third source of institutional influence on the fortunes of political parties derives from the organization of governmental powers between levels of government. Canada has a federal system like the United States, but there are only ten provinces in Canada. Two of the provinces, Ontario and Quebec, contain about 60 percent of the population and economic activity in the country. Further, federalism has acted to organize and reinforce regionalism in Canada.[6] As the provincial governments have become more powerful and aggressive political actors in Canada since 1960, regional tensions have grown. Moreover, the presence of a large French-speaking population in Quebec, with some historic concerns for their cultural and linguistic future, has also increased regionalism. The federal system can have an impact on the future of a party in at least two ways. First, a party can maintain a presence in provincial politics even though it has no presence at the national level, or almost none. Second, by reinforcing regionalism, the federal institutions may make it difficult for a regional party to establish itself successfully as a national party with support across the country. Thus, whereas the electoral system may make it easier for a regional party to establish itself, the operation of the federal system in Canada may prevent the party from extending its influence across the country. All of these institutional factors are largely constant in their form, but they do have the capability of affecting a party's fortunes. If a political party should experience serious electoral difficulties, these institutional structures can speed its decline or block its revival. At the same time, a party may be able to retain a niche in Canadian party politics by remaining important in one or more of the provincial party systems. This would give it the opportunity to reemerge as a national force at a later time.

The third type of explanation for party decline focuses on the strategy and tactics of the party and its leaders. This category would include the choice of party leader, the prevalence of scandals or other events that have an impact on the moral standing of the party, and the choice of issues on which to base an election campaign. Canadian voters have been described as "flexible partisans" in voting studies. This refers to the presence of a less intense, stable, and consistent partisan identification among Canadian voters. The result is that voters may be more responsive to issues and events in Canada than voters are in the United States.[7] These factors are most likely to threaten the future of a party when they occur in combination with some of the other factors described earlier. In the next section, I will examine each of these types of explanation separately in trying to assess why the Conservatives collapsed in the 1993 election, how permanent this collapse is likely to be, and, because they share a largely common constituency, what impact the Reform and Conservative Parties will have on one another.

Explanations for the Conservative Collapse and the Rise of Reform

Cultural and Structural Explanations

Any discussion of the fate of the Conservative Party must give substantial attention to its leadership role in two attempts to reform Canada's constitution as well as its negotiation and signing of a wide-ranging trade agreement with the United States. These three initiatives raised virtually every theme of division and conflict that has existed in Canadian politics over the country's history. The constitutional negotiations attempted to reconstruct Canada's political institutions so that decades of regional and ethnic conflict would finally be resolved. Unfortunately, the result of these initiatives was to worsen rather than improve these relations. For its part, the Canada-United States Free Trade Agreement raised not only regional tensions but also ideological issues; it focused attention on the country's historic relationship with the United States, its much larger neighbor to the south.

The first of the constitutional reform efforts is commonly referred to as the Meech Lake Accord. The justification for this attempt began with a May 1980 promise made to the Quebec electorate by the prime minister at the time, Pierre Trudeau. He promised that if voters rejected the proposal for an independent Quebec in the referendum being held then, the national government would work to reform the existing federal system. This led eventually to the passage of the Charter of Rights and Freedoms and an amending formula for constitutional change. However, in the process of getting provincial support for the constitutional changes, the government of Quebec was isolated and refused to support the changes. While the new constitutional provisions were legally binding in Quebec, the province refused to give them legitimate standing by denying its consent. Quebecois nationalists feared that the individual rights protected in the charter might threaten provincial legislation protecting Quebec's French language and culture. Moreover, it was felt in Quebec that, as one of the founding nations of Canada, the consent of the province where most French Canadians lived should be necessary to make such important constitutional changes. Several years later, the new Conservative government, elected with strong representation from the west and from among Quebec nationalists, initiated another attempt at constitutional reform. This round of talks focused on Quebec's concerns, although as the negotiations unfolded, western concerns also received attention. The result was an accord that, among other things, proposed changes on how members of the upper house of Parliament—the Senate—and the justices of the Supreme Court were chosen; it also made several changes in the formula for constitutional amendment. However, the most controversial proposal designated Quebec as a "distinct society" within Canada and gave the Quebec provincial government the responsibility for preserving and promoting this reality. This agreement generated extensive and heated debate over three years, as it made its way through the federal and provincial parliaments. Eventually, it was defeated when the Manitoba and Newfoundland legislatures failed to ratify it. The defeat of the accord produced an explosion of nationalist outrage in Quebec and led a small group of Quebecois MPs to split from the Conservatives and form their own party called the Bloc Quebecois (BQ).

The resulting fiasco was blamed on the Conservatives, and Prime Minister Brian Mulroney in particular, as support for independence reached new highs in Quebec. At the same time as the Quebecois were reacting with rage at the defeat of the agreement, there was strong sentiment against it outside Quebec. Many believed, especially in the west, that Quebec was getting constitutional advantages that all provinces should receive. The Meech Lake Accord generated great anger throughout the country.

This constitutional crisis led to another round of negotiations that resulted in a new agreement called the Charlottetown Accord. This accord was supported by all three of the traditional national political parties: the Liberals, the Conservatives, and the New Democrats. It was also supported by all ten of the provincial premiers, each of whom took part in the negotiations, as well as by the leadership of the organization that claimed to speak for the indigenous peoples of Canada. The Charlottetown Accord included provisions to reform the Senate, a longtime goal of reformers from the Canadian west, as well as provisions to recognize the "inherent right to self-government" of the aboriginal population and a distinct-society clause to establish constitutional recognition of Quebec's uniqueness within Canada. This accord was to be approved through a referendum held on October 23, 1992. Despite the support of all the elected political leaders in the country, the Charlottetown Accord was rejected by the Canadian electorate by a margin of 54.4 percent to 44.5 percent. The accord was decisively rejected in Quebec and the four western provinces—all areas of Conservative strength in the two previous national elections—and was only narrowly accepted in Ontario. The opposition to the accord in English Canada was led by a new political leader from western Canada, Preston Manning, the leader of the Reform Party and a politician often compared with Ross Perot in the United States. A major consequence of these two constitutional failures was to arouse deep and sharp regional antagonisms toward the national government and toward the Conservative government and its leader, Brian Mulroney.

A third policy initiative of this period that aroused strong antipathy toward the Conservatives was the negotiation of the Free Trade Agreement (FTA) with the United States. This trade agreement, which served as a model for the North American Free Trade Agreement (NAFTA), was implemented about one year before Canada, and especially Ontario, entered a major recession. The FTA provided the United States with a guarantee of continuing access to Canada's energy resources, put new restrictions on the operation of the existing automobile pact, and generally established a framework for the increased economic integration of the two countries. The trade treaty directly confronted and attacked the established Canadian nationalist understanding that Canada was a political creation that used government policies to resist the natural north-south flow of economic pressures. It did so by putting constraints on the capacity of the government to continue these policies. There were also fears that the trade deal would devastate Canadian manufacturing, fears that seemed to be being borne out during the recession of the early 1990s. As with the two constitutional initiatives, the FTA hardened a substantial number of Canadian voters against the Conservative Party, especially in the province of Ontario, the manufacturing center of Canada, where the party had usually enjoyed considerable influence and where voters felt particularly vulnerable to the possible consequences of the trade treaty.

These three initiatives, along with some others, helped to exacerbate regional tensions in Canada. Westerners in particular were angered, despite the major role for western-based politicians in the Conservative governments of the period 1984–1993. The Conservative policies, according to western opponents, seemed to remain broadly similar to those of previous Liberal governments, favoring Quebec and Ontario. Mulroney's first cabinet contained thirteen westerners among the thirty-nine members, and seven of these people sat on the inner cabinet of fifteen ministers where the real power lay. Yet in a 1986 decision early in the Conservative mandate, the government decided to contract for the repair of Canada's CF–18 fighters with a Montreal firm rather than with a western-based firm in Winnipeg, the lowest bidder in the tender.[8] This seemed to confirm the western belief, especially strong in Alberta and British Columbia, that no national government, including a Conservative one, could be trusted. The anger was not confined to the west, however. In Quebec anger over the constitutional failures had led to the creation of the Bloc Quebecois, which was committed to Quebec's secession from Canada. In Ontario the unhappiness had contributed, in 1990, to the unexpected defeat of the seemingly invincible provincial Liberals who had been strong defenders of the Meech Lake Accord.

The Conservative Party of the 1980s was built around three foundations of support. The first was strong support in the west, which, since the record-breaking victory of John Diefenbaker and the Conservatives in 1958, had been a solid source of Conservative electoral support. After their defeat in 1963, the Conservatives were in power again, although only briefly for nine months in 1979–1980. As a result, the sense of ongoing exploitation of the west by national governments and the belief that the Conservative Party would make a difference were sustained and not tested as widely shared beliefs. When the new Conservative government itself, despite its strong western representation, came to be perceived as not adequately representing western interests and being too solicitous of Quebec interests, the electorate in the west became increasingly fertile ground for new electoral forces. It was into this space that the Reform Party appeared, arguing that the Canadian state had been captured by special interests and that an elected, effective, and equal Senate needed to be created in order to counter the pervasive influence of the large populations of Ontario and Quebec in the House of Commons. Reform support came overwhelmingly from former Conservative voters, and its success clearly threatened the Conservatives in the west. In the 1993 election, despite efforts to adopt some of Reform's policy positions, the Conservative Party lost support in its western stronghold: from over 40 percent of the vote and 48 seats Conservative support fell to 13 percent of the vote and no seats whatsoever. Reform won 38 percent of the vote and 51 of 86 seats in the west and was especially successful in prosperous Alberta and British Columbia, where it won 46 of 58 seats.[9]

The second part of the Conservative foundation of support was in Ontario. Canada's most prosperous province had traditionally divided its support between the Conservatives and the Liberals, with a smattering of support for the NDP. The province itself elected Conservative provincial governments every election between 1943 and 1985 when, surprisingly, the government was defeated. In changing leaders just prior to the 1985 election, the provincial Conservative Party had chosen a new leader who was too right-wing for the provincial electorate. A reaction against the established Conservative Party leadership set in and the provincial party, long a major source of national Conservative votes, money, and personnel, was reduced to a third party in the next two provincial elections. The federal party was the object of great anger for the economic difficulties that beset Ontario during the early 1990s at the time of the passage of the FTA and for its part in the constitutional fiascoes that had revived Quebec separatism. With the provincial electorate that is most concerned with national unity issues, the Conservatives fared badly in Ontario in the 1993 election. The Conservatives won only 17.6 percent of the vote in Ontario with no seats—

a drop from 38 percent of the vote in 1988—while Reform won 20.1 percent and 1 seat. Most of the Reform votes came at the expense of the Conservatives. The Liberals swept the province winning 98 of 99 seats and 52.9 percent of the vote. The right-wing vote in Ontario was now more or less evenly split between two parties, rendering it ineffective.

The third foundation of support for the Conservatives in the 1980s was in Quebec. Historically, the Quebec electorate had given overwhelming support to the Liberals, helping them to dominate national politics from the mid-1930s to the mid-1980s. Mulroney's great achievement in the 1984 election was to persuade many Quebecois to vote Conservative. Many of the new Conservative MPs were strong nationalists and, provincially, they were supporters of the separatist Parti Quebecois. The constitutional failures in the Meech and Charlottetown Accords and the breakaway of the Bloc from the Conservatives in 1990 set the stage for Conservative voters in 1984 and 1988 to switch to the Bloc in 1993. Moreover, the signing of the FTA, which was very popular in Quebec, was interpreted by Quebec nationalists as assuring a viable Quebec economy after independence through secured access to the U.S. economy. This would make independence a more attractive option for Quebecois, who were undecided and fearful for the economic future of a separate Quebec. The Conservative share of the vote in Quebec fell dramatically from 53 percent in 1988 to 13.5 percent in 1993, and the party won only 1 of 75 seats. The big winner in Quebec was the Bloc, which took 54 seats and 49.3 percent of the vote, with its support coming largely at the expense of the Conservatives. The Bloc, a party led by a former Conservative cabinet minister, was now the strongest party in the province.

The net result of these developments was a collapse in Conservative support nationwide. The Conservatives were reduced from 157 seats at the time of the dissolution of Parliament to 2 seats after the election. The beneficiaries of the collapse in Conservative support were the Reform Party in the west especially and, to a lesser extent, in Ontario and the Bloc in Quebec. Former Conservative voters were now flooding the ranks of these new parties. The threat posed by Reform was particularly serious. The Conservatives had only done well in Quebec recently, and the support of nationalists in the province was generally considered to be a marriage of convenience. The loss of support in the west and in Ontario constituted a loss in long-term core supporters. There is room for only one successful party on the Right in Canada, and after the election the Reform Party seemed poised to take over this role. The demise of the Conservatives is largely explained by these structural and cultural factors, but other sources need to be considered in understanding both why the Conservatives collapsed and why it may be hard for the party to be revived. At the same time, certain institutional factors could provide a springboard for a Conservative revival over the longer term.

Political Institutions as Explanations

The first institutional factor that needs to be considered is the impact of the executive and legislative branches within Canada's parliamentary system. This system of government tends to concentrate power when the government has a majority. At the same time, it also concentrates responsibility. Under the U.S. system of government, it is less clear which institution should receive the blame or credit for a failure to act. In recent decades, one party has not controlled both the presidency and the two houses of Congress except briefly during the first two years of the Clinton administration. The institutions of the U.S. federal government are designed so that the power and responsibility are shared. In Canada these powers are fused. If the capacity to act lies with the constitutional powers of the national government, there can be no doubt as to whether the government will receive the blame or credit. The Conservatives were the main recipients of the blame for the policy initiatives that we have described. By 1993, Mulroney was the most unpopular prime minister in Canadian history. During the election of 1988 and thereafter, the FTA was commonly referred to by its opponents as the "Mulroney trade deal." In the run-up to the referendum on the Charlottetown Accord, the opponents constantly called it "Mulroney's deal." The institutional structure allowed the Conservatives to be marked as the villain for the many unpopular deeds of the previous decade, and the success of this marking was clearly reflected in the sharp collapse in Conservative voter support.

A second institutional factor contributing to Conservative weakness, and likely to be a continuing influence in the future, is the electoral system. Canada's electoral system works to exaggerate the strength of the strongest party, commonly translating a minority in the popular vote into a majority of seats. In the 1993 election, the victorious Liberals won 177 seats, 60 percent of the seats in Parliament with only 41.3 percent of the popular vote.[10] The system also benefits parties with a regionally concentrated vote. In this fashion, the Bloc, which contested seats only in Quebec, won 54 seats or 18.3 percent of the total seats with what constituted only 13.5 percent of Canada's popular vote. For its part, Reform won 17.6 percent of the seats with 18.7 percent of the vote, but its voter support in Ontario, with 20.1 percent of the vote, generated only 1 seat. In Alberta and British Columbia, however, Reform was able to translate 9 percent of Canada's popular vote into 16 percent of the parliamentary seats. Finally, the system penalizes nondominant parties that receive their support more or less evenly across the country. Apart from the victorious Liberals, the Conservatives were the only party to receive at least moderate support across the country. The Conservatives won less than 1 percent of the seats despite winning 16 percent of the vote, with a provincial vote share ranging from 11.3 percent to around 26 percent in each of the Atlantic provinces. The success of Reform may have cost the Conservatives their regional stronghold in the west, where for years Conservatives could count on receiving at least a solid block of seats. If this is true, then the electoral system may finish the job of eliminating the Conservatives, which began with the 1993 election. It will do this by making support for the Conservatives unlikely to produce seats. This will encourage voters on the Right of the political spectrum to concentrate their support on the Reform Party, where the prospects for winning seats are much brighter.

One institutional feature of the Canadian political system, however, may work toward keeping the Conservative Party alive and contending for office. Canada has a federal system of government and it is quite possible for a political party to continue as a viable entity in one or more provinces even though it is weak in national politics. In Canadian party politics, the Reform and the Conservative Parties are largely competing for the same constituency in national elections. However, Reform remains only a national party and, as of Reform's October 1994 convention, this concentration on national politics will continue. This means that there will be no official Reform Parties in provincial politics in the near term and the Conservatives will have an opportunity to rebuild at the provincial level and hope that an attractive leader with national appeal emerges. Reform leader Preston Manning believes that if Reform were to try and mount provincial wings, the capacity of the party to win at the national level would be compromised.[11] However, if the Conservatives are able to rebuild at the provincial level, the reverse may be equally true. The Reform Party's preoccupation with national politics may allow a beaten opponent the opportunity to regroup and rebuild. There are presently three provinces with majority Conservative governments and one of these is Ontario, the most populous of Canada's provinces. It is not only the fact that Reform does not currently have a presence at the provincial level that makes this possibility of a Conservative Party rebirth a credible one. The party is also both built on a foundation of alienation in western Canada and tightly controlled by its leader. It appears that Manning is attempting to moderate the appeal of Reform in order to increase its appeal in Ontario. Whether he will be able to reach this goal without alienating his supporters in the west remains to be seen. The fact that Reform's level of support in the public opinion polls began to slip in the first year after the 1993 election suggests that the transition from protest party to established national party may not be all that easy to achieve.

Tactical and Strategic Factors in the Demise of the Conservatives

The fate of a political party can also be influenced by tactical and strategic factors. In June 1993, the Conservatives chose a new leader to replace Mulroney. Both the choice of the leader to replace Mulroney and the strategy adopted in the subsequent election were factors that contributed to the Conservative defeat.

There were two main candidates in the June leadership convention that chose Kim Campbell. While both were relatively young and fresh faces in national politics, the one chosen was the one with the least experience. Campbell was relatively new to national politics, having been first elected in 1988. However, many among the party leaders felt that she was the appropriate choice for the 1990s. She had two factors in her favor: her gender (she became Canada's first female prime minister) and her reputation as an intellectual, having taught part-time at the University of British Columbia. She promised that her government would practice "new politics," but what this meant was left unclear. The choice of Campbell was, in retrospect, to be combined with an electoral strategy that showcased the new prime minister as a fresh and dynamic political leader and one who marked a sharp change from the previous Mulroney administration, which had become extremely unpopular. Little attention was paid to the policies that would be part of the "new politics." The lack of policy preparation and content for the campaign eventually undermined her image as an intellectual during the election. Further, her lack of political experience became a great liability. However, during the summer months leading up to the fall election, this strategy seemed to be working as Campbell was leading all her competitors in the public opinion polls at the time the election was called, except the leader of the Bloc in Quebec. It seemed possible that the dark cloud that Mulroney represented might be lifted.

Nevertheless, the electoral campaign was a disaster for the Conservatives from the beginning. At her first press conference, the prime minister commented that she did not expect any reduction in unemployment before the year 2000. The fact that she did not seem to be overly disturbed by this situation, when the opposition Liberals were focusing on the need to create jobs, generated a storm of criticism of the new Conservative leader in the media. It also suggested that the "new politics" were not so new after all.

Campbell was unwilling to explain how her government would reduce the deficit over five years, although this claim was a major part of the Conservative platform that was quickly put together in mid-campaign. She claimed that she was unable to discuss social policy issues during an electoral campaign because such discussions were inappropriate in an electoral setting. In general, she appeared poorly informed and unprepared to be challenged by her critics. Her campaign was also not well coordinated. Well into the campaign, when Conservative support was dropping in the polls, one of the party's leading organizers released several television advertisements directed at the facial disabilities of the Liberal leader Jean Chretien. The ads focused on the partial paralysis of one side of Chretien's face and asked the voters in effect whether this man would make a suitable prime minister. The public reaction to these negative advertisements was swift and scathing from both supporters and opponents of the Conservative Party; the ads were quickly withdrawn. These are but a few of the many gaffes that marred the electoral campaign from the start. The fact that the Conservatives raised and spent more money on the campaign than any other party in Canadian history and still suffered an ignominious defeat is a reminder that there are limitations to what money can buy in a democracy.

How does one pull together the cumulative impact of all these factors in attempting an overall assessment of the decline and future of the Conservative Party? The issues that we discussed under the grouping of structural and cultural explanations were all of a fundamental nature, proposing a substantial redefinition of Canada. The constitutional accords would have significantly changed Canada's political institutions, and the FTA was viewed by opponents as leading to ever closer economic and eventually political integration with the United States. These policy proposals aroused deep divisions in Canadian society, especially those concerning region and ethnicity. With the rise of the Bloc and the September 1994 election of the Parti Quebecois in Quebec—both parties committed to breaking up the Canadian federation—the issue of independence for Quebec must now be squarely faced. The Conservatives under Mulroney were held largely responsible for these developments. Any government suffering electoral defeat has likely pursued a number of highly unpopular policies. These three policies were more than just unpopular. They proposed to, and actually did, change Canada forever. They changed the institutions and their capabilities and, in the process, the culture of the country by giving political weight to new groups and weakening the positions of other groups. While it would have been a near miracle if the Conservatives had made a good showing, there was no expectation of the rout that took place.

The structural and cultural factors generated the electoral weakness of the Conservatives. The political institutions helped to exaggerate them and make them more serious. The electoral system in particular translated the 16 percent of the popular vote won by the Conservatives to less than 1 percent of the seats. The sharp decline of the Conservative Party was made even more impressive in the process. The fact that the Conservatives lost their main regional stronghold of Alberta and British Columbia to the Reform Party makes this defeat that much more serious. The Reform Party largely shares the same constituency as the Conservatives and the electoral system will tend to over-reward Reform as a regional party as long as it continues to play that role. If the Conservatives have lost their regional stronghold in the west, the relatively even but modest representation of the party in the rest of the country may result in very few seats in the House of Commons. If this scenario is correct, a revival of the Conservative Party may not come quickly, if at all.

Another feature of Canada's political institutions may save the Conservatives from this fate in the long run. This is the federal system of government. The Conservatives may yet revive as a strong party through success in provincial politics. This possibility continues to exist because the Reform Party has decided not to contest provincial elections for fear of dividing its resources too thinly. Given Canada's large debt and deficit, the fiscally conservative position of the Conservatives has good potential for renewed popularity at the provincial level. If Reform has difficulty transforming itself from a regional to a national party, with significant support across the country, and if the Conservatives can produce an attractive national leadership candidate, its current state of decline may be reversed.

An alternate scenario might see the national Reform Party go into coalition with some or all of the provincial Conservative Parties, especially the Alberta- and Ontario-based parties. In 1942, the former Liberal-Conservative Party became the Progressive Conservative Party at an earlier time of great electoral weakness. Its new leader, in 1942, was the Liberal-Progressive Party leader from the province of Manitoba. It is possible that some variation on those events of the 1940s may be played out in the 1990s. Thus, one might speculate that a future Reform-Conservative Party may emerge, combining in some manner the national Reform Party with some or all of the provincial Conservative Parties. In this way, the Conservative Party presence would be maintained while the Reform Party national leadership could abandon its provincial ambitions and become the national organization of a renewed party.

Relevance of the Canadian Experience for the United States

What relevance does the recent demise of the Conservatives have for understanding U.S. political parties and elections? Canada has a different set of political institutions from the United States and, as we have argued in this chapter, these institutions have an appreciable impact on party behavior and fortunes. In this final section, I will argue that institutional differences between the two countries, which otherwise share so much in common do not make the experience of the Conservatives in Canada overly relevant to the U.S. situation. While the Democrats suffered a severe setback in the 1994 midterm congressional elections, the political institutions cushioned that impact by affecting the reelection prospects of only one-third of the senators and sparing the president at least until 1996. The fact that political institutions can, on their own, have an important and independent impact on the party system is an important reminder.

Canada and the United States have more in common than almost any other two countries. They were both settled by Europeans and, apart from most Quebecois, speak a common language. Social movements, new ideas, and social changes have always flown easily (and continue to do so) across the long and undefended border between the two countries. While there appears to be more ideological diversity in Canada compared to the United States, neither country has experienced much in the way of class voting. The electorates in both countries have been expressing considerable disenchantment with politicians, and each country faces serious problems with their annual deficits and their accumulated total debt, although the problem is more severe in Canada. While the United States has not faced the kind of constitutional acrimony that Canada has had to confront in the Quebec crisis, each country is facing serious changes in the composition of its economy and workforce, as international trade and investment are liberalized. Canadians and Americans both share a common unease about the future. Yet, despite these commonalities, differences in political institutions make it unlikely that a defeat such as that suffered by the Democrats in 1994 threatens the political future of the Democratic Party. It only poses a threat to the party as it is presently constituted.

Electoral Behavior

A concept that has historically received a great deal of attention in U.S. voting literature is partisan identification. This concept is also used in studying voting patterns in other countries, but its significance is not always as great. While Canadian voters do identify with political parties, their commitment tends to be weaker and more readily subject to change. There is a tendency for partisanship to change comparatively easily in Canada and to do so over short periods of time.[12] In the United States, the realignment thesis of voting and party behavior suggests that when change occurs, it sustains itself for some time. The existence of a weaker partisanship in Canada suggests that the possibility of the revival of a party is greater in Canada than in the United States. Further, the pattern of supporting different parties at the national and provincial levels, which is less common in the United States than in Canada, may allow a Canadian party a better opportunity to regroup and return to the electoral battle.

Another feature of U.S. elections that differentiates them from those in Canada is that all voters get to vote for their national leader, the president. This means that voters can express their displeasure with the president while continuing to support local candidates from the president's party. In Canada this is not possible. In the parliamentary system all candidates, including the prime minister, are elected only in their constituency. Consider the case of a voter who is disenchanted with the prime minister and lives in a constituency where the elected MP, whom he/she favors, is of the same party as the prime minister. This voter is faced with the choice of voting against the favored local member in order to try and defeat the prime minister and his/her party or to help reelect the disliked prime minister by voting for the favored local member. This ballot rigidity may help explain some of the sudden shifts in party support and partisan identification in Canada as compared to the United States. These differences suggest that the recent dramatic shifts in party fortunes in Canada are not likely to be replicated in the United States. U.S. institutional factors permit a voter to differentiate more precisely between individual candidates and the party itself by separating each choice. However, if such change were to occur in the United States, it would likely be more conclusive than in Canada because the party identification of voters is more durable. As a result, there would be less likelihood that the party's fortunes could be reversed.

Party System

The political parties in both countries have been regarded as brokerage-type parties, attempting to pragmatically bring together a range of interests in order to create a winning coalition. In neither country are political parties good policy-making vehicles, and the mandates of parties after an election are difficult to determine. In both countries, class voting is relatively unimportant (even less so in Canada) and regional influences have been important. Yet there are important structural differences between parties in the two countries. It is probably safe to say, however, that U.S. political parties are more permeable to outside groups than their Canadian counterparts. It is more likely that disgruntled voters in the United States will seek to infiltrate and transform one of the existing parties rather than attempt to set up a new party. This reality has been reflected in the realignment thesis about adaptation over time within the U.S. party system. It is also apparent in the loose structure of U.S. political parties. The recent success of religious groups in taking control over parts of the Republican Party is a reflection of this process. In Canada, in contrast, political parties are more centrally controlled. The political leader has more control over the party organization, and new or disgruntled groups have less room to take over and dominate parts of the organization. Canadian political parties seem less open to ideological transformation as a result of the influence of new members or outsiders than U.S. parties. At the same time, this greater central control on the part of Canadian party leaders may make it easier for them to change the policy direction of their party if they feel it is necessary. Nevertheless, Canadian political parties are more politically autonomous than their U.S. counterparts.

A second institutional feature of U.S. party politics that makes the Canadian experience less relevant is the combined impact of only one-third of all senators being up for election every two years and of the President being directly elected only every four years. This means that U.S. parties are somewhat less exposed at each election than their Canadian counterparts. If a Canadian party faces a hostile electorate, the results can wipe it out. In the U.S. setting, a disaffected electorate will only directly affect some of a party's representatives, especially in an off-year congressional election. This gives the party time to adapt to the new environment.

These are only some of the institutional differences between Canada and the United States. The overall point, however, is that despite the close social, economic, and political interdependence of the two countries and the many demographic similarities of their populations, the differences in their political institutions are significant. The experience of the Conservatives in Canada is not particularly relevant for U.S. party politics.

Conclusion

This chapter has asserted that there are some good reasons to believe that the recent collapse of the Conservative Party in Canada will be permanent. This would constitute a major transformation of Canada's party system since the Conservative Party has been one of Canada's two major political parties since the founding of the country in 1867. At the same time, it has been argued that Canada's federal system and the strategy of the Reform Party may provide the Conservatives with an opportunity to rebound. The federal structure will provide the Conservatives with opportunities to succeed in provincial elections and the decision of the Reform Party not to contest elections at the provincial level will leave open to Conservative strategists the issues associated with fiscal restraint, an agenda that is in ascent in Canada. Finally, it was argued that the Conservative experience in Canada was not overly relevant for the U.S. scene because of the greater fluidity of Canadian voting behavior and differences in the structure of political parties in the two countries.

Notes

1. William R. Brock, *Conflict and Transformation: The United States, 1844–1877* (New York: Penguin Books, 1973), pp. 121–169.

2. Samuel H. Barnes, "Italy: Oppositions on Left, Right and Centre," in *Political Oppositions in Western Democracies,* ed. Robert H. Dahl, pp. 303–331 (New Haven: Yale University Press, 1966); F. Roy Willis, *Italy Chooses Europe* (New York: Oxford University Press, 1971); and Adrian Lyttleton, "Italy: The Triumph of TV," *New York Review of Books* 41, no. 14 (1994): 25–29.

3. R. K. Webb, *Modern England* (New York: Dodd, Mead and Company, 1970) and Giovanni Sartori, *Parties and Party Systems: A Framework for Analysis* (Cambridge: Cambridge University Press, 1976), pp. 190–191.

4. Keith Archer and Faron Ellis, "Opinion Structure of Party Activists: The Reform Party of Canada," *Canadian Journal of Political Science* 27, no. 2 (1994): 277–308.

5. Douglas Rae, *The Political Consequences of Electoral Laws* (New Haven: Yale University Press, 1967).

6. Alan C. Cairns, "The Governments and Societies of Canadian Federalism," *Canadian Journal of Political Science* 10, no. 4 (1977): 695–725.

7. H. D. Clark, J. Jenson, L. LeDuc, and J. H. Pammett, *Absent Mandate: Interpreting Change in Canadian Elections* (Toronto: Gage, 1991), pp. 46–49.

8. Robert M. Campbell and Leslie A. Pal, *The Real Worlds of Canadian Politics* (Peterborough, Ontario: Broadview Press, 1988).

9. Archer and Ellis, "Opinion Structure"; D. Laycock, "Reforming Canadian Democracy? Institutions and Ideology in the Reform Party Project," *Canadian Journal of Political Science* 27, no. 2 (1994): 213–247.

10. Canada, *Official Voting Results: Thirty-fifth General Election, 1993* (Ottawa: Elections Canada, 1993).

11. Archer and Ellis, "Opinion Structure," and Laycock, "Reforming Canadian Democracy?"

12. Clarke, Jenson, LeDuc, and Pammett, *Absent Mandate,* pp. 47–151.

2

PUBLIC POLICY AND ELECTIONS

The Republican Party clearly set the agenda in the 1994 election, and their ideas will likely set the agenda in the near future. The Democratic Party desperately needs an equivalent to the "Contract with America," which sets out its proscriptions for the future. This conclusion is advanced by analysts associated with both major parties and reflects important changes that have occurred in U.S. political life. No longer is there a bifurcation between national and subnational elections; the Republican sweep in 1994 indicated this. Indeed, even before that election, Republican victories in such unlikely races as the New York and Los Angeles mayoralty campaigns were construed in national terms—even though the Republican victors stood far to the Left of their party's mainstream.

One clear result of this linkage is that voters increasingly see connections between policies at the national level and those at lower levels. For example, public assistance is increasingly seen as a linked issue. Similarly, the entire gamut of traditionally local issues such as illegal drugs, quality of education, crime, and so on, are viewed as linked issues. Even a typically local problem such as spousal abuse is now seen as linked. But linking the two levels does not imply that voters prefer a solution based on the concept of cooperative federalism in which federal, state, and local public officials participate in attempting to achieve solutions. One of the contentions in post-1994 U.S. politics will be which level of government is best equipped to deal with a particular set of issues. The Republicans have clearly moved in the direction of sending the issues back to the states. Whether the Democrats will develop a coherent pattern in this respect remains to be seen.

Pre-1994 politics is also challenged by other recent developments that will influence elections and public policy in the future. The most important of these stems from the dramatic international events that occurred during the Bush administration. The fall of the Berlin Wall and the collapse of the Soviet Union not only brought disrepute to the ideology of communism but raised the fundamental issue of what governments should do. Public policies today are designed with a bigger role for private markets and voluntary arrangements than they were in the past. Most Americans feel that there is a role for government, but they increasingly must be shown that it is necessary in each specific issue that reaches the public agenda.

In these ways and others that are discussed in the essays in this section, the connections between elections and public policy will be different in post-1994 United States than they were in the past.

2.1

Busted

Government and Elections in the Era of Deficit Politics

Daniel Wirls

It was awkward to follow Reagan and claim success. We couldn't say we'd be cleaning up the Reagan mess. We would just have to do it without talking about it.
—Aide to President George Bush; quoted in Michael Duffy
and Dan Goodgame, *Marching in Place:*
The Status Quo Presidency of George Bush

Nobody knows we have any spending cuts. . . . We've got the worst of all worlds. We've gotten all this deficit reduction. We've made all the hard painful choices, and nobody even noticed.
—President Bill Clinton; quoted in Bob Woodward,
The Agenda: Inside the Clinton White House

Elections matter insofar as they can lead to significant change. Sometimes, however, the consequences of electorally driven policy change then render subsequent elections less meaningful. We are living through such an era— the era of deficit government. The elections of 1980 brought on the Reagan revolution, which in turn produced dramatic and durable budgetary consequences. From a broad perspective, the fiscal vise created by those budgetary consequences made the elections of 1988 and 1992, nearly inconsequential. Despite their differences, the Bush and Clinton presidencies fell victim to the politics created by deficit government. This essay examines the nature and consequences of the era of deficit government, which began, roughly, with Reagan's second term and the passage of the Gramm-Rudman Act. Despite the congressional realignment in 1994, the effects of deficit government will constrain governmental action (even some of the Republican version) for years to come. The politics of retrenchment differ conspicuously from the politics of growth that characterized most of the postwar period. We are in the middle of a governmental transformation unlike any in the postwar era, a transformation driven, to a significant extent, by the deficit and debt and the politics they helped to create.

The New Era in U.S. Politics

Since Ronald Reagan's election in 1980, various attempts have been made to characterize what seems to be a new era in U.S. politics. The New Deal era was ending and something else was emerging, with the timing and scope of the change depending on the characteristic one concentrated on. Most descriptions focused on electoral behavior and derived from the theory of partisan realignment in U.S. politics. The elections of 1980 prompted some to conclude that a Republican and conservative realignment was finally in the making. With the persistence of Democratic control of the Congress, and the apparent failures of the Reagan administration, many scholars returned to the idea that we remained stuck in an era of dealignment.[1] Concern mounted that the concept of realignment had lost its utility.[2] We had entered an era of coalition government or even postelectoral politics.[3] The election of George Bush prompted many to adopt a new description: an era of divided government.[4] A consequence of manifold trends in U.S. politics, divided government, as a description, avoided the expectations and problems inherent in realignment theory and put more attention on governmental consequences.

A different characterization, implicit in much of the discussion of U.S. politics since 1980 but never explicitly stated, is more policy oriented. This is the era of deficit government.[5] The dominance of party and electorally oriented descriptions clouded this way of looking at the last decade, even though we refer to the previous era as the New Deal era. Perhaps that is precisely the point. The New Deal era was arguably characterized less by consistency in voting behavior than by the dominant focus of governmental policy—the twin revolutions of the welfare and warfare states. And if the New Deal is being replaced by something, then it might be worth noting that so far it is characterized less by a regular pattern of voting behavior than by a trend in public policy or, to be more precise, the politics of public policy. Just as the New Deal was followed by World War II, the fall of the New Deal domestic system under Reagan was soon followed by the demise of the Cold War system under Bush. In their wake has come an era dominated by red ink and retrenchment. The politics of growth has been replaced by the politics of contraction.

In the long run, we may look back and see a Republican realignment (if the 1994 Republican congressional takeover is followed in 1996 by a presidential victory). For now, I would argue, the budgetary tail is wagging the dogs of policy and politics. While certainly not the only significant force at work, the twin engines of the deficit and the debt are driving key elements of national politics. Though their origins may be linked to relative economic decline, dealignment, increased conservatism, and divided government, they have become causes in and of themselves. As a result, they have helped to create a whole package of post-Reagan characteristics of the U.S. political landscape: the real and perceived fiscal crisis in government, the resulting negative-sum effect on political choices, and the bleak public mood about government and the U.S. future. The debt and deficit dominated both the Bush and (at least the first two years of) the Clinton administrations. And should the Republicans complete a realignment, they will in large measure owe their success as much to the deficit politics that they, under Reagan, helped to create and then benefited from as to any other source of ideas, frustrations, and social change. It took a world depression and war to inspire and institutionalize the New Deal era. This time around, it is the fiscal crisis of the state—a crisis of governance itself, not the economy or world strife—that is helping to forge a new regime to replace the old one.

The Reagan Legacy and the Onset of Deficit Government

Though various fiscal and budgetary pressures had been increasing for several years at the level of the national budget, the sea change began with the so-called Reagan revolution and its budgetary consequences. At the core of the Reagan revolution was the most significant alteration of governmental programs and priorities since the New Deal and World War II. Reagan seized on widespread discontent with the economy, waste in governmental programs, and taxes to effect a reversal of much of the mathematics of the Democratic welfare state that had dominated the federal budget.

The budgetary revolution of the Reagan era was a combination of large tax cuts, a massive defense buildup, and reductions in domestic spending. The only way the budgetary equation could stay in balance, however, was for the domestic cuts to be large enough to offset both the defense increases and the tax revenue losses. But the combination of the largest tax cuts in the country's history and the largest peacetime defense spending increases could not be offset by cuts in domestic spending. Reagan did not even propose cuts sufficient to prevent a growing deficit. Though Reagan blamed Congress for the deficit, Congress gave the president much of what he wanted. Congress may have refused to make some domestic cuts Reagan requested, but the Democrats also cut defense spending as compensation. After fiscal year 1982—Reagan's first complete budget period—Congress decreased his military spending requests every year. From fiscal year 1982 through 1985, Congress trimmed over $69 billion, or an average of $17 billion for each of the four years. Moreover, Congress compelled President Reagan to agree to several tax increases to offset some of the revenue losses from the 1981 cuts. The budgetary contradictions were built into the Reagan revolution.[6]

Despite congressional resistance, Reagan engineered a dramatic revision of the federal budget. Discretionary domestic programs fell from 4.9 percent of gross domestic product (GDP) in 1981 to 3.3 percent by 1987. In the same period, defense spending rose from 5.1 to 6.3 percent. In budgetary terms, this change was more striking. From 1981 to 1987, discretionary spending on domestic programs decreased by 19 percent, while defense outlays increased by 50 percent, adjusted for inflation. Despite several tax increases, especially those in 1982, 1983, and 1984, which slowed the revenue losses, taxes decreased from 20.2 percent of GDP to 18.2 percent from 1981 through 1986. The only major tax that rose in real terms was the regressive Social Security tax. Meanwhile, federal spending continued to increase in real terms.[7]

As a result of the growing gap between revenues and spending, the budget deficit skyrocketed, the debt exploded, and interest payments on the debt became the fastest growing expenditure. In this way, the era of deficit government began with Reagan's second term and was marked by these three interrelated developments as well as by the passage of the Gramm-Rudman Act (see below). First, the annual budget deficit more than doubled in real terms in three years, leaping from $78.9 billion in 1981 to $127.9 billion in 1982 and $207.8 billion in 1983, and showed no signs of slowing down by 1985. Even adjusted for inflation, the difference between the deficits of the 1980s and earlier decades is still astounding (Figure 1). Second, the explosion of deficits doubled the total federal debt by 1986 (from $1,003.9 billion in 1981 to $2,130 billion in 1986). By this time, the debt was approaching 50 percent of GDP for the first time since 1964, when the debt was in the middle of its long-term decline as a percentage of the economy to a low of 33 to 34 percent in 1980 and 1981 (Figure 2). Finally, interest payments on the debt, which increased from $52.5 billion in 1980 to $136 billion by 1986, became the fastest growing governmental expendi-

Figure 1. **Deficits by the Decade** (per year average in constant dollars)

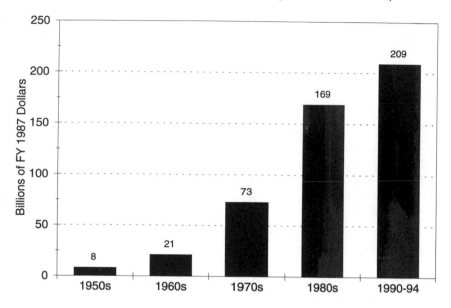

Figure 2. **Growth of the Debt** (in dollars and as percentage of GDP)

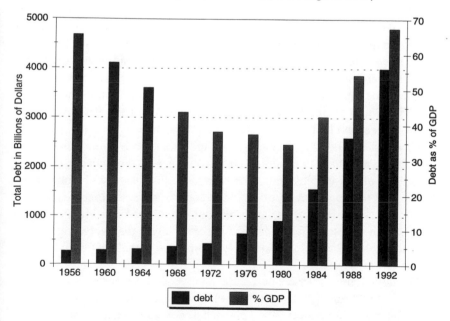

Figure 3. **Five Largest Budget Outlays, 1980 and 1990**

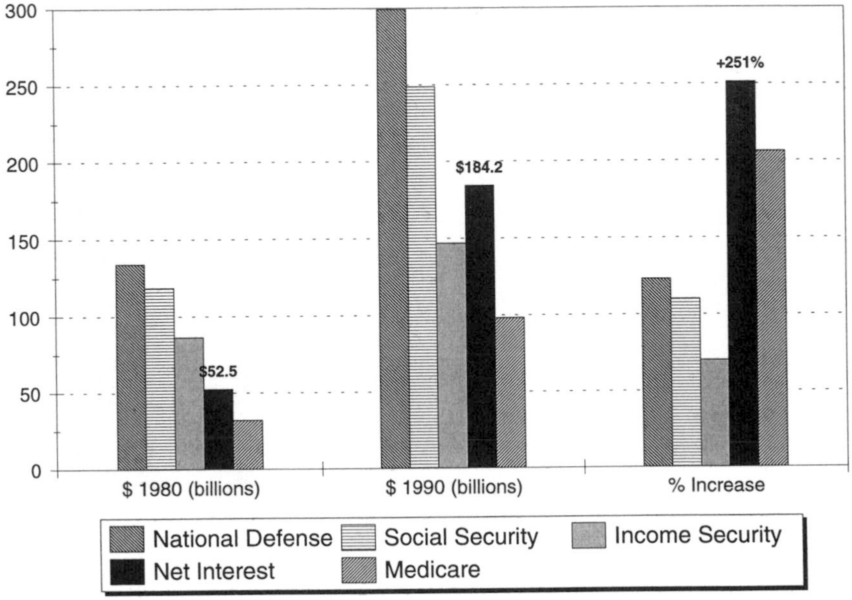

ture, on their way to nearly doubling as a percentage of federal spending and becoming the third largest outlay in the national budget (Figure 3).

The 1980s represented a clear departure from earlier periods of governmental red ink. Prior to the 1970s, deficits were largely cyclical, meaning they were the product of economic slumps and war. When times were bad, governmental revenues fell; good times often produced surpluses. Likewise, deficits from war rose and fell. World War II produced a mountain of deficit spending, but it disappeared soon after the war's end. The Korean and Vietnam Wars produced much smaller deficits in the first half of the 1950s and second half of the 1960s. The 1970s showed the first signs of a persistent structural deficit, that is, a deficit produced by a systematic gap between revenues and expenditures that would not be eliminated even under conditions of full employment. The change became starkly obvious in the 1980s with the combination of record peacetime deficits coincidental with sustained economic growth. The structural deficit was now the governing factor. Even after the effects of inflation are removed, the twelve years from 1982 through 1993 produced eleven of the twelve highest deficits since the end of World War II.

The deficit and debt were becoming major public concerns by the end of Reagan's first term. The fiscal crisis was a vulnerability for Reagan and the Republicans as November 1984 approached and a formidable constraint on the possible responses by the Democratic Party. The interrelationship of the three (deficit, debt, and interest payments) created a fiscal vise on governmental action that tightened as the decade wore on. Foreign policy, including Iran-Contra and the new relationship with the Soviet Union, dampened the political importance of the deficit and the effects of deficit politics. Nevertheless, struggles over the budget, with the deficit always the crux of the issue, dominated congressional politics in these years.

Nothing demonstrates this better than the Gramm-Rudman Act of 1985, which sought to redirect the budget process toward the single goal of deficit reduction and to mandate and enforce step-by-step progress toward a balanced budget. No law, especially its failure, better characterizes the onset and nature of deficit government. "A bad idea whose time has come" was how Senator Warren Rudman characterized the law he helped to create.[8] He might have added that its time came on rather quickly. The Gramm-Rudman Act (officially, the Balanced Budget and Emergency Deficit Control Act of 1985) was a swiftly conceived and hastily considered measure. As finally passed, it mandated annual $36-billion-dollar reductions in the deficit until the budget was balanced in six years. The most controversial aspect was the enforcement provision, which gave the comptroller general the power to order the cuts if Congress failed to do so. It was, as Senator Robert Byrd put it, a "hybrid item veto and a constitutional amendment to balance the budget, combined."[9] It was never considered as a separate bill; it never went through standard committee hearings. Instead, it was offered in the Senate as an amendment to legislation to raise the debt ceiling. The bulk of congressional deliberation took place during two House-Senate conferences on the debt ceiling bill, in an atmosphere of fiscal crisis.

What motivated such extraordinary legislation and procedures was the need to pass a debt ceiling extension that would allow the debt to exceed the $2 trillion mark, double what it was when Reagan was elected less than five years earlier. The explosion of the deficit and the debt had Congress thinking about the potential for economic and political fallout. In particular, Senate Republicans did not want to sign the debt ceiling extension without any action to show they were doing something about the deficit. In this way, the must-pass debt extension was used as a vehicle to insure that the Gramm-Rudman bill would be voted on. It also insured that it would not be subject to the kind of scrutiny and debate such portentous legislation typically receives. Despite some resistance from House Democrats, and despite protracted conference negotiations, Gramm-Rudman ultimately passed both chambers by overwhelming margins.

Ultimately, the Gramm-Rudman Act never worked. After the Supreme Court voided the key enforcement provision, Congress revised the law. But the revision failed as well. The six years from 1986 through 1991, during which Gramm-Rudman mandated a decline from $180 billion to a balanced budget, saw instead an average deficit of $195 billion, ending with a new record high in 1991 of nearly $270 billion. By this time, the debt had hit $3.5 trillion.

Regardless of its ultimate failure, both constitutionally and politically, the origins and passage of the Gramm-Rudman Act signaled the arrival of deficit government. From that time onward, Congress and the president more often than not were consumed by the budgetary predicament. The nation had turned a corner and was heading in a different direction.

The First Victim: Bush and the Reagan Legacy

Bush may have never gotten the "vision thing" down. He certainly lacked Reagan's passion. Maybe he did just want to be president. But the critique of the Bush presidency based on personality and ideology misses the larger point. While the immediate successors to regime-builders usually suffer politically, Bush, more than any of his "faithful son" presidential ancestors, was hamstrung by the legacy of his predecessor.[10] Bush had to obscure or clean up the "Reagan mess" referred to in the quotation at the beginning of this essay. Though it included such things as the Savings and Loan industry bailout, the core of the Reagan mess was, of course, the budgetary crisis of deficits and debt.

Bush was between a rock and a hard place. The country was weary of the Reagan revolution and its consequences and seemed to be swinging back toward expectations of governmental action in certain areas, including the environment and education. But the deficit overwhelmed everything else. More tax cuts were impossible. The discretionary budget had been slashed repeatedly. The defense budget was decreasing steadily. Only entitlements, a politically intractable issue, loomed large as an object of reform and source of revenue. As a result, Bush had precious little room to maneuver, even if he had mastered the vision thing. (As we shall see, Clinton was a master of the vision thing and look how far it got him.)

Bush contributed to his personal leadership dilemma before it had even officially begun by asking Congress and America, during his nomination acceptance speech, to read his lips: "no new taxes." Not only that, Bush promised no cuts in core entitlement programs. The "read my lips" vow was, as we learned later, the subject of heated debate among his advisers because, even then, they knew he probably could not hold to such a commitment. The election might demand this sort of grandstanding, but after the election the budgetary and political realities would require some sort of tax increase. It was, some felt, only a matter of time, a matter of how long the inevitable could be postponed.[11]

The inevitable was delayed until about eighteen months into Bush's administration. By this time, the 1990 budget was turning a deep shade of red, heading for a new record of $221 billion, after three years at the relatively manageable level of $150 billion. Everyone knew that the initial rosy projections for the 1991 budget, then being debated in Congress, were hogwash. The faltering economy was taking care of that. Something had to be done. Democrats would not agree to a package of spending cuts alone, and Bush was not willing to propose cuts deep enough to make a serious dent in the problem. Tax increases were both politically and fiscally necessary. The president would have to compromise. The protracted and contentious negotiations between the White House and the Democratic congressional leadership eventually produced a budget agreement in late 1990, which sought to reduce the deficit through a combination of tax increases and program cuts. Despite (or because of) the fact that the relatively rich bore the brunt of the new tax burden, this became the single greatest mistake and regret of the Bush administration. In the weeks before the 1990 elections the deficit and debt made significant headway against what had been the dominant issue of the late summer and early fall—the Persian Gulf crisis following Iraq's invasion of Kuwait. Following the desperate and messy budget negotiations between Congress and the president, the deficit pulled nearly even with the Persian Gulf crisis as the most important problem, ahead of the economy, drugs, spending, and taxes.[12]

Though voters failed to throw the congressional bums out that November in what had been billed as the "Year of the Angry Voter," discontent grew, especially with the worsening economy, as the 1992 presidential campaign approached. Voters were angry about governmental performance in general, and the deficit was the symbol, if not the substance, of these frustrations. Though the economy would become the major issue, the capitulation or deception on taxes stuck around like nothing else that was under Bush's control. The Persian Gulf War triumph faded into relative insignificance next to the tax betrayal.

When recession set in, the deficit tightly constrained options at Bush's disposal, including any possible stimulus package. Instead, the White House and Congress had to rely on the Federal Reserve for any help with the recession by easing up on interest rates. But even the Federal Reserve's efforts were hampered by the effect of the deficit on long-term interest rates, which stayed stubbornly higher than anticipated in spite of the Fed's twenty-three cuts in short-term rates between mid-1989 and mid-1992. As a result, a fiscal stimulus could not be mustered and a monetary stimulus was dampened by the deficit.[13]

The recession was probably the downfall of the Bush presidency. Throughout 1992, the economy always ranked first in public opinion polls as the most important issue facing the country, but the debt and deficit were a close second and were factors, as we have seen, in the impact of the recession as a political issue. Though difficult to measure in its impact on votes, Bush's broken promise on taxes alienated well-to-do supporters who were not so adversely affected by the recession. More importantly, H. Ross Perot made the debt and deficit the cornerstone of his presidential campaign and offered these disaffected Bush voters an alternative. While candidate Bill Clinton also had to talk about the deficit and debt, his campaign centered on the economy. In fact, the most famous catch phrase to emerge from the race came from James Carville, one of the political architects of Clinton's campaign, who hung a sign in the Arkansas campaign headquarters to remind everyone not to get diverted from the core issue: It's "the economy, stupid."[14] Clinton's campaign largely succeeded in sticking to that message and making it stick with the American people. Clinton would learn once he got to Washington, however, that it isn't the economy; it's the deficit, stupid.

The Characteristics and Consequences of Deficit Government

President Bush lived the consequences of deficit government; President-elect Clinton was about to. On the eve of Clinton's inauguration, the nature of the U.S. government had been altered significantly. The politics of deficit government had become the unspoken law of the land. The fiscal vise had been turned so tightly for long enough that the discomfort and pain were taken for granted. Zero-sum politics and budgeting had been supplanted by negative-sum politics and budgeting. The political and fiscal problems entailed by the debt, deficit, and interest burden were so prominent and persistent that they were changing characteristics of government and politics in several areas, from institutions and procedures to public opinion and trust. What had been in part caused by underlying socioeconomic trends and political choices was now a cause in and of itself, shaping politics and producing significant consequences for the U.S. government.

The Deficit as One of the Most Important National Problems

A signal event in the onset of deficit government was the appearance of the deficit and debt in public opinion surveys as one of the leading problems facing the nation. Prior to the mid-1980s, surveys did not even include the deficit and debt as an independent response to the typical question, "What do you think is the most important problem facing the nation?" If any surveys did include it, it did not appear in the results because so few of those surveyed chose it. The only choice that came close was "excessive governmental spending," which was clearly intended to measure the more Reaganesque sentiment that government was spending too much in general on programs, rather than to measure concrete concerns about the debt and deficit. When the structural deficit began to emerge as a problem, the choice, at least in Gallup polls, was modified to "excessive governmental spending/the deficit." This confusion of two related but different issues was resolved by pollsters in 1985 and 1986, when the debt and deficit were finally recognized as a separate problem and source of public concern. Excessive spending was no longer the appropriate label—the debt and deficit in and of themselves were problems.

Once surveys began to include the debt and deficit as a response, especially from 1986 onward, they maintained a status that few other issues could match in scale and consistency. For example, in the polls from 1987 through 1994 done for the Times Mirror Center for the People and the Press, the debt and deficit (as a single response) was selected as the most important national problem by an average of 10.3 percent of respondents.[15] This was lower than only three others: drug and alcohol (13.9 percent), unemployment and jobs (13.6 percent), and the economy in general (12.6 percent). Both the economy and drugs varied substantially in the level of response, while the deficit, though never exploding to a peak as the others did during times of perceived or real crisis, maintained a more stubborn consistency.[16] Similarly, when asked about their top priorities for presidential action, respondents consistently placed reducing the deficit among the top two or three choices.[17] Here, in an unprecedented fashion, a problem of governance itself, rather than yet another social, economic, or geopolitical issue, was among the major national problems.

From Zero-Sum to Negative-Sum Politics

Public opinion about the importance of the deficit and debt put added pressure on Congress and the president to act. However much economists might disagree about the effect of deficits on the economy, politicians knew the debt and deficit were ruining government and damaging their public standing. Something had to be done. But the choices were difficult and painful.

Even prior to the era of deficit government, the budget had been the alpha and omega of Washington politics. The yearly struggle consumed

much of the energy on Capitol Hill, leaving little time to consider funda-
mentals—what programs to terminate, plans for innovative new programs,
and so forth. Deficit politics aggravated and transformed what was already a
nearly all-consuming process. It was hard enough to make choices and
trade-offs in the increasingly zero-sum world of the 1970s; the shift to
negative-sum budgeting—where any cuts, however painfully extracted,
shrank into insignificance when measured against the size of the problem—
made things that much more difficult.

As we have seen, the Gramm-Rudman Act of 1985 codified the negative-
sum budget and symbolized all its impact. Though a failure, the law indicated how far we had come in so little time and how far we were willing to
go (so far as to write unconstitutional procedures into law) to effect—or at
least to appear to be serious about—deficit reduction. The Gramm-Rudman
Act was replaced by the budget agreement of 1990, the one in which Bush
reneged on his "read my lips" pledge. In place of Gramm-Rudman's mandatory deficit reduction levels, the budget agreement produced a five-year deficit reduction package of tax hikes and spending cuts. But it also set in place
budgetary procedures that further restricted discretionary action, all in the
name of deficit reduction discipline and enforcement. The two principal
procedures were the budget caps on, and "fire walls" between, major discretionary spending categories—Pay-As-You-Go (PAYGO) requirements for
any changes in taxes and entitlements—and the automatic cuts by the Office
of Management and Budget (OMB) for any violations of the caps or
PAYGO rules. All this substantially circumscribed congressional discretion
in the budget process. Negative-sum budgeting had already made the choices
extremely tough to make. The 1990 agreement made sure there were fewer
options, less leeway in making the decisions. Some choices were simply
removed from the table; the remaining ones were politically painful, at best.

The Gramm-Rudman Act and the 1990 budget agreement were part of a
larger trend in policy making provoked by deficit government—procedural
government or government by commission. The budgetary crisis and the
politics of retrenchment compelled Congress, which is far better at sharing
the wealth than spreading the pain, to seek ways of shifting responsibility
for tough decisions to non-legislative entities. One of the first examples of
this was the Social Security Commission of 1983, which led to the tax
increase and a few minor adjustments supposedly necessary to salvage the
system. Perhaps the most successful and prominent example is the military
base closure law of 1988, which mandated that an independent commission
be the principal vehicle for producing lists of military bases to close or
realign. Congress could only vote up or down on the whole list, with no
amendments. Decisions too difficult for the legislative process were given

over to commissions to provide political cover and procedural shortcuts to reduce, once again, congressional discretion.[18]

The failure of procedural devices such as the Gramm-Rudman law and the 1990 agreement to reduce the deficit fueled support for the serious reconsideration of an old but rarely considered idea—a balanced budget amendment to the Constitution. Congress did not even look at such an amendment until 1936, after the New Deal had begun the first sustained period of deficit spending.[19] The proposal died in the House Judiciary Committee. A few other attempts were made in the 1940s and 1950s, but none went as far as a floor vote in either chamber. Not until the fiscal crisis of the 1980s produced enough congressional support did the balanced budget amendment get to the floor of Congress. The Republican Senate led the way in 1982 with a vote of 69–31, two more than necessary for such an amendment, but it fell well short of two-thirds in the House. By 1984, thirty-two states (two shy of two-thirds) had submitted calls for a constitutional convention to consider a balanced budget amendment. In 1986, the amendment fell one vote short in the Senate; the loss was attributed not only to a stronger Democratic minority but also to the passage of the Gramm-Rudman Act. Impetus shifted to the House in the 1990s, with two floor votes in 1990 and 1992 that came within seven and nine votes, respectively, of two-thirds. During the 103rd Congress, at least twenty-six balanced budget measures were introduced, and a version received strong support in both chambers but in each case just short of the requisite super-majority.

The elections of 1994 augured that a balanced budget could be one Senate filibuster away from being sent to the states. The amendment was the top priority of the House Republicans' "Contract with America," and the changes in the partisan and ideological makeup of both chambers indicated probable passage. In fact, the House did pass the amendment by a comfortable margin, but it fell one vote short in the Senate on its first try.[20] In effect, a balanced budget amendment would be an attempt to take what failed as ordinary legislation (Gramm-Rudman) and see if it works as higher law. Should the balanced budget amendment become part of the Constitution, it would be the ultimate consequence of deficit politics—the first substantive policy amendment to the Constitution since the income tax and probably the most disruptive and profound of them all in its immediate consequences on government and politics nationwide.

The Cynical Civic Culture

Just as deficit government is producing a de facto and possibly de jure constitutional transformation, it is likewise influencing the political attitudes that shape U.S. political culture. Though the assertion is difficult to prove, I would argue that the mounting cynicism of Americans toward their national government has been driven as much by the deficit and its consequences as by, for example, real perceptions of failures in the programs of the welfare state. That is, one can argue that the fiscal crisis and the deadlock it produced conveyed or confirmed an impression of government gone bad that then infected or aggravated sentiments about governmental activism and specific programs. If nothing else, and however simplistic, the average American could point to the debt and deficit as the concrete and undeniable measure of government's failure.

The interaction between deficit government and public opinion created a quandary for Congress and the president. At the same time that public opinion placed the debt and deficit among the most pressing national problems, the public also clamored for governmental action on pressing problems and opposed many specific areas for cuts (including Social Security, Medicare, the environment, education). To make matters worse, they wanted Congress to cut spending, rather than increase taxes, to lower the deficit.[21] In polls, for example, the overwhelming majority support for a balanced budget amendment dwindles rapidly when respondents are informed that a balanced budget would require deep cuts in particular programs.[22]

Politicians were faced with a dilemma. What did the majority really want? In the world of negative-sum politics, it was certainly impossible to successfully balance all the competing and contradictory preferences. These pressures facilitated the bipartisan cooperation in some budgeting legerdemain from the mid-1980s onward. For example, Congress at times resorted to smoke and mirrors to find "cuts" that would lower the deficit for that fiscal year by pushing the problem onto the next year. Politicians tried to square the circle; the press would report on the ugly process and its consequences; and the public would be outraged. Eventually the public realized that the deficit was not going down and perceived that it was business as usual in Washington (but the same public was also often asking for business as usual). In this way, the public's increase in cynicism during the 1980s and early 1990s can be linked to deficit politics and the dysfunctional relationship it set in motion among politicians, the media, and public opinion. Deficit politics had created a self-perpetuating civic cynicism.

As the 1992 election campaign got underway, there was no more stark and significant manifestation of that public cynicism and frustration than the independent candidacy and campaign of H. Ross Perot. Though obviously drawing on the general discontent of voters, Perot centered his campaign on what he and his supporters saw as the signal failures of government: the trebling of the debt and the inability to significantly reduce the deficit and balance the budget. The debt and deficit were the measure of government's failure and the threat to our future. They were also the starting point for fixing the economy.

Bill Clinton's triumph after twelve years of Republican presidents, however, briefly eclipsed the cynicism and the significance of Perot's unprecedented candidacy; it fostered illusions that Clinton had a significant mandate from the American people and that we could begin anew.

It's the Deficit, Stupid: Assessing the Clinton Presidency

Public expectations were high following the 1992 election. Though based perhaps more on hope than hard facts, optimism about the prospects for fruitful united government was widely shared. Twelve years of divided government, the level of partisan hostility, the lack of a clear mandate in the election, all tempered expectations among informed observers, but Clinton and the Democratic majority in Congress presaged, if nothing else, a respite from the last several years of political acrimony and frustrations.[23]

The optimism was rewarded by a productive first session of the 103rd Congress. Several bills that Bush had vetoed, including the one on family leave and the Brady gun control bill, were easily enacted. Despite difficulties, Clinton pushed through the bulk of his "economic plan." He then won a difficult fight to approve the North American Free Trade Agreement (NAFTA). Clinton's 1993 success rate on congressional votes (86.4 percent) nearly matched the best first-year presidential performances, which are Dwight Eisenhower's 89 percent in 1953 and Lyndon Johnson's 88 percent in 1964.[24] Within the administration, the move to "reinvent" government, led by Vice-President Al Gore, was implementing plans to reduce the federal workforce by over 250,000 positions.

But each victory seemed to be bracketed by problems or mistakes. The early legislative triumphs were at times overshadowed by the months-long imbroglio over gays in the military.[25] The economic plan, which had combined deficit reduction (a combination of spending cuts and tax increases) with economic investments, became all of the former and virtually none of the latter as a result of a protracted and bitter fight within and between the parties in Congress. Later, the initial triumph of the Clinton speech and agenda-setting in health care was quickly diminished, then completely dissipated as Congress struggled with the details. Ultimately, Congress failed to produce a health care bill and, at the same time, brought the 103rd Congress to a lackluster finish when several bills failed to pass for various reasons, including several Republican filibusters in the Senate. Clinton was forced to bring them back for a lame-duck session to pass the General Agreement on Tariffs and Trade (GATT) in an attempt to finish on a high note.

Though media attention often focused on "mistakes" or "misjudgments" by Clinton or his aides or on the occasional intrusions by the culture wars, the first two years of legislative work were dominated by the politics of the debt and deficit. And this was not just the case with the economic plan. The vast majority of Clinton's legislative triumphs did not involve any direct governmental spending, including family leave, the Brady bill, NAFTA, and GATT. Only the crime bill cost real money. Clinton's small stimulus package could not survive cost-cutting politics. Even Clinton's health care plan, which was vulnerable on so many points, was doomed, I would argue, because it would cost billions in the short run. Savings would come only later, if at all. The problem was that the deficit was such a tight political vise that we could not afford short-term costs, no matter what the eventual gains. This was true as well, although in a smaller way, with campaign finance reform, which foundered on the inability of Congress to find an acceptable method to self-finance the small system of public funding.

The 1994 elections, stunning in and of themselves, were read as a decisive verdict that Clinton and the Democratic majority failed to produce significant change. In a year, the presidency and the Democratic Congress had gone from a rousing success to a government in crisis. Following the election, the Clinton presidency seemed a shambles. In early January 1995, at the start of the 104th Congress, his presidency was characterized as a sideshow to the actions of the new Republican majority. Never in the era of the modern presidency had the locus of political initiative and action shifted so suddenly and decisively to Congress. Clinton may be able to work his way back by his own efforts or through the possible failures of the Republicans, but the two-year descent from electoral triumph to political tragedy merits consideration and analysis regardless of what transpires by the next presidential election.

The problem is that, as with Bush, not enough attention has been paid to the more historical or contextual causes of the problems that Clinton has faced. Instead, as with any presidency, there has been a decided tendency to ascribe success or failure of the Clinton administration to the personality and character of the president himself or the strategy and tactics employed by the White House in general.[26] Whether justified or not, Clinton has suffered constantly from the image that he is indecisive, inconsistent, and generally lacking an ideological anchor. While these accusations might be valid descriptions, they might not be good explanations. This mode of analysis might be mistaking cause for what could be mostly effect. The charge that Clinton has waffled or vacillated is unfair to the extent that he has shown a readiness to compromise in order to deal with a difficult political situation (one caused largely by the nature of deficit politics). Personality and strategy are often circular, and therefore too convenient, forms of explanation—Carter's failures stemmed from his excessively hands-on approach; Reagan's detachment was an asset. In each case, an easy link is made to fit the personality or behavior to the outcomes. Personality and strategy may be important but their impact are conditioned by circumstances. Deficit government and the other signal features of this political era would diminish the ability of any personality to successfully manage Clinton's agenda. Instead of the tendency to look to personality and strategy in assessing the success and failure of Clinton's presidency, we must pay more attention to the underlying political realities, especially the intractable politics of deficit government. Clinton is more like Bush than like Kennedy or Johnson, because both Clinton and Bush have governed in a period when governing has been more difficult. Clinton, like Bush, has been hamstrung by the legacy of the Reagan era.

Deficit government, as a contextual explanation, does not preclude other historical or situational factors. Clinton has also faced a society rent by certain sharp cultural cleavages that cannot be attributed to deficit politics. Nevertheless, the combination of historical circumstances (of which I would rank the budgetary crunch first and foremost) that constrain government might warrant a reconsideration of the current relevance of traditional perspectives on presidential and congressional power. For example, the literature on the presidency and the legislature frequently emphasizes the struggle between both branches for power. Some presidents dominate Congress; others are dominated; a few reach deadlock. One is often seen as being powerful at the expense of the other. Historically, this has been an often instructive insight. Deficit government, however, has been coincidental with, and a major cause of, a period in which both institutions appear indecisive and ineffectual. The president may be "tethered" and "fettered" but not by Congress; Congress is just as encumbered.[27] The weightiest of these mutual shackles are the debt and deficit and the politics they have fostered. The character and significance of the separation of powers are being shaped by the last decade of budgetary politics.

The Era of Deficit Government

A funny thing happened while we were waiting for a partisan realignment. U.S. politics and policy underwent a profound transformation in a relatively short period without a classic electoral realignment to make it happen. As was noted earlier, we may look back from the year 2000 and see a Republican realignment, but we should not forget that much of the political and policy character of that regime was forged before 1994 signaled potentially broad and enduring electoral change. The politics created by the deficit and debt had already put its stamp on the nature of the U.S. government.

The era of deficit government encompasses a whole range of afflictions that confound U.S. politics, including the fiscal deficit and debt, the deficit of public trust and patience, the deficit of new political ideas, and how they are all interrelated and mutually reinforcing. Manifestations are everywhere—in the nature of congressional lawmaking, the loud but unspecified or contradictory public demands for change (as long as it happens quickly), the appeal of term limits and the demagoguery of Ross Perot, and the relentless government-bashing in the media and by the public.

The era of deficit government is an accurate description or label to attach to U.S. politics from 1984 through, most likely, the end of the century. But it is also an explanation for the kind of politics we are experiencing and will continue to experience. Theodore Lowi has argued that a particular type of public policy or policy regime produces consonant politics.[28] The distributive or patronage policies of the nineteenth century engendered a party system and relationship between Congress and the president harmonious with that system of policy. The New Deal and World War II, by creating the welfare and warfare states, produced a new kind of politics. The era of presidential government was predicated on the shift from a largely distributive federal system to the redistributive and regulatory state.

In contrast to Lowi's perspective, the logic of electoral realignment theory focuses on the more intuitive democratic model of the relationship between policy and politics. That is, that politics (social change and elections) produces changes in policy. The policies in turn affect the nature of the budget and, in large measure, whether there is a budgetary surplus or deficit. The election of 1980 effected such an electorally driven shift in policy. But the results of the policy changes produced budgetary consequences that then began to reverse the chain of cause and effect. The fiscal vise created by the deficit and debt began to squeeze policy discretion, which in turn shaped politics. Just as distributive, redistributive, and regulatory policies manifest particular kinds of politics, especially under conditions of growth, the shift to negative-sum budgeting mandated by the fiscal crunch has created its own kind of politics. Deficit-driven retrenchment is producing a policy regime and politics consonant with itself.

In many ways, the Republicans are the natural beneficiaries of deficit government, and might be able, therefore, to gain and maintain a united government and majority support if their changes appear to "work." The fiscal deficit and debt inhibit new national programs, which the Republicans are against, and remain powerful arguments for cutting any and all existing programs, which they are for. Deficit politics eliminates much of the need for a positive agenda. Instead, the agenda is retrenchment and the transfer of federal power and responsibilities to the states. The core of the "Contract with America" are items predicated on the existence of deficit politics, including the balanced budget amendment, unfunded mandates, and the line-item veto. The divisive social issues such as abortion restrictions and repeal of gun control, in contrast, were on hold through 1995. The Democrats, in turn, have simply not developed an answer to the constraints of the debt and deficit and the perceived limits of national public policy.

Then again, the Republicans must govern amid the profound frustrations and anxieties they helped to foster and flourish. The Republicans are the short-term beneficiaries of unprecedented public disgust with politics and political institutions, but that, of course, could come back to haunt them. The self-perpetuating cycle of cynicism, the lack of patience and trust, might be hard to reverse. Americans could just as quickly lose patience with Republican retrenchment and decentralization, if they are perceived to be little more than strategies to shirk responsibility for national problems or if tax cuts, unmatched by spending cuts, exacerbate the deficit. The backlash against the magnitude of the reductions necessary to approach a balanced budget could be as swift as the cuts are large. The testy American voter might throw the new bums out and put other bums in. It is possible that no set of bums (at least under the same party) will be able to stay in office and stay the policy course long enough to see whether anything can work.

Thus, the circumstances of the era make an enduring realignment unlikely. Americans may no longer have the politics required to support a regime long enough for effective government. And if the nasty, brutish, and short world of deficit government and politics simply reinforces the electoral chaos that has been the U.S. norm for some time, then the ability of U.S. politics to cope with its national problems, not to mention the problems of the post–Cold War world, will remain in jeopardy.

Notes

The author gratefully acknowledges Hans Riemer's able and timely research assistance.

1. Everett Carll Ladd, "The 1988 Elections: Continuation of the Post-New Deal System," *Political Science Quarterly* 104 (spring 1989): 1–18.
2. Everett Carll Ladd, "Like Waiting for Godot: The Uselessness of Realignment for Understanding Change in Contemporary American Politics," *Polity* 22 (spring 1990): 511–525; James L. Sundquist, "Needed: A Political Theory for the New Era of Coalition Government in the United States," *Political Science Quarterly* 103 (winter 1988/1989): 613–635.

3. Sundquist, "Needed: A Political Theory"; Benjamin Ginsberg and Martin Shefter, *Politics by Other Means: The Declining Importance of Elections in America* (New York: Basic Books, 1990).

4. See Morris P. Fiorina's "An Era of Divided Government," *Political Science Quarterly* 107 (fall 1992): 387–410, and *Divided Government* (New York: Macmillan, 1992).

5. About the only parallel to this perspective is in Lawrence J. Haas, *Running on Empty: Bush, Congress, and the Politics of a Bankrupt Government* (Homewood, Ill.: Business One Irwin, 1990). The parallel is implicit in his excellent descriptive account of the Bush presidency. I located Haas's work after I was well into the research for this essay and regret the nearly unavoidable similarity in the titles.

6. David Stockman, *The Triumph of Politics: The Inside Story of the Reagan Revolution* (New York: Avon Books, 1987). In fact, Stockman argues that deficits would have been much larger without tax increases and defense cuts forced on the president by Congress (p. 450).

7. All budgetary figures were taken or calculated from data in the *Budget of the United States Government, Fiscal Year 1995* (historical tables 1.3, 8.2, and 8.4).

8. Quoted in "Congress Enacts Strict Anti-Deficit Measure," *Congressional Quarterly Almanac, 1985* (Washington, D.C.: Congressional Quarterly Press, 1986), pp. 459–468. Lawrence D. Longley and Walter J. Oleszek, in *Bicameral Politics* (New Haven: Yale University Press, 1989), pp. 305–334, provide a fine account of Gramm-Rudman's legislative history.

9. Longley and Oleszek, *Bicameral Politics,* p. 309.

10. Stephen Skowronek, *The Politics Presidents Make* (Cambridge: Harvard University Press, 1994), pp. 429–430. This section parallels Skowronek's analysis of Bush's dilemma, but whereas Skowronek is a bit vague I am explicit about what I see as the principal source of the dilemma—the debt and deficit.

11. Bob Woodward, "Origin of the Tax Pledge: In '88 Campaign Bush Camp Was Split on 'Read My Lips' Vow," *Washington Post,* October 4, 1992, 1, and Duffy and Goodgame, *Marching in Place,* pp. 233–234.

12. For example, in a CBS/*New York Times* poll from October 28–31, 1990, the eve of the elections, majority disapproved of the deficit reduction/budget agreement and 14 percent chose the deficit as the most important problem, compared to the Persian Gulf crisis (15 percent), the economy (12 percent), and drugs (10 percent). In August, 21 percent chose the Persian Gulf crisis and 8 percent, the deficit. "CBS News/*The New York Times* Poll," October 28–31, 1990, press release dated November 3, 1990.

13. John P. Frendreis and Raymond Tatalovich, *The Modern Presidency and Economic Policy* (Itasca, Ill.: F. E. Peacock Publishers, 1994), pp. 280–281.

14. As Woodward points out, the famous sign in the Arkansas "war room" said a few things, including "The economy, stupid." This was later popularized as "It's the economy, stupid." Woodward, *The Agenda,* p. 54.

15. "The People, the Press, and Politics: The New Political Landscape," Times Mirror Center for the People and the Press, news release, September 21, 1994, pp. 121–122.

16. The standard deviation for the surveys for each item were as follows: debt and deficit (5.05), economy (13.9), drugs and alcohol (12.1), and jobs and unemployment (5.2).

17. For example, in late 1993 and early 1994, deficit reduction (20–22 percent) ranked just behind "improving the job situation" (26–28 percent) and was, with "reducing crime" (20–23 percent), the second highest priority for Clinton. Health care was fourth with 14–16 percent. See "The People, the Press, and Politics," p. 123.

18. The best analysis of how congressional politics can lead Congress to procedural solutions is in Douglas Arnold, *The Logic of Congressional Action* (New Haven: Yale University Press, 1990). See pp. 139–141 for his discussion of military bases specifically.

19. Sondra J. Nixon, "Balanced Budget Amendments: An Idea That Never Goes Out of Style," *Congressional Quarterly Weekly Report,* January 14, 1995, 142–143. See also Richard B. Bernstein, *Amending America* (New York: Times Books, 1993), pp. 181–185.

20. At the time of this writing, Senate Majority Leader Bob Dole was retaining the option to bring back the amendment for another vote.

21. For a review of the contradictions in public opinion and their consequences for elections, see Gary C. Jacobson, *The Electoral Origins of Divided Government* (Boulder, Colo.: Westview Press, 1990), pp. 105–137.

22. For example, see Maureen Dowd, "Americans Like G.O.P. Agenda But Split on How to Reach Goals," *New York Times,* December 15, 1994, 24. Some 81 percent of those polled favored a balanced budget amendment, but that support dropped to 41 percent if it would be necessary to raise taxes, 30 percent if it would require cuts in Social Security, and 22 percent if it would require cuts in education.

23. Everett Carll Ladd, "The 1992 Vote for President Clinton: Another Brittle Mandate?" *Political Science Quarterly* 108 (spring 1993): 1–28.

24. Phil Duncan and Steve Langdon, "When Congress Had to Choose, It Voted to Back Clinton," *Congressional Quarterly Weekly Report,* December 18, 1993, 3427–3431.

25. Indeed, the administration's attempt to change the military's policy on homosexuals sparked the first filibuster of the session when some Republican senators sought to attach an amendment about the policy to the Family Leave Act.

26. The emphasis on personality or style and/or White House strategy has come in several forms both academic and journalistic. See, for examples, Fred I. Greenstein, "The Presidential Leadership Style of Bill Clinton: An Early Appraisal," *Political Science Quarterly* 108 (winter 1993–94): 589–601; Woodward, *The Agenda;* and Elizabeth Drew, *On the Edge: The Clinton Presidency* (New York: Simon and Schuster, 1994).

27. Thomas M. Franck, ed., *The Tethered Presidency* (New York: New York University Press, 1981); L. Gordon Crovitz and Jeremy A. Rabkin, *The Fettered Presidency* (Washington, D.C.: American Enterprise Institute, 1989); and Joseph A. Califano, Jr., "Imperial Congress," *New York Times Magazine,* January 23, 1994, pp. 40–41. For a recent review of the debate about the balance between presidential and congressional power, see Robert J. Spitzer, *President and Congress: Executive Hegemony at the Crossroads of American Government* (New York: McGraw-Hill, 1993).

28. See Theodore J. Lowi's "American Business, Public Policy, Case Studies, and Political Theory," *World Politics* 16 (July 1964): 677–715, and *The Personal President* (Ithaca, N.Y.: Cornell University Press, 1985).

2.2

The 1994 Explosion

Thomas Ferguson

> Our issues are basically safe now, the health mandates, the employer
> mandates, the minimum wage. . . . I don't think those will be high pri-
> orities in a Republican Congress.
> —GOPAC contributor Thomas Kershaw

Down through the ages, survivors of truly epic catastrophes have often
recounted how their first, chilling presentiment of impending doom arose
from a dramatic reversal in some feature of ordinary life they had always
taken for granted. Pliny the Younger's memorable account of the destruc-
tion of Pompeii and Herculaneum by an eruption of Mount Vesuvius in
A.D. 79, for example, remarks how, in the hours before the volcano's final
explosion, the sea was suddenly "sucked away and apparently forced back . . .
so that quantities of sea creatures were left stranded on dry sand."[1]

Sudden, violent changes in an ocean of money around election time are
less visually dramatic than shifts in the Bay of Naples. But long before the
Federal Election Commission (FEC) unveils its final report on the financing
of the 1994 midterm election, it is clear that in the final weeks before the
explosion that buried alive the Democratic Party, changes in financial flows
occurred that were as remarkable as anything Pliny and his terrified cohorts
witnessed two thousand years ago: A sea of money that had for years been
flowing reliably to congressional Democrats and the party that controlled
the White House abruptly reversed direction and began gushing in torrents
to Republican challengers.

Throughout most of the 1993–1994 election cycle, a reversal of these
proportions seemed about as likely as the sudden extinction of two important Roman towns in Pliny's time. The Republican Party, virtually everyone

agreed, normally enjoyed a lopsided overall national advantage in campaign fund-raising. But in the Congress, incumbency was decisive. Because big business, the Democratic Party's putative opponent, ultimately preferred "access" to "ideology," Democratic congressional barons could reliably take toll—enough to make them all but invulnerable for the indefinite future.[2]

In addition, the Democrats now also controlled the White House. By comparison with its recent past, the Democratic Party was thus exquisitely positioned to raise funds for the 1994 campaign. The party could extract vast sums of "soft money" from clients (i.e., patrons) in the business community, funds allegedly raised for state and local party-building purposes but, in fact, closely linked to national campaigns. It could also exploit the unrivaled advantages occupants of the Oval Office enjoy in hitting up big ticket individual contributors.

The glib contrast between "access" and "ideology" was always, at best, a half truth. Particularly if one reckons over several election cycles, the differences in total contributions flowing to a Democratic leader who literally opened for business, such as former House Ways and Means chair Dan Rostenkowski, and a populist maverick, such as outgoing House Banking Committee chair Henry Gonzalez, are quite fabulous.

Between 1982 and 1992, for example, FEC figures indicate that Rostenkowski succeeded in raising more than $4 million in campaign funds. Over the same period, Gonzalez's campaigns took in less than $700,000. (Among Democratic congressional leaders, Rostenkowski's was far from a record-setting pace. Not including funds formally raised for his forays into presidential politics, Richard Gephardt, formerly House majority leader and now minority leader, raised over $7 million in the same stretch.)[3]

Differences of this order demonstrate that in the long run, "access" eventually leads to favorable policy outcomes, or the money goes elsewhere. Airy talk about mere "access" also subtly diverted attention from the historically specific stages of the accommodation between the Democrats and big business as the New Deal system died its painful, lingering death of 1,000 contributions.[4]

Early reports by the FEC for the 1993–1994 election cycle appeared to confirm the conventional wisdom. In August 1994, the FEC released a survey of national party fund-raising efforts—a much narrower category than the name suggests, since it takes no account of, for example, the separately tabulated efforts of individual campaigns for Congress, where the consolidated totals run far higher. The survey indicated that the Republicans were continuing to cling to their overall lead. Fund-raising by the national Democratic Party, however, was up by 34 percent compared to the same period in 1991–1992, when George Bush was president.[5]

In the bellwether category of soft money (one of the best available indicators of sentiment among the largest investors of the United States), the contrast in regard to the same period was even sharper: Democratic receipts had doubled to $33 million, while GOP receipts were down 28 percent to a mere $25 million.[6]

Early statistics on congressional races indicated much the same trend. One FEC report released during the summer of 1994 showed the early flow of contributions to Democratic candidates in all types of races—incumbents, challengers, and especially open seats—running well above the levels of 1991–1992. By contrast, House Republican candidates in every category trailed well behind their Democratic counterparts in average (median) total receipts. Other FEC statistics also indicated that in House races, corporate political action committees (PACs) were tilting strongly in favor of Democratic candidates.[7]

As late as October, reports continued to circulate in the media of persisting large Democratic advantages in fund-raising in regard to both congressional races and soft money.[8] By then, however, little puffs of smoke were appearing over Mount Vesuvius. Leaks in the press began to appear suggesting that the Republicans, led by the redoubtable Newt Gingrich, were staging virtual revivals with enthusiastic corporate donors, lobbyists, and, especially, PACs.[9]

On November 2 came what could have become the first public premonition of the coming sea change: New figures for soft money published by the FEC indicated that between June 30 and October 19, the Democrats had managed to raise the almost laughable sum of but $10 million, while the Republicans had pulled down almost twice that much. Alas, the media and most analysts concentrated on each party's now closely similar take during the full two-year cycle. No one asked what had happened to dry up money for the Democrats in a period in which most observers still took for granted the continued Democratic control of at least the House. Neither did anyone think to project the new trend, which was undoubtedly gathering additional fierce momentum in the final, delirious weeks of fund-raising as the GOP scented victory.[10]

Two days later, the FEC published data on congressional races through October 19. Though almost no one noticed, the new data pointed to a startling turnabout: Funds to House Republican challengers and candidates for open seats were now pouring in at twice the rate of 1992. Democratic totals were up only slightly, save for a somewhat larger rise among candidates in races for open seats (that, unlike 1992, left their median receipts well behind their GOP counterparts).[11]

The ceaseless drumbeating by Newt Gingrich and other Republicans was beginning to pay off. Only a few months before, for example, corporate PACs investing in House races had been sending 60 percent of their funds to Democrats. By October, however, the PACs, along with other donors, were swinging back toward the GOP.

The trend was strongest where it probably mattered most: in races waged by challengers and candidates for open seats. A study by Richard Keil of the Associated Press (AP) indicates that in 1992 PACs as a group favored Democratic challengers and open-seat aspirants by a 2–1 margin. By October 1994, however, the AP found that PACs had switched dramatically: More than half of their donations to challengers and open-seat aspirants were going to GOP candidates. (The AP figures are for PACs as a group. They thus include contributions from labor PACs, which give lopsidedly to Democrats. The real size of the shift within the business community and related ideological PACs is, accordingly, significantly understated.)[12]

Pressed by Gingrich, who wrote what the AP described as a "forceful memo" on the subject to would-be Republican leaders of the new House, the GOP also made efficient use of another emergency fund-raising vehicle: the shifting of excess campaign funds from Republican incumbents with a high probability of reelection. Additional last-minute spending against Democratic candidates also appears to have come from organizations "independent" of the parties but favoring issues firmly associated with Gingrich and the Republicans, such as the recently founded Americans for Limited Terms.[13]

With so many races hanging in the balance (the Republicans, in the end, garnered only 50.5 percent of the total vote, according to a study by Stanley Greenberg for the Democratic Leadership Council), the tidal wave of late-arriving money surely mattered a great deal. But the AP's striking analysis of the effects of this blitz underscores just how wide of the mark were the establishment pundits who rushed to claim that "money can't buy everything" in the wake of (razor thin) defeats suffered by high-visibility, high-spending Republican Senate candidates in California and Virginia.[14]

The AP examined sixteen House contests decided by 4 percentage points or less. Campaign funds from Republican incumbents to other Republican candidates came in at three times the rate of donations from Democratic incumbents to their brethren. The Republicans won all sixteen. Even more impressive, of the 146 Republicans who the AP estimated had received $100,000 or more in PAC donations, 96 percent were victorious—a truly stunning result when one reflects that much of the late money was clearly funneled into close races.[15]

Most election analysts in the United States habitually confuse the sound of money talking with the voice of the people. Thus, it was only to be expected that as they surveyed the rubble on the morning after the election, many commentators gleefully jumped to the conclusion that the electorate had not merely voted to put the Democratic Party in Chapter 11, but had also embraced Newt Gingrich's curious "Contract with America."

But the evidence is strong that "it's still the economy, stupid" and that the 1994 election was essentially the kind of massive no-confidence vote that would have brought down the government in a European-style parliamentary system.

Let us start with some obvious, if once again relatively neglected, facts. As an anointed representative of massive blocs of money, Newt Gingrich may indeed be on his way to becoming a figure of towering significance in U.S. politics. But until the sunburst of publicity that followed the election, he was just another face in the crowd to most Americans. In a Yankelovich poll of eight hundred adult Americans taken for *Time*/CNN immediately following the vote, 68 percent of respondents said they were not familiar with him. (Another 3 percent were unsure of their response; of those who were, slightly more people—16 percent vs. 13 percent—viewed him unfavorably rather than favorably.)[16]

It is true that a few late Democratic advertisements targeted the Contract and that the White House briefly attacked it. But the Contract itself was essentially an inside-the-beltway gimmick, publicized in the closing weeks of the campaign to answer the charge—coming mostly from desperate rival elites who saw all too clearly what was happening—that the GOP stood for nothing in its own right and was simply trying to win by opposing Clinton and the Democrats. Based on what we know about the way ideas play off personalities in U.S. politics, it is hard to believe that in such a short, distracted time the Contract could have become more visible or attractive than Gingrich himself.[17]

Neither does survey evidence about the public's attitudes support sweeping claims about a sharp new "right turn" by the public. Virtually all the polls released so far rely on various forms of so-called forced choice questions. Because these questions pressure respondents to choose among alternatives selected by the survey designer, they are not always appropriate tools for sorting out the opinions that are actually important to voters as they make up their minds, especially considering the welter of other convictions that they entertain, which are irrelevant to specific voting decisions. For example, it does not automatically follow that because voters do not care for a president's foreign policies, that their distaste will actually carry over to their voting decisions. Many may simply vote their pocketbooks; their truthful answer to a foreign-policy question might be irrelevant.[18]

Forced choice questions also lend themselves to misinterpretation, by posing choices that the electorate (or pollsters) may not realize are, in fact, incompatible or by omitting alternatives that voters consider important. Depending on which responses receive emphasis, the electorate can appear to be moving in almost any direction.

Eighty-five percent of those interviewed in the Yankelovich poll, for example, attached "high priority" to reducing the federal budget deficit, while 75 percent attached a similar priority to a constitutional amendment to balance the budget. Fifty-four percent agreed that legislation to limit the terms of members of Congress to twelve years was also a "high priority" item; 82 percent thought tougher crime enforcement legislation was too. The same poll showed large majorities favor placing a "high priority" on actions to limit welfare payments (66 percent) and a line item veto for the president (59 percent).[19]

But this particular survey, which is well crafted by the standards of the trade, did not ask voters a number of other questions. Respondents were not asked, for example, whether they ranked economic growth above deficit reduction. In all polls known to me, whenever that question is asked, growth is the landslide winner.[20]

Nor was the public asked its views about cutting social security or about the wisdom of making many specific budget cuts (e.g., in Medicare and Medicaid) that the affluent sponsors of the balanced budget are seeking to impose by what is, in reality, stealth. (In a postelection poll by Greenberg for the DLC of people who said they had voted, 62 percent of those interviewed indicated that protecting Social Security and Medicare should be either the "single highest" or one of the "top few" priorities of the president and the next Congress. Sixteen percent placed increasing defense spending within those two categories.) Gingrich's and the GOP's stalwart opposition to raising the minimum wage is also unlikely to be echoed strongly by most Americans.[21]

One also needs to remember that many Americans have been ideologically conservative and programmatically liberal for decades. At no time before, during, or after the New Deal were new taxes, more bureaucracy, or "big government" ever anyone's idea of shrewd political appeals. This is one of several reasons for skepticism about the meaning of Greenberg's discovery, in his survey for the DLC, that if respondents are forced to choose between "traditional Democrats who believe government can solve problems and protect people from adversity" and "New Democrats who believe government should help people equip themselves to solve their own problems," 66 percent say they identify with the latter.[22]

To the extent the answer does not reflect unalloyed familiarity with beltway buzzwords, I suspect strongly that one would find roughly the same pattern of responses at any point in the high New Deal. Who now remembers, for example, that in the first Gallup poll published in 1935, 60 percent of respondents said that too much money was being spent on "relief and recovery"? On the other hand, Greenberg's survey does show clearly enough that whatever the popular mood about government action (which, as indicated below, has hardened), a majority of respondents flatly reject what certainly qualifies as the guiding idea of the Contract: that "government should leave people alone to solve their own problems."[23]

Nor is this all. Fifty-four percent of respondents in the Yankelovich poll came out for tougher legislation to regulate lobbying, which Gingrich staunchly opposed as he solicited corporate cash. (This news was reported in a preelection leak to the *Washington Post;* a Democratic Party less hopelessly mortgaged to pecuniary interests could have trumpeted it until the heavens resounded.) Moreover, 45 percent indicated campaign finance reform as another "high priority." In the great tradition of predictive social science, one can venture that Mount Vesuvius will freeze over before House Republicans offer anything except cosmetics on this decisive issue.[24]

Surveys also suggest that the Clinton administration's own Rube Goldberg scheme for health care reform did finally become unpopular with many voters. In the later stages of the mammoth onslaught against health care reform by industry groups, opinion likewise wavered on related health issues. Still, 72 percent of those polled by Yankelovich wanted health care "reform" to be a "high priority" in the next Congress. Health care reform also topped all other responses in the poll when respondents were asked to pick one issue as the top priority of the new Congress. Whatever senses of "reform" respondents read into those questions, most surely intend something quite different from anything Gingrich and the new GOP majority in Congress have in mind.[25]

More abstract—and hence, perhaps, less clearcut—benchmarks also show no sudden new turn to starboard. While election day surveys do not exhaust the complicated question of how the public labels itself, the party identification figures in the (massive) *New York Times* (*NYT*) election day exit poll actually moved the wrong way for a new "right turn" hypothesis: In 1994 the percentage of self-described Democrats was 39 percent, compared to 38 percent in 1992. (The percentage of self-described Republicans declined by one percent, as did the percentage of Independents.)[26]

Based on the percentages of the mass population who—in contrast to Democratic presidential candidates—remain willing to identify themselves with a specific political ideology, even the dreaded "L-word" does not yet seem ready to join the spotted owl on the list of politically endangered species. In 1994, 17 percent of respondents in the *NYT* election day survey described themselves—or perhaps, confessed to being—"liberal." A drop of 4 percent from 1992, this looks provocative, until one realizes that the figure in, for example, 1988 was again 18 percent. The trend in the percentage of self-described "conservatives" was essentially a mirror image of these small zigs and zags: 34 percent in 1994, 29 percent in 1992, but 33 percent in 1988. The only other choice given in all three years was "moderate."[27]

It may also be suggestive that some Democrats who were sagging dangerously in the polls, including Massachusetts Senator Edward Kennedy, but who still commanded sufficient financial resources to make effective counterarguments rallied to victory as they attacked the Contract.

Polls by the Los Angeles-based Times Mirror Center for the People and the Press suggest that strong opinions about race have receded since 1992, when the publicity and protests surrounding the Rodney King case led to sharp increases in the percentages of respondents reacting sympathetically to African American concerns. Yet, despite the noise about Republican gains in the South (which have a solid basis in that region's changing industrial structure—and institutional obstacles to unionization and community organizations—that the press and most scholars virtually ignore), one cannot plausibly blame the staggering Democratic losses nationwide on some inchoate perception that the administration was "excessively" partial to minorities or even to cities. The Clinton administration too obviously turned its back on all such concerns and people associated with them.[28]

A number of Republicans, of course, made a major issue out of illegal immigration. But this scarcely explains the across-the-board GOP victory. First, the issue in fact cuts across party lines, both in Congress and the states (as in Florida). During the campaign, Republican elites divided sharply on the question, not least because so many see it as intimately bound up with "economic growth" (translated into plain "English only": low wages).[29]

Most fatefully, however, immigration's emergence as an object of mass political concern in U.S. politics strongly resembles the gathering trend toward greater hostility to government activity or the various other (mostly far smaller) rightward shifts in public opinion mentioned above or documented in other recent polls.[30] It is essentially a reactive phenomenon, an emergent, constructed reality that grows out of the persisting failure by (money-driven) governments to do more than talk about problems such as high unemployment, which, along with the federal reluctance to share revenues with states receiving large numbers of immigrants, surely is the key to the upsurge of anxiety about immigration.

Senator Dianne Feinstein's narrow victory in the California senatorial race, which will—at least until 1996—go down in the *Guinness Book of World Records* as the most expensive non-presidential campaign in world history, is one more proof that, where there are resources and a will to counterargument, issues of this sort can be effectively engaged.

What destroyed Bill Clinton and the Democrats in 1994, however, was precisely what derailed his Republican predecessor only two years ago: In the midst of a steadily deepening economic crisis, it is impossible to beat something—even a fatuous, heavily subsidized something—with *nothing*.

But this was the hopeless task Clinton set for himself and his party after he—precisely as some of us predicted on the basis of the outpouring of Wall Street support for his "New Democrat" candidacy in 1992—betrayed his campaign promise to "grow out" of the deficit by "investing in America" as he assumed office in 1993. By deciding to make the bond market the supreme arbiter of economic policy, by ostentatiously refraining from jawboning the Federal Reserve Board to restrain rises in interest rates, by abandoning his much touted plan for an economic stimulus and instead bringing in a budget that was contractionary over the medium term, the president embraced precisely the program of continuing austerity that the electorate elected him to break with.[31]

Once he had embarked on this course, most, if not all, of his subsequent endeavors were doomed. No amount of politically correct posturing, homilies about values, or pathetically funded demonstration schemes for worker training or education could long disguise the fact that 5.5 or 6 percent unemployment is not really full employment and, a fortiori, not a "boom." (Note that, as usual, no one in the administration spoke up in public to support Alan Blinder, the president's own nominee to the Federal Reserve Board, during the firestorm of criticism that followed his few brief remarks in a non-public speech about the weakness of the case for the much-touted [high] "natural rate of unemployment" hypothesis. Because of this incident's chilling effect on future discussions of Fed policy, it may well be every bit as significant as the 1994 election itself.)[32]

By some estimates, based on census data, the economic situation of as much as 80 percent of the population has not substantially improved since 1989. Such statistics may slightly underestimate the real distribution of economic welfare, particularly as this is affected by the thorny problem of valuing new products and changing quality.[33]

But this is arguing about decimal points. What matters is the real "chain reaction" that now threatens to blow apart the political system. This chain reaction begins with the desperate economic squeeze a largely unregulated world economy now places on ordinary Americans. It leads next to the decay of public services and nonprofit institutions that sustain families and communities, including schools, court systems, and law enforcement. In the end, it makes the daily life of more and more Americans increasingly unbearable.

Given that the Democrats controlled both the White House and Congress, it is scarcely surprising that so many Americans are fed up with them. Or that substantial numbers of citizens should be increasingly attracted to the only public criticisms of the system that they are consistently allowed to hear (particularly on talk radio or the generally right-wing "new media")—that their real problem is the bell curve, immigrants, welfare, or, indeed, the very notion of government action itself, which does inevitably cost money.[34]

That the system is so obviously money-driven and frequently corrupt only enrages people, while the administration's all-out efforts for NAFTA and GATT underscored the fact that Clinton's priorities and his real constituency were somewhere else.

Sixty percent of those in the Yankelovich poll expressed the belief that the outcome of the 1994 election was "more a rejection of Democratic policies" than "a mandate for Republican policies." Fifty-six percent of the voters in the Greenberg survey claimed that they were "trying to send a message about how dissatisfied [they] were with things in Washington." Invited to be more specific, 15 percent said the message referred to "Bill Clinton," 15 percent pointed to "Congress," 5 percent each indicated "Republicans" and "Democrats"; while *45 percent* said the problem was "politics as usual."[35]

But the most striking evidence about what is now happening in the U.S. political system comes from the *NYT* election day exit poll. This broke down the vote in terms of whether the respondent reported that his or her standard of living was becoming better or worse. The results are astonishing in the light of the publicity garnered after the election by the eight-point spread in the overall party vote by men and women, as well as conventional views that the Democrats mobilize less well-off voters.

In both the overall national vote and major state campaigns that were separately reported (including the New York gubernatorial and Massachusetts senatorial races), those whose standard of living was improving voted roughly 2–1 (66 percent vs. 34 percent in the national sample) for the Democrats. By contrast, those whose standard of living was getting worse went roughly 2–1 (65 percent vs. 35 percent in the national sample) for the Republicans, while the group in the middle split virtually down the middle (48 percent for the Democrats vs. 52 percent for the GOP).[36]

The contrast with the 1992 data is glaring. At that time, according to the *NYT* exit poll, Clinton lost support from those whose living standard was improving 62 percent to 24 percent (with 14 percent going to Perot). He split the group in the middle 41 percent to 41 percent (with 18 percent voting for Perot). But he swept the group whose standard of living had declined by an overwhelming 61 percent to 14 percent (with, suggestively, 25 percent going to Perot).[37]

The 1994 surveys still show a sizable pocket of people with low incomes and relatively little schooling who remain stalwart Democrats, when they do vote. But these numbers show just how upside down patterns of mobilization are now becoming in the United States. Essentially, the 1994 elections suggest that the party that commands by far the most money is now succeeding by mobilizing increasing numbers of disenchanted poor and middle-class voters against their traditional champions.[38]

This is a voting pattern more reminiscent of some European elections in the 1930s than most U.S. elections. It ought to ring some alarm bells. Asked whether the Republicans would do a better job of running Congress than did the Democrats, 61 percent of respondents in the Yankelovich poll declared that they would either do a worse job (16 percent) or make no difference (45 percent). Sixty-one percent, in other words, expect no major improvement.[39]

A full analysis of Newt Gingrich's Contract with America is not possible here. There is space only to observe that the voters may well be right. Nothing in the Contract really addresses the problems of a world economy in which many of the biggest U.S. businesses increasingly do not need most of the American workforce or even the infrastructure—apart from the defense and foreign relations establishments—for anything. Nor will the suggestion by Gingrich and other Republican leaders after the election that price stability should perhaps be legally enshrined as the sole target for Federal Reserve policy.[40]

What will happen as the economic crisis deepens and voters discover that their suspicions were right? Perhaps for a while, the merry-go-round in Washington will spin with the speed of light.[41] But in the long run? In all probability, I suspect, Mount Vesuvius's greatest blowouts are still to come. As in the thirties, those who scorn John Maynard Keynes will be astonished at the outcomes for which they will have to accept responsibility.

Notes

This chapter is a slightly revised version of the postscript to Thomas Ferguson, *Golden Rule: The Investment Theory of Party Competition and the Logic of Money-Driven Political Systems* (Chicago: University of Chicago Press, 1995). © 1995 by the University of Chicago. Slight alterations in style, punctuation, and grammar have been made to the version that appears here. I am grateful to Richard Keil, Benjamin Page, Robert Shapiro, and seminar audiences at Columbia University and the New School for Social Research for comments on early versions of this postscript.

As this version of the essay goes to press, the Federal Election Commission has not yet published a final report on the financing of the 1994 election. But a later FEC press release of December 22, 1994, "1994 Congressional Spending Sets Record," strongly confirms the essay's central conclusions about the tidal wave of GOP money. The figures contained in an FEC press release of April 13, 1995 also bear out this essay's contention that trends in soft money after the late spring of 1994 strongly favored the GOP (cf. the earlier figures reported in the FEC press release of November 2 and August 8, 1994 discussed in note 10 below).

The Kershaw quotation appears in an article in the *Boston Globe,* November 20, 1994. The article described Kershaw as "a $10,000-a-year charter member" of Newt Gingrich's "grand effort to engineer a Republican takeover of Congress." The article also notes that Kershaw's holdings include the Bull and Finch Pub of Boston, which inspired the "setting of the 'Cheers' television show." The GOP action committee (GOPAC) has been a vehicle for various organizing efforts of Gingrich's.

1. Pliny's description appears in his letter to Cornelius Tacitus, in *Pliny Letters and Panegyricus,* vol. 1, trans. Betty Radice (Loeb Classical Library; Cambridge: Harvard University Press, 1969), p. 443.

2. On the expected primacy of incumbents, see, for example, the *Washington Post,* November 3, 1994. Note also that, of course, the advantages entrenched incumbents enjoyed were considered to be stronger in the House; many recognized that the Senate could easily go Republican.

3. The campaign finance totals come from the FEC; they are arrived at by summing the appropriate figures for total receipts in the commission's various final reports on financial activity for the years indicated. Note that fees received from giving speeches, stamp sales, and other activities are not included in these figures. These would almost certainly increase the disparities considerably.

4. See the discussion in chapters 5 and 6 in Ferguson, *Golden Rule.*

5. See the statistics presented in the FEC press release of August 8, 1994.

6. Ibid.

7. For the congressional races, see the FEC press release of August 12, 1994, especially the comparative figures on median receipts for House candidates on p. 4. For the party balance among (House) corporate PAC contributions, see the FEC release of September 19, 1994 (the data reflect contributions through June 30; the exact percentage varies slightly depending on whether one calculates figures for only 1994 or through the whole cycle to that point), especially p. 4. Note that donations to GOP candidates in the Senate, where many observers saw a chance of a GOP turnaround, unsurprisingly held up very well.

8. In a spirit of collegial goodwill, let us dispense with specific references. See, instead, the surprise various commentators registered after the election in, for example, Richard Keil's story of November 17, 1994 for the Associated Press (AP). (My reference is to the full text supplied to me by the AP; AP stories are often edited severely before running in local papers.)

9. For example, *Washington Post,* October 14, 1994.

10. See the FEC press release of November 2, 1994, which focused on the two-year totals. However, the real news comes when one goes back and compares these statistics to those in the earlier FEC press release of August 8, 1994. It then becomes fairly clear that the real "break" in the trend of soft money probably came in the late spring or early summer. This was well before any widespread anticipation of the GOP takeover of the House and is, thus, of considerable interest. What happened?

In the absence of the FEC's final report on the 1994 election, it is difficult to be sure. Because the available evidence defies brief summary, all that is possible here is to record my belief that two developments, which were closely related to the majestic bond crash that roiled world markets in the spring of 1994, played important roles in this shift of funds. First, the administration's policy of talking down the dollar against the yen drove a wedge between Clinton's administration and many of its supporters on Wall Street, as Ferguson, *Golden Rule,* chapter 6, note 47 suggested might happen. Second, congressional inquiries into hedge funds led other Wall Street supporters of the president to either switch to the GOP or simply withdraw from previously made commitments to help finance the Democrats.

11. See the FEC press release of November 4, 1994, especially pp. 3 and 8. This constitutes the truly clinching evidence for the late turn in funding House races, since it can be compared cautiously, but directly, with the earlier FEC release of August 11, 1994.

12. See the AP story of November 15, 1994 by Richard Keil. I rely here on the full text the AP supplied me. I took considerable pains to resolve various ambiguities in statistics the story reported. I am grateful to Keil for the patience and good humor he displayed in dealing with my queries.

13. On the excess campaign funds, see Keil's story for the AP of November 17, 1994, which also alludes to the Gingrich memo. Again, I rely on the uncut text supplied me by the AP. On the independent organizations, see, for example, *Wall Street Journal,* November 4, 1994.

14. See p. 1 of the draft dated November 17, 1994 of Greenberg's "The Revolt Against Politics," which accompanies his survey for the DLC discussed here.

15. See (the uncut text to) Richard Keil's stories for the AP of November 9, 15, and 17, 1994.

16. See the "Memorandum" to "Data Users" from Hal Quinley of Yankelovich Partners, November 11, 1994, which reports the poll in detail. See p. 5 for the question on Gingrich.

17. In a press release of November 29, 1994 released over a computer network, Kathy Frankovic of CBS News reports that 28 percent of those polled by CBS in late November had heard of the Contract with America.

18. See the discussion of the work of Stanley Kelley, Jr. and John Geer in chapters 5 and 6 of Ferguson, *Golden Rule.* Some recent work using panel data that is critical of Kelley or Geer's reliance on open-ended questions relies on statistical assumptions that simply cannot be accepted. But this controversy exceeds the scope of this discussion.

19. See pp. 14–17 of the Quinley memorandum cited in note 16 above.

20. See the discussion in note 5 of chapter 6 in Ferguson, *Golden Rule.*

21. For the Greenberg poll, see Greenberg Research, Inc., "Survey of Voters, with Figures and Tables," November 8–9, 1994, p. 32. The Yankelovich survey, reported in the Quinley memo, p. 15, found slightly more support for increasing defense spending— 31 percent thought it should be a "high priority." But compare that to the other numbers quoted earlier.

I think we can safely conclude that the rush by both Democrats and Republicans to raise defense spending after the election has nothing to do with satisfying public opinion.

22. See Greenberg Research, "Survey of Voters," pp. 12–13.

23. See George Gallup, *The Gallup Poll Public Opinion, 1935–71* (New York: Random House, 1972), p. 1. For the Greenberg data, see his "Survey of Voters," p. 13.

24. For the Yankelovich data, see the Quinley memo, pp. 16–18; for the *Washington Post* article, see its October 14, 1994 issue.

25. The "single highest" Yankelovich result is on p. 18 of the Quinley memo; for the "high priority" statistic, see pp. 14 and 16. In addition to supporting data in the Greenberg survey already cited, see, among many other analyses, Lawrence R. Jacobs and Robert Shapiro, "Public Opinion's Tilt Against Private Enterprise," *Health Affairs,*

spring (I) 1994: 285–298, and Lawrence R. Jacobs, Robert Shapiro, and Eli Schulman, "Medical Care in the United States—An Update," *Public Opinion Quarterly* 57 (1993): 394–427.

26. For the *NYT* exit polls, see the paper for November 13, 1994 and November 5, 1992; the later *NYT* revisions are discussed in notes 27 and 36 below.

27. See the poll results reported in the *NYT* for November 13, 1994 and November 5, 1992; for 1988, see the press release to the *NYT/CBS* exit poll dated November 8, 1988. The latter year, of course, saw the question emerge as a campaign issue. The figure for 1994 used in this version of the essay follows the slightly revised table issued in the form of a press release by the *NYT* poll, 3/1/95. The figures for liberals differ by (a trivial) 1 percent from the earlier published version. See also the discussion below in note 36.

28. Along with the discussion in chapter 6 in Ferguson, *Golden Rule,* see also the critical discussion of claims that reapportionment explains the GOP gains in the South by Allan J. Lichtman, "Quotas Aren't the Issue," *NYT,* December 7, 1994. This is an effective critique of suggestions advanced by other analysts quoted in news sections of the *NYT* for November 13. On recent trends in opinion on racial issues, see, for example, Larry Hugick and Andrew Kohut, "Taking the Nation's Pulse," *The Public Perspective* 6, no. 1 (November/December 1994): 4.

29. For GOP differences on immigration, see the *Boston Globe,* November 22, 1994; cf. also Thomas Ferguson, "From Boiling Pot to Melting Pot: The Real Lessons of the American Experience of Immigration and 'Assimilation,' " in *Between States and Markets: The Limits of the Transatlantic Alliance,* ed. Roger Benjamin, C. R. Neu, and Denise Quigley (New York: St. Martin's Press, 1995).

30. As indicated in the postscript to *Golden Rule,* I would follow Robert Shapiro's tentative formulation (offered in conversation) that, in broad terms, opinion drifted somewhat to the Right around the time Clinton entered office, after mostly moving the other way for a long time. A number of obvious exceptions to this generalization exist on both sides of the time line, and the shift in question is usually, though not always, of a minor sort, but this topic simply cannot be developed any further here. Note, however, the time trends of the data discussed in Hugick and Kohut, "Taking the Nation's Pulse," pp. 3–6; their material omits discussion of health care, where "self-reliance" usually looks hollow. Compare also the shifts in the Times Mirror Center press release of September 21, 1994, "The People, the Press, and Politics: The New Political Landscape," for example, the small shift in environmentalism (p. 41) between 1992 and 1994.

31. See the discussion in the introduction and chapter 6 of Ferguson, *Golden Rule.*

32. See chapter 6 in Ferguson, *Golden Rule,* especially the reference to Robert Eisner's evidence against the "natural rate" hypothesis.

33. Cf. the data presented in Lawrence Mishel and Jared Bernstein, *The State of Working America, 1994–95* (Washington, D.C.: Economic Policy Institute, in press), especially chapters 1, 3, and 4. For an explicit 1989–1994 comparison from Census data, see e.g., Table 1.6. Note that the downturn in the early 1990s influences the trend of virtually all such data. The widespread switch to variable rate mortgages in the United States may also be a factor in the 1994 outcome, as an earlier move to them appears to have influenced British politics in the previous decade.

In a mid-October 1994 Times Mirror survey cited in Hugick and Kohut, "Taking the Nation's Pulse," p. 5, 50 percent of respondents could not name a single achievement of the Clinton administration. However, Robert Samuelson, in "False Economic Report Card?" *Boston Globe,* November 1, 1994, offers several criticisms of the pessimistic critique of the U.S. economy's recent trend. Mishel and Bernstein, I believe, provide a convincing (implicit) rejoinder, along with the fact that, as suggested, many of the proposed corrections do not add up to a major difference. I would also emphasize the negative effects on individual lives of the decay of the nonprofit sector, which is not really reflected in any of the usual statistics.

A *NYT* report of October 17, 1994 that recent jobs data did not support the pessimists' position(s) appears to have rested on a statistical confusion. See the Letters to the Editor by Lawrence Chimerine and Edward S. Herman in the *NYT* of October 24, 1994 and Robert Kuttner's "Inequality Sours Economic Recovery," *Boston Globe,* October 24, 1994.

34. A Gallup poll taken on the eve of the 1994 election suggested that voters who listened frequently to talk radio disproportionately favored Republican candidates. See *USA Today,* November 10, 1994. It seems clear that save for a few exceptions, talk radio and most cable television shows have taken advantage of the new, less-regulated climate (and the shift rightward by most of the owners of the media since the sixties) to move much further to the Right than the major television networks. See the longer discussion in the postscript to *Golden Rule.*

35. See Greenberg Research, "Survey of Voters," pp. 8–9; for Yankelovich, see the Quinley memo, p. 7.

36. These 1994 figures reflect a slight revision of the original exit poll issued in the form of a press release by the *NYT* poll of 3/1/95. They hardly differ from the numbers originally published in the newspaper on November 13, 1994, on which the original version of this essay was based. Michael Kagay kindly made the exact form of the question available to me. For results in particular state elections, see the polls printed in the *NYT* of November 10, 1994.

37. See *NYT,* November 5, 1992.

38. One should note the possibility that a form of "rationalization" perhaps influenced some pro- or anti-Clinton voters in making their minds up about the economy or vice versa. But the numbers in the exit poll are far too large for that to be the main explanation.

39. For the Yankelovich results, see pp. 9–13 of the Quinley memo.

40. For the story on Gingrich, the GOP, and the Fed, see *Wall Street Journal,* November 18, 1994.

41. On the one hand, it is clear that the midterm election results considerably complicate any hopes the Clinton administration entertains for a political business cycle in 1996, since it has lost control of Congress and does not firmly control the Fed. On the other hand, postelection polls also suggest that much of the population credits the president with good intentions, if not with any results. See, for example, the Greenberg "Survey of Voters," pp. 10–11, where 73 percent of voters say "It is too early to tell" if Clinton will fail as a president; 68 percent assert that they are still hopeful Clinton "can succeed"; and 64 percent agree that Clinton "has tried to move the country in the right direction."

In the absence of the FEC's final report on the midterm election, it is impossible to characterize the investor coalition that is lining up behind Newt Gingrich and his wing of the GOP. It is obvious that most of the health industry and many opponents of Clinton enlisted early. So, also, have some finance and many service-sector firms, but more of this another time. I think, however, that, as the quotation that opens this postscript suggests, one fundamental result of the 1994 election will be a powerful reinforcement of existing trends for a "low wage" strategy of international competition.

2.3

Issues, Elections, and Political Change
The Case of Abortion

Timothy A. Byrnes

In 1973, the Supreme Court declared in *Roe v. Wade* that the constitutional right to privacy, found in the Fourteenth Amendment's guarantee of liberty, was "broad enough to encompass a woman's right to terminate her pregnancy."[1] Nineteen years later, in 1992, a very different Supreme Court held in *Planned Parenthood of Southeastern Pennsylvania v. Casey* that "the essential holding of *Roe v. Wade* should be retained and once again reaffirmed."[2] In between these two landmark decisions, however, lay two decades of intense political battle.

Over that time period, abortion was often at the center of U.S. national politics. In each presidential election, the major party candidates sharply differed over abortion. Speeches were made, positions taken, and, in some cases, abortion came to play a central role in framing the campaign debate between the candidates. Political strategists sought to use abortion as a tool for voter mobilization either, in the Republican case, to attract voters anxious to restrict abortion or, in the Democratic case, to retain voters committed to preserving abortion rights. In fact, from 1980 onward, the Republican and Democratic Parties officially held radically divergent positions on abortion. The Democrats defended abortion's status as a fundamental constitutional right; the Republicans condemned abortion as a moral abomination, called for a constitutional amendment banning it, and promised the selection of federal judges who would work to overturn *Roe* and read abortion out of the United States Constitution.

Now, looking back on this period of political struggle between *Roe* and *Casey,* it is appropriate to ask what all this activity amounted to. There was, to be sure, a lot of noise surrounding the politics of abortion in the 1970s and 1980s, but exactly what role did abortion play in U.S. electoral politics during this period? Did abortion significantly influence electoral outcomes? Did those outcomes, in turn, significantly affect national policy on abortion? How important was abortion in determining the terms of the political debate during these years and in shaping the nature of the partisan alignment? This chapter will offer answers to these important questions.

Put more generally, this chapter will use an examination of abortion politics to shed light on the relationship between issues and elections in contemporary U.S. politics. One of the central projects of modern political science concerns the relationship between the positions people take on the issues and the candidates those people choose in the voting booth. Is there such a thing as "issue voting?" Can issues supersede other voting cues such as partisan affiliation? Can the so-called social issues compete with economic interest in determining partisan affiliation, voting behavior, or the relationship between the two? I do not hope to offer here definitive answers to these large questions. But I will survey the copious literature on the relationship between attitudes on abortion and the vote, and I will assess the degree to which national elections of the 1970s and 1980s were influenced by the issue of abortion.

I will also examine the other side of the relationship between issues and elections. That is, after the balloons have dropped and the bunting has been put away, do the results of national elections tangibly affect particular public policies? Our most fundamental notions of democracy require an affirmative answer to this question. But the case of abortion reveals that the relationship between elections and issues is more complex than we might originally think. The national government, for example, can do precious little about some issues that nevertheless come to dominate national debate. Or the differences between the candidates on a given issue may not be clear enough to allow for confident electoral explanations of policy developments. And, sometimes, candidates run on platforms that stress issues to which they pay little attention once in office. Promises, to put it another way, often are not kept. I will argue here that abortion *policy* was relatively unaffected by the great ferment of abortion *politics*. Opponents of abortion "won" elections in the 1980s, but they derived little policy satisfaction from their victories.

Having examined the relationship between abortion and elections from both sides of the equation, I will then turn to a final series of questions. Regardless of abortion's direct effect on the vote, and regardless of the vote's direct effect on abortion policy, what role did abortion play in building what we might call the structure of national politics during these years?

How central was abortion in this period as a symbolic and rhetorical tool for coalition building? I will argue that conservative strategists, seeking to re-align the U.S. party system, placed abortion at the center of their political agenda. They tried to use abortion to mobilize evangelical Protestants, con-vert conservative Catholic Democrats, and knit together a fractious but potentially powerful electoral coalition. I will conclude by affirming that for this reason, if for no other, abortion was, between *Roe* and *Casey,* a power-ful force for political change in the United States.

Do Elections Matter?

Between *Roe* and *Casey,* despite all the attention paid to the issue and all the political energy expended on it, national electoral politics did not funda-mentally alter public policy on abortion. *Roe* established a woman's consti-tutional right to terminate her pregnancy. And *Casey,* after twelve years of Republican presidents devoted to reversing *Roe,* reaffirmed that right. More restrictions passed constitutional muster in 1992 than did in 1973, but the basic right to an abortion endured.

In response to *Roe v. Wade,* the burgeoning antiabortion movement set out four closely related political and legislative goals. The first was to pass a constitutional amendment that would ban abortion altogether or, less am-bitiously, that would send the issue back to the states for restriction and regulation. This goal stands as the signal failure of antiabortion politics in the 1970s and 1980s. An antiabortion amendment reached the floor of the Republican-controlled Senate in the early 1980s, but it was defeated by lack of broad-based support and by fissures within the pro-life camp concerning the specific form that constitutional protection of the right to life should take.

Second, antiabortion forces sought to limit the use of public funds to pay for abortions for poor women. In contrast to the constitutional amendment, this goal has been achieved since 1976 through the various Hyde Amend-ments that have eliminated public funding of abortions with few excep-tions.[3] For most years during this period, federal funding of abortions was authorized only in cases where the woman's life would be threatened by carrying the pregnancy to term. The Hyde Amendments were passed with bipartisan support by appealing to the argument that taxpayers ought not to be forced to pay for a procedure that so many of them find fundamentally repugnant.

Third, antiabortion activists set the goal of pressuring state legislatures to pass restrictive abortion laws that either tested or flouted the parameters set out by the court in *Roe.* This strategy was also readily implemented after

1973 as a number of state lawmaking bodies from Pennsylvania to Ohio to Missouri to Utah proved willing to pass such laws in the hopes of granting the court an opportunity to reverse *Roe* explicitly or, failing that, to scale back the constitutional right to abortion by allowing for more restrictions on access to the procedure.[4]

The success of this strategy, of course, depended on achievement of the movement's fourth goal: the election of presidents who would appoint Supreme Court justices hostile to abortion rights and willing to reverse *Roe*. This goal seemed met with the election of Ronald Reagan in 1980. But during the ensuing twelve years of Republican, antiabortion administrations, the relationship between the political views of a president and the constitutional decisions of those he appointed to the federal judiciary proved to be considerably more complicated and problematic than antiabortion activists hoped.

As a matter of fact, right-to-life leaders actually opposed President Reagan's first appointment to the court, Sandra Day O'Connor.[5] As a legislator in Arizona, O'Connor had cast a number of votes that could be (and were) perceived as expressive of ambivalence regarding the legal and constitutional status of abortion.[6] Moreover, she did little to dispel that perception with her carefully guarded remarks at her confirmation hearing. "I am opposed to abortion as a matter of birth control or otherwise," she said in response to a question. "[It is] a valid [subject] for legislative action *subject to any constitutional restraint or limitation.*"[7]

Once on the court, Justice O'Connor proved through the 1980s to be neither the reliable vote to overturn *Roe* that the right-to-lifers had desired from Reagan nor the trojan horse of abortion rights that they had feared prior to her confirmation. In *City of Akron v. Akron Center for Reproductive Health* (1983), the first major case on abortion in which Justice O'Connor participated, she staked out her own ground on the constitutionality of restrictions on access to abortion. She proposed jettisoning the trimester framework established in *Roe v. Wade* and replacing it with a new "undue burden" standard. According to O'Connor, state restrictions on abortion ought to be deemed constitutional so long as they did not "drastically limit the availability [of abortion]. . . . That a state regulation may 'inhibit' abortions to some degree does not require that we find that the regulation is invalid."[8]

O'Connor continued to press the "undue burden" test in other cases throughout the decade. But her attempts to finesse the constitutional issues involved in abortion and her resulting refusal to countenance actually overturning *Roe* became more obvious with the arrival on the court of Antonin Scalia in 1986. Scalia, who replaced Associate Justice William Rehnquist when Rehnquist was elevated to replace the retiring Chief Justice Warren Burger, left no doubt where he stood on *Roe*. He wanted it overturned and the volatile issue of abortion sent back to the political and legislative processes in the states where he felt it belonged. Abortion, he argued in an opinion in 1989, was an area where the Supreme Court "has little proper business since the answers to most of the crucial questions posed are political and not juridical."[9] As for overturning *Roe* explicitly, Scalia wrote simply: "I think that [it] should be done."[10]

The central constitutional battle over abortion in the 1980s, however, took place not in the Supreme Court itself but, rather, in the chambers of the United States Senate. The Senate's rejection of President Reagan's appointment of Judge Robert Bork to replace the retiring Lewis Powell not only kept Bork, a devoted and energetic opponent of *Roe*, off the court but also led to the subsequent appointment and confirmation of a little known Californian named Anthony Kennedy. In time, Kennedy would become a pivotal figure in the court's handling of abortion. At the time of his appointment, however, many observers on both sides of the controversy assumed that the new Justice Kennedy shared Judge Bork's basic views on the constitutionality of antiabortion legislation. Kennedy lacked Bork's incendiary rhetorical style and his voluminous paper trail (those attributes probably got him confirmed, in fact), but that did not necessarily mean that his *votes,* on abortion as well as on other issues, would differ substantially from the votes a Justice Bork would have cast.

In the first abortion case in which Kennedy participated, *Webster v. Reproductive Health Services, Inc.,* the new justice joined with two of the court's three committed opponents of abortion rights, William Rehnquist and Byron White, in a plurality opinion that upheld a restrictive abortion law passed by Missouri's state legislature. Though the opinion, written by the Chief Justice, stopped short of actually overturning *Roe,* it upheld several provisions of Missouri's law and suggested portentously that "the key elements of the *Roe* framework—trimesters and viability—are not found in the Constitution or in any place else one would expect to find a constitutional principle."[11]

As Ronald Reagan was succeeded by George Bush in 1989, then, the constitutional right to abortion was just barely surviving. Three members of the court (Rehnquist, Scalia, and White) were on record as willing to overturn *Roe* explicitly; one new member, Kennedy, based on his vote in *Webster,* appeared to be similarly disposed; and Justice O'Connor continued to confound simple characterization. She clearly did not believe that the Constitution required abortion on demand, but she refused to tip her hand on the *central* constitutional question of whether the Constitution contained within it any right to abortion whatsoever. She would not address that question, she said, until "the constitutional invalidity of a State's abortion statute actually turns on the constitutional validity of *Roe v. Wade*."[12] Observers who could count, however, could see in 1989 that the right to abortion was at best one vote away from being extinguished. Four votes to overturn seemed assured, and as Harry Blackmun wrote in dissent in the *Webster* case: "the signs are evident and very ominous, and a chill wind blows."[13]

In response to shifts on the court, and in hopes of testing further the emerging new parameters of acceptable restrictions on access to abortion, a number of states passed laws in the late 1980s that were, on their face, inconsistent with the court's holdings in *Roe* and later in *Webster*.[14] Louisiana, Utah, and the territory of Guam passed particularly restrictive statutes that would have, if upheld by the courts, virtually eliminated legal abortion within their borders. But it was Pennsylvania's Abortion Control Act, involving a much less sweeping retrenchment of abortion rights, that made it to the high court first.[15] This law, though not a direct assault on the right to abortion as such, placed a number of barriers in the path of access to abortion, such as informed consent, a twenty-four-hour waiting period, and spousal notification, that were unmistakably disallowed by *Roe's* trimester framework and that had been declared constitutionally infirm before Presidents Reagan and Bush refashioned the court in the 1980s.

This time, however, the constitutionality of most of these provisions was upheld by the Supreme Court in *Planned Parenthood of Southeastern Pennsylvania v. Casey*. In an unusual joint opinion penned by Justices O'Connor and Kennedy, and their new colleague Justice David Souter, the court applied the "undue burden" test that O'Connor had been advocating for a decade:

> Only where state regulation imposes an undue burden on a woman's ability to make this decision [to have an abortion] does the power of the State reach into the heart of the liberty protected by the Due Process Clause.[16]

Under this new test, restrictions such as waiting periods and mandatory counseling sessions are deemed constitutional. But perhaps more importantly, sweeping restrictions on abortion, limitations that in practice would actually prevent large numbers of women from procuring abortions, are *disallowed* by the test. The court, using O'Connor's standard, found that these types of restrictions place an "undue burden" on a woman's exercise of her constitutional liberties by placing "substantial obstacles" in her path. In fact, instead of reversing *Roe v. Wade* and overturning abortion rights, the joint opinion in *Casey* actually offered a ringing endorsement of a woman's constitutional right to terminate her pregnancy.

> The essential holding of *Roe v. Wade* should be retained and once again reaffirmed. . . . Constitutional protection of the woman's decision to terminate her pregnancy derives from the Due Process Clause of the Fourteenth Amendment. It declares that no State shall "deprive any person of life, liberty, or property, without due process of law." The controlling word in the case before us is "liberty." Although a literal reading of the Clause might suggest that it governs only the procedures by which a State may deprive persons of liberty, for at least 105 years . . . the Clause has been understood to contain a substantive component as well, one "barring certain government actions regardless of the fairness of the procedures used to implement them."[17]

Readers familiar with the sketchy argumentation contained in Harry Blackmun's majority opinion in *Roe v. Wade* will recognize that in *Casey* Justices O'Connor, Kennedy, and Souter actually provided the most detailed defense of abortion's place in the Constitution ever offered in a Supreme Court decision. This despite the fact that all three of these justices were appointed by presidents who had run for office pledging their commitment to the right to life and who were widely expected to use their power of judicial appointment to effect the reversal of *Roe v. Wade*. Many observers assumed *Casey* would be the occasion for that reversal and for the demise of the constitutional right to abortion. Instead, *Casey* led to an unmistakable endorsement of Blackmun's claim that the right to privacy, created by the liberty guarantees of the Fourteenth Amendment, is "broad enough to encompass a woman's decision to terminate her pregnancy."[18]

I do not mean to minimize by this argument the obstacles that now lie in the path of a woman seeking to terminate her pregnancy. It is true that abortions are somewhat more difficult to procure after *Casey* than they were before. Waiting periods and "informed consent" may pose "substantial obstacles" for some women, regardless of the court's arguments to the contrary. I also do not wish to minimize the real burdens placed on women by the myriad issues related to access to abortion. Radical elements of the right-to-life movement have succeeded in terrorizing abortion providers and their patients and in effectively reducing the number of physicians willing to engage in the practice of providing abortions.[19] Nevertheless, I think it is important that we do not minimize the extent to which a Supreme Court dominated by appointees of Presidents Reagan and Bush upheld the constitutional right to abortion. Abortion was the subject of a tremendous amount of political posturing, maneuvering, and plotting over the course of the twenty years preceding *Casey*. But at the end of those years, despite all the drama and all the "victories" by the pro-life side, the right to abortion was arguably more secure after Reagan and Bush than it was before. The tone and content of the joint opinion in *Casey* make it abundantly clear that a solid majority of the current court now views the constitutional right to abortion as settled law:

> Liberty finds no refuge in a jurisprudence of doubt. Yet 19 years after our holding that the Constitution protects a woman's right to terminate her pregnancy in its early stages, . . . that definition of liberty is still questioned. . . . The essential holding of *Roe v. Wade* should be retained and once again reaffirmed. . . . Before viability, the State's interests are not strong enough to support a prohibition of abortion or the imposition of a substantial obstacle on the woman's effective right to elect the procedure.[20]

Do Issues Matter?

While it is fair to say that public policy on abortion was not *fundamentally* changed by presidential politics between *Roe* and *Casey,* it is equally fair to say that the opposite is true as well. Despite all the attention paid to abortion during the 1970s and 1980s, the issue apparently had little direct effect on national elections during that period. Political scientists have used a number of techniques in efforts to uncover such an effect, but those efforts have been notable only for their failure.

Of the many studies published on this question, the most comprehensive was "Presidential Politics and Abortion, 1972–1988," by Byron W. Daynes and Raymond Tatalovich.[21] In this article, the authors not only reviewed the relevant literature on the subject, they also performed their own analysis of the relationship between abortion attitudes and the vote. What they found, in short, is that the data "do not support the interpretation that abortion attitudes had much effect on how voters differentiated between Republican and Democratic presidential candidates" between 1972 (just after *Roe)* and 1988 (just before *Casey).*[22] In 1976 and 1980, the candidates' positions on abortion, and the distinction between them, were not well understood by the electorate. And in 1984 and 1988, the differences between the candidates, though stark and well understood by most voters, were overshadowed by other considerations and voting cues.

These general conclusions are well supported by more targeted analyses of particular elections. The first presidential election year to follow *Roe v. Wade* was 1976, and a good deal of attention was paid to abortion and to the candidates' positions on the issue during the campaign. Nevertheless, Maris Vinovskis found that "voters did not divide in any consistent pattern for Carter or Ford on the basis of their own attitudes on abortion."[23] In fact, Vinovskis found abortion to be the weakest of all the potential voting predictors he included in his study.[24]

By 1980, 17 percent of respondents to a CBS News/*New York Times* poll listed abortion as one of the three most important issues facing the country.[25] However, the electorate still did not align itself according to its views on the issue. One explanation for this outcome was Jimmy Carter's success at straddling both sides of the abortion controversy during his presidency. The parties' platforms sharply differed on abortion in 1980, but according to one empirical examination of voter attitudes, "substantial ignorance and misperception persist[ed]" regarding the candidates' own positions and proposed policy reforms.[26]

Of course, it would have been difficult to misinterpret the differences over abortion that characterized the 1984 presidential campaign. President Reagan emphasized his opposition to abortion as an indicator of his commitment to religious principles and traditional values. And Geraldine Ferraro's public dispute with John Cardinal O'Connor in New York clearly emphasized the Democratic ticket's commitment to defending abortion rights.[27] Despite all the drama, however, the issue of abortion apparently played only a marginal role in directly determining individual votes. A mere 1 percent of survey respondents that year cited abortion as one of the three central issues in the election.[28]

Similarly, George Bush and Michael Dukakis differed in their publicly expressed views on abortion in 1988. But abortion was superseded as a central element of the Republican Party's social agenda that year by the issues of crime and patriotism. Willie Horton and the pledge of allegiance pushed abortion to the margins of presidential politics.

One of the reasons that abortion did not correlate closely with candidate preference between *Roe* and *Casey* is that the parties, seeking to define themselves on the issue and curry favor with powerful but narrow interests on either side of the dispute, radicalized their positions on abortion and spoke past the generally moderate views that the mass electorate holds on abortion. Only narrow bands of the electorate agree with *either* the Republican position that there should be a virtual ban on abortion *or* the Democratic defense of abortion on demand. Given that the bulk of public opinion falls within these two poles, voters have in a sense rejected both parties on the issue and voted according to other considerations.

Some recent studies have sought to take account of this disjunction between public opinion on abortion and the major parties' positions on the issue, by restricting their focus on those elements of the electorate that do hold extremist views of any kind. Kevin B. Smith, for example, examined the 1984 and 1988 presidential elections and found a moderate, though statistically significant, relationship between abortion attitudes and voting behavior among voters who hold "extreme" pro-choice views. "Pro-choice attitudes," he found, "appear to be enough to pull some Republicans into voting Democratic and to prevent some Democrats from voting Republican. There is not evidence that pro-life attitudes create similar effects."[29]

Smith's findings are interesting and a bit surprising, but they are nevertheless limited in their significance. His analysis is straightforwardly narrow, and he admits that abortion's influence on the vote disappears when viewed in aggregate terms. He does not suggest, in other words, that abortion on its own had a significant effect on the election itself.

Throughout the period between *Roe* and *Casey,* some voters on either end of the spectrum may have been motivated primarily by the candidates' positions on abortion. And some single-issue abortion groups on both sides of the question clearly provided organizational and financial support to their favored candidates. But based on the best empirical evidence currently available, the tremendous attention paid by politicians, strategists, and commentators to the issue of abortion and to the sharply divergent positions taken by the major parties and their presidential candidates masks the fact that abortion played, between *Roe v. Wade* in 1973 and *Planned Parenthood of Southeastern Pennsylvania v. Casey* in 1992, a sharply limited role in determining the outcome of presidential elections. Cut it any way you like (and there is a growing cottage industry devoted to doing just that) and you end up agreeing with Wattier, Daynes, and Tatalovich: "The electorate has NOT been choosing between presidential candidates from a single-issue perspective on abortion."[30]

That does not mean, of course, that the national political process was not influenced at all by the issue of abortion during these years. Elections may not have been swayed, but political rhetoric, electoral strategies, and mobilization efforts most certainly were. In fact, abortion as a centerpiece of the Republican Party's "social agenda" was at the heart of the most significant and concerted effort at systemwide political change since the 1930s.

Abortion and Political Change

As originally devised by V. O. Key, Jr., realignment theory holds that U.S. political history is punctuated by critical elections "in which the depth and intensity of political involvement are high, in which more or less profound readjustments occur in the relations of power within the community, and in which new and durable electoral groupings are formed."[31] Realignments, the theory states, are the results of tensions that develop in a governing political coalition over time. Divisions *within* a party become sharper than divisions *between* parties, and finally those tensions and divisions bring about dramatic shifts in both the subject matter and voting patterns of national electoral politics.

Realignment theory may have been the subject of more books and articles over the last forty years than any other theory of U.S. political behavior.[32] But over at least the last decade or so, almost all of these writings have focused on the fact that we have not had a critical election, or resulting realignment, since Franklin Roosevelt's formation of the powerful New Deal coalition in the 1930s. Walter Dean Burnham pointed out in a highly influential book in 1968 that critical elections have not occurred in U.S. history at random. "Instead," he noted, "there has been a remarkably uniform periodicity in their appearance."[33] The elections of 1800, 1828, 1860, 1896, and 1932 are widely recognized as the critical starting points of the five "party systems" that comprise U.S. political history. Based on Burnham's periodicity, both political scientists and practitioners of U.S. politics had reason to look to the 1960s as a decade of potentially historic and enduring political change.

In some ways, of course, those expectations were met and even exceeded. Some of the social changes associated with "the sixties" have indeed been historic and more or less enduring. But in terms of *political* change, in the way the phrase is used by realignment theorists, the 1960s were a bust. Richard Nixon's election in 1968 inaugurated a powerful Republican hold on the White House. But the Democrats retained control of Congress; they remained the clear plurality party among the electorate; and the issues and cleavages of the New Deal era refused to give way to new divisions and agenda the way that critical issues like extension of slavery and commitment to the Gold Standard had in other realigning eras. In short, there was no realignment. And predictably, scholarly journals burst with articles offering explanations for the nonevent.[34]

But while legions of analysts were dissecting, rejecting, and reinventing realignment as a *theory* of political change, politicians and political operatives were busily employing realignment as the basis for a *strategy* designed to bring about political change. By the late 1960s, Republican pols and conservative activists who either had read Key, Schattschneider, Burnham, and the others, or had recognized the same historical patterns themselves surmised that their time was at hand. They were not content, however, to trust the periodicity of historic trends and passively benefit from the tensions that inevitably form in any long-governing majority coalition. Rather, they set out self-consciously to aggravate those tensions and to raise issues that, in the lexicon of realignment theory, would cause "a substitute of one conflict for another" and would cause the party system to "shift on its axis."[35] As part of these efforts, these strategists turned, in time, to abortion. The issue of abortion, they found, could create and exacerbate tensions within the Democratic coalition at the same time that it could mobilize and energize the emerging conservative wing of the Republican Party.

At first, however, abortion was far from the minds of these realignment strategists. In fact, the tensions within the New Deal coalition, based largely though not exclusively on race, first emerged without any help from Republican strategists. Barry Goldwater stressed in 1964 his support for "states' rights," and as a result he won five states in the old confederacy. But Goldwater's candidacy was more the result of a coup at a national convention than it was a carefully planned strategy to build a new national majority. It was not until Richard Nixon's campaigns of 1968 and 1972 that Republican leaders really latched onto the theory of realignment and placed its dynamics at the heart of their political strategies.

Nineteen sixty-eight was potentially the pivotal year. It had been thirty-six years, after all, since the last critical election, and the Democratic Party was badly splintered over race and other noneconomic issues. Tensions and divisions within the Democratic coalition were sharp, and George Wallace's third-party candidacy posed a direct challenge to the New Deal political order. In the end, however, race and Wallace were not enough to bring about the realignment that Burnham's periodicity predicted for 1968. Just as Goldwater's rout had revealed the limits of ideological conservatism (in 1964), so the results of 1968 uncovered the limited electoral utility (outside the South) of overt racial appeals. Wallace carried his native region, but segregation evidently was not powerful enough on its own to rend the Democratic Party completely or to install the Republicans as the new majority party.

The deep fissures in the Democratic coalition were enough, however, to deny the presidency to Hubert Humphrey and to elect Richard Nixon. Moreover, the results of 1968 were portentous enough to set the strategic direction of U.S. national politics for the following two decades. As Kevin Phillips pointed out in his justly famous analysis of the 1968 election, if the Republicans could find a way to hold their own partisan base and add to it the "Wallace vote" of disaffected Democrats, then they could form a new electoral coalition that could reasonably expect to dominate U.S. politics for, say, the next thirty-six years.[36]

The fact remained, however, that a Republican appeal to disaffected Democrats could not be based on race alone. As Phillips and others recognized at the time, Republican inroads among conservatives in both the North and the South would require a much broader agenda. Ironically, it was two Democrats, Richard Scammon and Ben Wattenberg, who most clearly directed the Republicans toward the outline of what that agenda could be. In a book called *The Real Majority,* Scammon and Wattenberg pointed to the tremendous electoral potential of something they called the "social issue."[37] This issue, or set of issues, tapped into the voters' fears concerning race and crime, their anxieties in the face of declining traditional values and sexual mores, and their anger at the anti-American tone of the opposition to the war in Vietnam.

Scammon and Wattenberg saw the "social issue" as a powerful engine of emerging political change in the United States. It was potentially so powerful, they argued, that it could "rival bimetallism and depression in America's political history, an issue powerful enough that under certain circumstances it [could] compete in political potency with the older economic issues."[38] Clearly, Scammon and Wattenberg hoped that the Democratic Party would turn away from the dead end of the New Politics movement (feminism, environmentalism, peace activism, etc.) and ride the social issue to renewed vigor and success. But in fact it was the Republicans, rather than the Democrats, who were positioned to benefit from the increasingly vocal social conservatism of large segments of the U.S. electorate. The "social issue" was primarily a cluster of resentment directed at national elites who had foisted rapid social change on reluctant local communities. Since the Democrats, rather than Republicans, had been in firm control of the federal government for almost forty years, it was no surprise that they bore the brunt of social conservatism's wrath. The "social issue" became a central feature of U.S. politics in the 1970s and 1980s as Republican candidates and strategists argued that working and middle-class Americans should consider not only their economic interests but their social, moral, and religious interests as well. They should, the argument went, turn away from a Democratic Party led by radical feminists, homosexual activists, secular humanists, and black agitators, and toward a Republican Party recommitted to family, church, and traditional values.

Abortion was tailor-made for use by political operatives seeking to make this argument and to use the Republican Party as a vehicle for conservative political change. First of all, abortion had the potential to serve as a wedge issue that could help convert some socially conservative Roman Catholics to the Republican Party. Republican candidates, for example, could emphasize their agreement with Catholic teaching on abortion (broadly defined) as part of an effort to break the traditional and familial links between the Democratic Party and U.S. Catholicism.

At the same time, abortion also had the potential to help mobilize politically inactive Evangelical Protestants who deeply resented what they took to be federal imposition of secularist values on their communities, schools, and families. For Evangelicals, *Roe v. Wade* was a particularly egregious example of the federal government's unwillingness to allow local communities to govern themselves. Even some who were not particularly energized by the moral issues involved in early-term abortions recognized the threat that federal judicial power, starkly represented by the creation of a constitutional right to abortion, posed to local autonomy.

Finally, abortion was virtually unique in that it also had the potential to draw these two traditionally antagonistic religious populations into a single "pro-family" coalition.[39] Evangelical Protestants and Catholics viewed each other across wide historical and cultural divides. In fact, it is fair to say that for much of U.S. history, these two traditions had been in open and often violent conflict with each other. But, by the late 1970s, Evangelical and Catholic leaders began to draw tentatively closer together. Relations between bishops and preachers remained strained in some ways, but prominent spokespersons from each tradition came to recognize a common threat posed by secularism and the decline of traditional values. Nothing symbolized that threat more clearly than the federal judiciary's insistence on a fundamental constitutional right to terminate a pregnancy. And for religious leaders from Jerry Falwell to John Cardinal O'Connor, nothing more clearly identified the Republican Party with church, community, and family than the party's increasingly strident opposition to abortion.

For abortion to play this specific political role between *Roe* and *Casey,* it was not necessary for Catholics or Evangelicals actually to vote in large numbers on the basis of abortion as such. Nor, particularly in the case of Catholics, was it even necessary for them to accept fully their church's teachings on the subject. For politicians, it was enough that abortion could be used as a symbol with which conservatives and Republicans could identify themselves and, by implication, distance their opponents from, the moral concerns, social values, and religious beliefs of Middle America. Abortion was not particularly powerful as a direct determinant of individual votes. But it was indispensable as a symbolic, rhetorical tool in the Republican effort to redefine the agenda of U.S. politics and realign the U.S. party system.

Richard Nixon, as always an early practitioner of these realignment strategies, was the first national candidate to make partisan use of the issue of abortion. Just before the 1972 presidential vote, Nixon disavowed the pro-choice findings of his administration's commission on population issues. More importantly, he communicated that disavowal in an open letter to Terence Cardinal Cooke, the Catholic archbishop of New York and one of the leading advocates for his church's opposition to abortion.[40] Like all of his Republican successors since, Nixon used his stated opposition to, or even qualms about, abortion to drive a wedge between the Democratic Party to which U.S. Catholics had been committed for decades and the central moral values espoused by the church's leadership.

The use of the abortion issue in this way was significantly more important to Gerald Ford in 1976 than it had been to Richard Nixon in 1972. Ford, after all, was opposed by Jimmy Carter, an ex-governor of Georgia and a born-again southern Baptist. President Ford knew that he had no chance of repeating Nixon's 1972 success in the South, so he pinned his electoral college hopes on sweeping the heavily Catholic states of the Northeast and Midwest. Nixon's "southern strategy," one could say, gave way to Ford's Catholic strategy, as Ford used the abortion issue to associate himself with Catholic leadership and to exacerbate the so-called Catholic problem faced by the Democrats' Evangelical candidate. Ford, not much of a right-to-lifer himself, acquiesced in a strongly antiabortion plank in the Republican platform; he declared his reverence for life at Catholic functions; and he stressed his support for an antiabortion constitutional amendment during a personal meeting with the executive committee of the National Conference of Catholic Bishops (NCCB).[41] In short, Ford did everything he could to loosen Catholic attachment to the Democratic Party by doing everything he could to express his own respect for the church and its moral teachings. This strategy was not successful, of course. Ford lost the election, and a narrow majority of Catholics cast their votes for Carter. But Ford's use of the abortion question in 1976 raised the profile of the issue in rhetorical and strategic terms, as it set the groundwork for Ronald Reagan's more expansive use of it in 1980 and 1984.

For Reagan, abortion was more than a wedge with which to distance Catholic leadership from the Democratic Party. It was also a centerpiece of a social agenda designed to (a) break disaffected Democrats free from the party for good and (b) mobilize new, primarily, Evangelical voters who believed that the country had lost its moral moorings. In Reagan, the Republican Party finally found a candidate who could use the social issues as Scammon and Wattenberg had originally imagined they could be used. Better than any candidate either before or since, Reagan was able to hold in a single coalition the traditional Republican base and the "Wallace vote," and he could do it without stooping to racial appeals. As I have already recounted, abortion was not, according to the poll data, a central issue in either of Reagan's victories. But abortion was nevertheless a central element of Reagan's definition of himself as the defender of moral standards and the champion of traditional values. Put another way, Reagan's position on abortion allowed him to present himself, a divorced ex-actor with at best a spotty record of church attendance, as the "religious" candidate in two national elections: the first against a Sunday School–teaching southern Baptist, and the second against the loyal son of a Methodist minister.

Conclusion

The Republican Party's use of abortion during the 1980s is not the whole story of the issue's role in U.S. politics between *Roe* and *Casey,* however. For toward the end of that decade, abortion began to cut politically against the Republicans rather than in favor of them. All along, national candidates like Ronald Reagan and George Bush had counted on traditional elements of the Republican Party accepting the presence of religiously motivated social conservatives in their midst. These social conservatives, after all, offered traditional Republicans their best chance of becoming the real majority party after decades in the political woods. In time, however, it became clear that these social conservatives expected a price to be paid for their support of Republican candidates. They expected, for example, that Republican political successes at the ballot box would actually translate into the recriminalization of abortion in the statute books. For conservative Catholics and Evangelical Protestants, the social issues were much more than a tool with which to build a political coalition; they were a moral crusade. By the time George Bush moved into the White House, some conservative leaders were openly expressing their disappointment with the paltry satisfaction they had derived from their years of supporting Republican candidates. The real problem for the party, however, was not just that the social conservatives made demands. It was also that, in response to those demands, other elements within the Republican coalition set out to mobilize and energize the theretofore silent pro-choice majority within the GOP's ranks.[42]

Not surprisingly, the first national leader to notice and act on these emerging new dynamics of abortion politics was Lee Atwater, George Bush's campaign manager in 1988 and a leading practitioner of "wedge" politics. In early 1990, Atwater called on the Republican Party to tone down its rhetoric on abortion so as to avoid a dangerous intra-coalition split on the issue. In a memorable and lasting metaphor, he described the GOP as a "big tent" that should be able to accommodate a number of different opinions on legal abortion.[43] As the 1980s gave way to the 1990s, however, the issue of abortion continued to drive a wedge between traditional Republicans and their more socially conservative coalition partners. Atwater may have been right in describing the GOP as a big tent, but within that tent a potentially ruinous debate over abortion was raging. In addition, as I alluded to above, some tentative evidence began to surface suggesting that pro-choice Republicans were more willing to vote on the basis of their views on abortion than were pro-life Democrats.[44] In the 1990s, in other words, abortion might actually cause the Republicans not only trouble in platform-writing sessions but also votes in general elections.

For my purposes here, however, the central point is that though political circumstances changed in the years just before the Supreme Court decided *Planned Parenthood of Southeastern Pennsylvania v. Casey,* the political role played by the issue of abortion remained remarkably consistent. It continued to be an issue of such symbolic power that it could serve to sow divisions within political coalitions of various types. In purely political terms, abortion was in 1992, as *Casey* was being decided, pretty much what it had been since *Roe* in 1973—an issue that cut across the prevailing cleavages of the New Deal political order and an issue that could confound a political party either trying defensively to rescue a majority coalition or trying creatively to forge a new one.

Notes

1. *Roe v. Wade,* 410 U.S. 113 (1973).
2. *Planned Parenthood of Southeastern Pennsylvania v. Casey,* 112 Sup. Ct. 2791 (1992).
3. For a straightforward account of the various Hyde Amendments, see Barbara Hinckson Craig and David M. O'Brien, *Abortion and American Politics* (Chatham, N.J.: Chatham House, 1993), pp. 119–137.
4. For an account and analysis of these laws, see Glen A. Halva-Neubauer, "The States After *Roe:* No 'Paper Tigers,' " in *Understanding the New Politics of Abortion,* ed. Malcolm L. Goggin (Newbury Park, Calif.: Sage, 1993), pp. 167–189.
5. *New York Times,* September 4, 1981, A8.
6. O'Connor had voted in 1970 to repeal Arizona's abortion law because the law disallowed dilation and curettage (D&C) procedures for rape victims. In 1974, she had voted against a resolution calling for an antiabortion constitutional amendment and against a bill that would have limited the use of state hospitals for abortions. See *New York Times,* September 10, 1981, B14.
7. Ibid., emphasis added.
8. *City of Akron v. Akron Center for Reproductive Health,* 462 U.S. 416 (1983).
9. *Webster v. Reproductive Health Services,* 492 U.S. 490 (1989).
10. Ibid.
11. Ibid. Justice O'Connor, in a separate concurrence, once again reiterated her "undue burden" standard. Scalia, also in an opinion that spoke only for himself, ridiculed O'Connor's timidity and called for the immediate reversal of *Roe v. Wade.*
12. *Webster v. Reproductive Health Services,* 492 U.S. 490 (1989).
13. Ibid.
14. For an analysis of a number of these laws, see Timothy A. Byrnes and Mary Segers, eds., *The Catholic Church and the Politics of Abortion: A View from the States* (Boulder, Colo.: Westview Press, 1992).
15. See Thomas J. O'Hara, "The Abortion Control Act of 1989: The Pennsylvania Catholics," in *The Catholic Church and the Politics of Abortion,* ed. Byrnes and Segers, pp. 87–104.
16. *Planned Parenthood of Southeastern Pennsylvania v. Casey,* 112 Sup. Ct. 2791 (1992).
17. Ibid.
18. *Roe v. Wade,* 410 U.S. 113 (1973).

19. For a discussion of these important issues concerning access, see Mary C. Segers, "The Pro-Choice Movement Post-*Casey:* Preserving Access," in *Abortion Politics in American States,* ed. Mary C. Segers and Timothy A. Byrnes (Armonk, N.Y.: M. E. Sharpe, 1995), pp. 225–245.

20. *Planned Parenthood of Southeastern Pennsylvania v. Casey,* 112 Sup. Ct. 2791 (1992).

21. Byron W. Daynes and Raymond Tatalovich, "Presidential Politics and Abortion, 1972–1988," *Presidential Studies Quarterly* 22 (summer 1992): 545–561.

22. Ibid., p. 556.

23. Maris A. Vinovskis, "Abortion and the Presidential Election of 1976: A Multivariate Analysis of Voting Behavior," in *The Law and Politics of Abortion,* ed. Carl E. Schneider and Maris A. Vinovskis (Lexington: Lexington Books, 1980), p. 199.

24. Ibid., p. 200. The strongest predictors were party identification and an index of "liberalism."

25. Cited in Mark Wattier, Byron W. Daynes, and Raymond Tatalovich, "Presidential Elections and Abortion, 1972–1992: Evaluating the Single-Issue Voting Thesis" (paper delivered to the Western Political Science Association, Albuquerque, New Mexico, 1994).

26. Louis Bolce, "Abortion and Presidential Elections: The Impact of Public Perceptions of Party and Candidate Positions," *Presidential Studies Quarterly* 18 (fall 1988): 826.

27. See Timothy A. Byrnes, *Catholic Bishops in American Politics* (Princeton, N.J.: Princeton University Press, 1991), pp. 119–126.

28. Daynes and Tatalovich, "Presidential Politics and Abortion, 1972–1988," p. 556.

29. Kevin B. Smith, "Abortion Attitudes and Vote Choice in the 1984 and 1988 Presidential Elections," *American Politics Quarterly* 22 (July 1994): 361.

30. Wattier, Daynes, and Tatalovich, "Presidential Elections and Abortion, 1972–1992," p. 9, emphasis in the original.

31. V. O. Key, "Theory of Critical Elections," *Journal of Politics* 17 (February 1955): 4.

32. For an excellent review of the voluminous realignment literature, see Harold F. Bass, Jr., "Background to Debate: A Reader's Guide and Bibliography," in *The End of Realignment? Interpreting American Electoral Eras,* ed. Byron E. Shafer (Madison: University of Wisconsin Press, 1991), pp. 141–178.

33. Walter Dean Burnham, *Critical Elections and the Mainsprings of American Politics* (New York: W. W. Norton, 1970), p. 8.

34. Again see Bass, "Background to Debate." I admit I have made my own contribution to the deluge. See Timothy A. Byrnes, "Realignment Theory and the Modern American Presidency: A Reformulation," *Congress and The Presidency* 17 (autumn 1990): 131–138.

35. See E. E. Schattschneider, *The Semisovereign People: A Realist's View of Democracy in America* (New York: Holt, Rinehart, and Winston, 1960), p. 81, and James L. Sundquist, *Dynamics of the Party System: Alignment and Realignment of Political Parties in the United States* (Washington, D.C.: Brookings Institution, 1983), p. 300.

36. Kevin B. Phillips, *The Emerging Republican Majority* (Garden City, N.Y.: Anchor Books, 1969).

37. Richard M. Scammon and Ben J. Wattenberg, *The Real Majority* (New York: Coward-McCann, 1970).

38. Ibid., p. 40.

39. For a discussion of the shift from a "pro-life" movement to a broader "pro-

family" coalition, see Connie Paige, *The Right to Lifers: Who They Are, How They Operate, Where They Get Their Money* (New York: Summit, 1983), p. 135.

40. Cited in Byrnes, *Catholic Bishops in American Politics,* p. 65.

41. Both Ford and Carter held meetings with the NCCB's leadership that year. Ibid., pp. 74–80.

42. For a discussion of the "Republican pro-choice insurgency," see Michele McKeegan, *Abortion Politics: Mutiny in the Ranks of the Right* (New York: Free Press, 1992), pp. 147–176.

43. *New York Times,* January 20, 1990, 10.

44. See Wattier, Daynes, and Tatalovich, "Presidential Elections and Abortion 1972–1992," pp. 5–6, and Alan I. Abromowitz, "It's Abortion Stupid: Policy Voting in the 1992 Presidential Election" (paper delivered to the American Political Science Association, Washington, D.C., 1993).

2.4

The Importance of Elections in a Strong Congressional Party Era
The Effect of Unified vs. Divided Government

Bruce I. Oppenheimer

The 1992 elections ended a twelve-year period of divided party control of the U.S. national government. With the election of Bill Clinton and the maintenance of Democratic majorities in the House of Representatives and the Senate, an extended period of polarized and, at times, stalemated struggles over policy between Republican presidents and Democratic congressional majorities (albeit with Republican majorities in the Senate for six of those years) ceased. Except during the four years of the Carter presidency, divided party control had been the rule since 1969. Importantly, the return of unified party government occurred when U.S. governing parties are more cohesive than at any point since the early part of the twentieth century. With unified party control and a more cohesive majority party, many believed that the potential to resolve a range of policy issues had greatly improved. The experience was, however, a short-lived one as the 1994 elections returned the United States to divided party government. Although this time the division is one with Republican majorities in the House and Senate and a Democrat in the White House, the expectation is that the resolution of major issues will again be difficult.

This perspective—that the existence of divided, as opposed to unified, party control of the U.S. government makes a substantial difference—is not without controversy. Some observers, such as David Mayhew, have carefully argued that there are few or no differences in terms of enactment of major policies during periods of unified and divided party control.[1] And although others have disputed Mayhew's position, they lacked a critical empirical condition to make a persuasive case.[2] That condition, a recent period of unified government, has not been available. Instead, one has to go back to the end of the Carter administration (1977–1980), or even further to the Kennedy and Johnson administrations (1961–1968), to find periods when elections resulted in unified party control.

Such comparisons are seriously flawed and not simply because of the time that has passed; the problem is that the political contexts differ in a critical way. The Kennedy, Johnson, and Carter administrations, along with those of Truman and Roosevelt after 1937, existed in a period when the governing parties—those composed of persons elected to office under a party label—were relatively weak. With weak governing parties, the effect of unified versus divided party control is severely diluted. From 1937 until the early 1980s, governing was largely done by cross-party coalitions of which the conservative coalition of Republicans and southern Democrats was the most prominent and durable. In that era, the conservative coalition would often block the policy initiatives of Democratic presidents during times of unified party control. The policy consequences of elections were muted by weak governing parties except in a couple of instances. The first exception was after the 1952 elections, during the 82nd Congress (1953–1954), when there was unified Republican control of government giving conservative dominance in both legislative and executive branches. But policy enactments were modest because of Eisenhower's limited agenda and his perspective about the appropriate presidential role.[3] The other exception was after the 1964 election, during the 89th Congress (1965–1966), when Democratic majorities were so extraordinarily large in both the House and the Senate that the lack of cohesiveness could not prevent the passage of a broad range of domestic programs that comprised the Great Society. In addition, there were some policy areas, such as agriculture, on which northern and southern Democrats remained linked against Republicans in the post-1937 period.[4]

Thus, for most of the era, Mayhew's analysis may well be correct. Whether voters' decisions resulted in unified or divided party control seemed to have had little effect on the capacity of the national government to resolve major policy issues. It would be difficult to argue that the U.S. government functioned any better or worse in resolving major policy issues with divided party control, rather than with unified party control, in the period from the late 1930s until the early 1980s. Republican presidents working with Democratic majorities in Congress could enact policies by combining the support they could attract from conservative southern Democrats with that of the minority Republicans to produce governing majorities. And Democratic presidents would struggle to hold enough support from southerners in Congress and from moderate Republicans to combine with northern Democrats to produce governing majorities. In the former case, as Gary Orfield analyzes during the Nixon administration, northern Democrats could sometimes block the efforts of Republican presidents, just as in the latter the conservatives in Congress could block the efforts of Democratic liberals.[5]

True, James MacGregor Burns and other advocates of "responsible party government" could criticize the lack of cohesiveness of U.S. parties and the policy deadlocks that they contended were a result of weak parties. But this was a problem of the party system first and existed whether there was unified or divided party government. In fact, the deadlock about which Burns was primarily concerned came about with a Democratic president and a Democratic Congress.[6]

Rarely then did the existence of unified versus divided party control of government have much impact. Since the early 1980s, this has been changing. The governing parties in Congress have become markedly stronger and more cohesive. The conservative coalition, for all practical purposes, had faded into history. And whether elections produce unified or divided party control has serious consequences for government's capacity to make policy.

Why Did U.S. Governing Parties Become More Cohesive?

One of the ironies of U.S. politics over the past two decades is that while political parties on one level, in the electorate, have become weaker, political parties on another level, in government, have become stronger. Since the late 1960s, the level of voter attachment to political parties has declined. Fewer voters describe themselves as strong identifiers, and more claim to be independents.[7] This has not been without its effects on politicians: the way they run for office and the stances they take after election. It has been argued that candidates run more individualistic campaigns that deemphasize their party attachment and that once elected to office they are more responsive to constituency-based interests than to party policy position when the two conflict.

But countervailing forces have been operating that have made the parties in Congress, especially the Democrats, more unified. The strongest of these has been the long-term impact of the 1965 Voting Rights Act and its subsequent revisions on the nature of southern representation in the House and Senate. With the enfranchisement of large numbers of African American citizens in the South following the 1965 passage of this civil rights law, the almost uniformly conservative voting records of southern Democrats in Congress began to change. This change involved three components. First, southerners in Congress were faced with altered reelection constituencies.

Table 1

Party Votes as a Percentage of All Roll Call Votes, 1971–1994

Year	House	Senate	Year	House	Senate
1971	38	42	1983	56	44
1972	27	36	1984	47	40
1973	42	40	1985	61	50
1974	29	44	1986	57	52
1975	48	48	1987	64	41
1976	36	37	1988	47	42
1977	42	42	1989	55	35
1978	33	45	1990	49	54
1979	47	47	1991	55	49
1980	38	46	1992	64	53
1981	37	48	1993	66	67
1982	36	43	1994	62	52

Sources: The data in this table for 1971–1992 are taken from Norman J. Ornstein, Thomas E. Mann, and Michael J. Malbin, *Vital Statistics on Congress, 1993–1994* (Washington, D.C.: CQ Press), p. 200. The data for 1993 and 1994 are from *Congressional Quarterly Weekly Report*, December 31, 1994, p. 3624. The latter have been rounded to the nearest percentage.

To represent the interests of newly enfranchised constituents, some of these members began taking more moderate positions on civil rights and a broad range of social welfare legislation. By the time the Voting Rights Act came up for renewal in 1970, many southerners who had voted against it in 1965 were among its supporters. Second, as this generation of southern Democratic members left Congress, they were usually replaced by Democratic nominees of a more moderate political persuasion. After all, to win contested Democratic primaries, candidates had to appeal for support to the growing number of African American voters in many southern constituencies. This became more pronounced as conservative, white voters increasingly moved to the Republican Party. Third, in some areas, conservative Republican candidates faced with more moderate Democratic opponents won seats that had previously been held by conservative Democrats.

The impact of these changes was gradual. By the early 1980s, however, it meant that conservative southern Democrats had become an endangered species in Congress. Democrats elected from the South voted more like their northern colleagues on most issues than had been the case previously. The data in Tables 1 and 2 trace the change from 1971 to 1994 in party votes and party unity scores.[8] Party votes, those on which majority of Democrats are opposed by a majority of Republicans, have risen from 30 to 40 percent of all roll call votes to a high of over 65 percent in 1993.[9] Party

Table 2

Mean Scores for Party Unity, 1971–1994

	House			Senate		
Year	All Democrats	Southern Democrats	Republicans	All Democrats	Southern Democrats	Republicans
1971	72	48	76	74	56	75
1972	70	44	76	72	43	73
1973	75	55	74	79	52	74
1974	72	51	71	72	41	68
1975	75	53	78	76	48	71
1976	75	52	75	74	46	72
1977	74	55	77	72	48	75
1978	71	53	77	75	54	66
1979	75	60	79	76	62	73
1980	78	64	79	76	64	74
1981	75	57	80	77	64	85
1982	77	62	76	76	62	80
1983	82	67	80	76	70	79
1984	81	68	77	75	61	83
1985	86	76	80	79	68	81
1986	86	76	76	74	59	80
1987	88	78	79	85	80	78
1988	88	81	80	85	78	74
1989	86	77	76	79	69	79
1990	86	78	78	82	75	77
1991	86	78	81	83	73	83
1992	86	79	84	82	70	83
1993	89	83	88	87	78	86
1994	88	83	88	86	77	81

unity scores—the percentage of the time members vote with a majority of their party on party votes—for southern Democrats increased markedly. The scores rose from the forties and fifties in the 1970s to the sixties in the early 1980s to the upper seventies and eighties by the late 1980s and early 1990s. Simultaneously, the difference between the mean score for southern Democrats and the mean score for all Democrats has declined. Party unity scores for Republicans have increased by modest amounts in part because they were higher at the start.[10]

Other explanations have been offered for the growing cohesiveness of parties in Congress. They include those related to the ideological position of presidents vis-à-vis that of the parties in Congress; the greater capacity of majority party leaders to structure and limit floor votes in the House than previously; and broader involvement of the national parties in the recruiting, training, and managing of congressional candidates.[11] Each of these may have contributed to stronger congressional parties but in a more mod-

Table 3

Members Voting with Opposition Party More Often on Party Votes

		House	Senate
95th Congress 1977–1978	Democrats	44	9
	Republicans	13	9
97th Congress 1981–1982	Democrats	26	3
	Republicans	14	2
99th Congress 1985–1986	Democrats	4	4
	Republicans	12	3
101st Congress 1989–1990	Democrats	1	1
	Republicans	14	2
103rd Congress 1993–1994	Democrats	3	1
	Republicans	2	2

est fashion than that resulting from the changing nature of southern Democratic membership in the Congress.

The data in Table 3 demonstrate the change that has occurred in the parties in Congress in dramatic fashion. It shows the number of Democratic and Republican representatives and senators who voted more frequently with members of the other party than with members of their own party on party votes. Note that in the 95th Congress (1977–1978) there was a substantial amount of overlap between the two parties. Eighteen senators and fifty-seven House members voted more often with the opposition party than with their own party. These members were often described as conservative Democrats and liberal Republicans. By the 103rd Congress (1993–1994) only three senators and five House members were voting with the other party more often than with their own party. And one of the senators, Richard Shelby (Ala.), switched parties at the start of the 104th Congress. There are few members whose voting records would still qualify as conservative Democrats or liberal Republicans, even among those who still accept one of those labels. Little overlap of the parties exists in Congress. They are more cohesive now than at anytime since the early years of Woodrow Wilson's presidency.

Significantly, more cohesive parties in the House and the Senate have had an important effect on the nature of party control of government. I will argue that when parties are relatively strong the existence of unified, as opposed to divided, party control has a sizable effect on how government confronts policy problems. Although Mayhew's analysis may be accurate in finding little difference between unified and divided party control in a period when the governing parties were weak, his conclusions are limited to that political context.

To demonstrate that elections that produce unified, as opposed to divided, party control have major effects on governing, it will be necessary to extend the time frame of previous analyses and to consider additional means for examining the impact of party control. As noted earlier, Mayhew and others did not have a period of unified party control to study during which the parties were strong. In addition to being deprived of a crucial set of conditions, it also made it more difficult to appreciate the problems faced by divided government operating with strong parties, as was the case from the mid-1980s through 1992. Thus, having the first two years of the Clinton administration to include in the analysis is valuable.

However, there is more to governing than the passage of major new laws.[12] The analysis of two additional facets of governing will provide a fuller picture of whether important differences exist in periods of unified and divided government. The first of these deals with the efficiency with which government performs routine, yet critical, activities. This is overlooked by those who only examine major undertakings. Yet it is another indication of governing effectiveness. The second deals with more general measures about the state of agreement between Congress and the president. Rather than being merely a measure of presidential success, such measures may indicate something about the capacity of Congress and the president to reach a consensus. It also provides a more generalized perspective on the government's ability to resolve conflicts beyond that measured by the passage of major new laws. With the use of these additional indicators, we will be able to develop a more comprehensive evaluation of whether significant governing differences exist during periods of unified as opposed to divided party control and whether the elections that produce these differing party conditions are of importance.

This analysis will largely focus on activity from the first two years of each of the past five presidential terms beginning with the Carter presidency in 1977–1978. Because the level of legislative activity may vary across a presidential term and because only two years of the Clinton presidency will be examined at this point, it is necessary to limit the analysis to the first half of the presidential terms to maintain comparability.

Lawmaking, 1977–1994

It is difficult to compare lawmaking across congresses. In his efforts to measure the number of important laws that were enacted, Mayhew recognizes the inherent methodological problems of the undertaking. But even his elaborate scheme misses some enactments that one might well deem important. For example, the establishment of the Department of Education makes the list but not the Department of Energy. Significantly, he relies heavily on major journalists' accounts supplemented by the writings of policy specialists, rather than on publications that may provide more comprehensive analysis of lawmaking activity. In addition, he recognizes the fact that in recent years there has been a tendency to enact omnibus legislation that contains a number of separate items.[13]

To develop a list of major laws enacted during the 103rd Congress, I used a different source than Mayhew had for earlier years, but I tried to apply similar criteria. I relied on the legislative summaries in *Congressional Quarterly Weekly Report* that are provided at the end of each session, rather than on summary articles by congressional correspondents from the *New York Times* and the *Washington Post.*[14] I was careful, however, to include only those enactments that could be reasonably described as important in the way Mayhew defines it as "both innovative and consequential."[15] And actions that Mayhew excluded, such as resolutions, annual appropriations, and routine extensions of existing laws, were also left out in developing the list for the 103rd Congress.

The data comparing the number of important enactments during the first congress in each of the past five presidential terms is presented in Table 4. Of immediate note is that the eighteen enactments in the 103rd Congress are twice that of the divided party governments in the 97th, 99th, and 101st Congresses, when Reagan and Bush were presidents, and 50 percent greater than that during the 95th Congress, when there was unified party control but the parties were weaker. The criticisms of the Clinton administration and the 103rd Congress for what they failed to achieve on issues such as health care, campaign financing, and lobbying disclosure may obscure their significant accomplishments. In Table 5, the eighteen major enactments are listed. Significantly, seven of them were achieved in 1994 when attention tended to focus on the legislative failures of the Clinton administration and Congress. The data suggest that media evaluations and conventional wisdom about the 1994 legislative achievements are not totally supported by the evidence.

The low level of enactments in the three congresses with divided party government is also worthy of comment. Mayhew largely attributes the drop in the number of important laws enacted in the 1980s compared to earlier years to the fact that legislation has become increasingly omnibus in nature. What in the past would have comprised several pieces of legislation is combined into a single bill. And at least a few of the enactments in the Reagan and Bush congresses fit the omnibus description. But if that were

Table 4

Number of Major New Laws Enacted

Congress	Major New Laws
95th (1977–1978)	12
97th (1981–1982)	9
99th (1985–1986)	9
101st (1989–1090)	9
103rd (1993–1994)	18

Sources: The entries for the 95th–101st Congresses are taken from David R. Mayhew, *Divided We Govern* (New Haven: Yale University Press, 1991).

Table 5

Major New Laws Enacted in the 103rd Congress, 1993–1994

1. Family and Medical Leave
2. Motor Voter
3. Budget-Reconciliation
4. Economic Stimulus
5. Thrift Bailout (sets up new deposit insurance fund)
6. Foreign Aid Authorization (includes Russian aid package)
7. National Institute of Health Reauthorization (family-planning funding and counseling)
8. National Service Corps
9. Handgun Waiting Period
10. Defense Authorization (cuts "star wars" and gays in military)
11. North American Free Trade Agreement (NAFTA)
12. Abortion Clinic Access
13. Independent Counsel
14. Interstate Banking
15. Omnibus Crime
16. School Improvement
17. Department of Agriculture Reorganization
18. General Agreement on Tariffs and Trade (GATT)

the sole or primary cause, how is one to explain the high number of major new laws in the 103rd Congress, several of which were omnibus?[16] The data on major enactments from the 103rd Congress make the effect of increasingly strong congressional parties more evident. Those stronger parties made the enactment of major new laws more difficult during congresses with divided government and easier in the one congress with unified government than had been the case when parties were weaker. The government during the Reagan and Bush presidencies produced fewer important laws than in previous periods of divided control because the majority party in the

Congress had become more cohesive. And with stronger parties, the unified government of the 103rd Congress was able to produce more major laws than the unified government in the first two years of the Carter administration. To see the effect clearly, however, one needed to have the data from these two years of unified control with strong governing parties.

Moreover, it took longer to enact a number of the major laws in the Reagan and Bush congresses because of divided party control. But the efficiency with which major enactments occur is difficult to measure. One cannot fairly compare the speed of enactment of an immigration bill in one congress with a voter registration bill in another congress. In rare instances, one can find major bills in two congresses that are sufficiently similar so that some conclusions about efficiency may be drawn. Such is the case with the Deficit Reduction Package of 1990 and the 1993 Budget-Reconciliation Bill. Both were tax and spending packages designed to reduce the deficit by about $500 billion over a five-year period. And both were the end step in an annual budget reconciliation process that began with the introduction of the president's budget in January. The 1990 bill was enacted during divided party control and was not completed until November 5 of that year. The 1993 bill enacted under unified party control was completed by and signed into law on August 10. Thus, the budget package comparison offers support for the claim that major enactments are handled more expeditiously under unified party government than under divided party government. Yet, even with the similarities, one might reasonably argue that the situations are not totally comparable, that factors unrelated to the state of party control affected the speed of enactment, or that a single case does not provide an adequate test of a hypothesis about the relationship between the state of party control and the efficiency of government decision making.

There is an alternative to using major enactments as a vehicle for measuring the efficiency of decision making under unified and divided party control. Instead of using major laws, one can examine the promptness with which required, major legislation is enacted. There are two vehicles that fit this description and allow us to examine whether the state of party control affects the efficiency with which government operates. The first of these involves the budget resolution. Under the 1975 Budget Act, Congress is directed to adopt a concurrent budget resolution each year to provide direction and parameters for its legislative work. The budget resolution is supposed to be adopted by May 15.[17] The adoption of the budget resolution has regularly been conflictual and highly partisan, especially in the House of Representatives. One might expect that during periods of unified party government, Congress is more supportive of the budget that the president sends to Congress and therefore finds it easier to construct its budget resolution.

Table 6

Date of Budget Resolution Passage

Year	Date
1977	May 17
1978	May 17
1981	May 21
1982	June 23
1985	August 1
1986	June 26
1989	May 18
1990	*
1993	April 1
1994	May 12

*In 1990, the House and Senate passed separate versions of the budget resolution but were unable to resolve the differences between them.

In addition, the resources of the presidency are available to the majority party in Congress to assist in the development and passage of the budget resolution. Does Congress find it easier to meet the May 15 deadline for adoption of the budget resolution when there is unified party government? The data in Table 6 suggest that it does. In the four unified years, the budget resolution was adopted as early as April 1 and no later than May 17. In only two of six years of divided government was the budget resolution completed in May. Twice it was adopted in late June, once in August, and in 1990 the difference between the House version passed on May 1 and the Senate version passed on June 14 were never really resolved.[18]

A second and perhaps more important indicator of the regular legislative activity of the national government comes in the form of the thirteen appropriations bills it has to address each year. Mayhew excludes these bills from his analysis of major laws in part because their passage is required. Yet, no one would deny their importance. Not only do these bills provide the annual spending for federal government agencies and their programs, but they may restrict the use of bureaucratic authority and, at times, actually grant or amend agency authority.[19]

To allow Congress more time to complete work on appropriations bills, the start of the fiscal year was moved from July 1 to October 1, beginning in 1975, as part of the Budget and Impoundment Control Act. One test of the efficiency of government operations can accordingly be obtained by looking at the record of enactment of appropriations bills under unified and divided party control situations. Does divided party control slow the com-

Table 7

Number of Appropriation Bills Enacted Within One Month of Fiscal Year Start by State of Party Control

Year	Party Control of Government	Appropriations Bills Enacted as of November 1
1977	Unified	11
1978	Unified	13
1981	Divided	1
1982	Divided	3
1985	Divided	1
1986	Divided	*
1989	Divided	2
1990	Divided	0
1993	Unified	11
1994	Unified	13

*In 1986, agreement could not be reached in a timely fashion on the separate appropriations bills so Congress passed a continuing resolution that combined the substance of the thirteen bills. President Reagan reluctantly signed it on October 30.

pletion of the enactment of appropriations? If these bills are not enacted by October 1, a continuing resolution must be passed to allow the affected agencies to operate until such time as the appropriations bill is enacted or those agencies will cease operation.

In Table 7, the record for enactment of appropriations bills is presented for the first two years of each presidential term from 1977 to 1994. Data is presented on the number of bills enacted by November 1. The reason for using the November 1 date is to allow any enactments that may have occurred shortly after the October 1 start of the fiscal year to be included and also to give some indication of the severity of the delay in enactment. The enactment of annual appropriations clearly has been more efficient during periods of unified party control than during periods of divided party control. In none of the six years of divided party control were more than three appropriations bills enacted by November 1. In 1986, the process became so bogged down on the individual bills that Congress finally presented President Reagan with one massive continuing resolution that was effectively an omnibus appropriations bill to sign or veto. It left many issues unresolved until Congress took up the supplemental appropriations bill after the new Congress began. By contrast, in the four years of unified party government, forty-eight of the fifty-two appropriations bills were enacted by November 1. In three of those years, the vast majority of the bills were actually complete by October 1.

Although the enactment of appropriations may be considerably less glamorous than the passage of major new authorizations, it may be no less important to the functioning of government. And the failure to complete the appropriations work on time creates uncertainty for government bureaucracies. More importantly, the clients of government programs are also affected. Decisions on the awarding of various contracts and grants are inevitably delayed, while agencies wait for the passage of appropriations. And the data suggest that the situation is more severe when Congress and the president are of opposite political parties than when they are of the same party. Certainly, the struggle between President Clinton and the Republican congressional majority over appropriations bills, which led to government shutdowns in 1995, indicates that the effects may be quite serious.[20]

In sum, even if one accepts the Mayhew position that major legislative enactments are no more likely during periods of unified government than during periods of divided government (a position that has been challenged in this article), there is a clear difference in the efficiency with which government handles the routine, yet important, legislative activity required of it depending on the state of party control.

Presidential-Congressional Agreement

Another aspect of governing that may be influenced by divided, as opposed to unified, party control is the state of presidential-congressional relations. It is only natural to expect higher levels of presidential-congressional agreement when there is unified party control. This has been fairly well documented by a number of scholars.[21] They have relied, to varying degrees, on the analysis of roll call votes in the House and the Senate on which the president has taken a position. *Congressional Quarterly Weekly Report* tracks these roll calls and computes an annual score for members of Congress, called the Presidential Support Score. The name is somewhat misleading because the scores are not merely a measure of whether the president gets what he wants from Congress. Many of the votes that are included in the analysis are on legislative initiatives of the Congress to which the president is reacting. Accordingly, the individual scores of members and the percentage of the time on which Congress supports the position favored by the president on these roll calls is more accurately a measure of presidential-congressional agreement.

What is important to note is that even during periods of divided party government, there has traditionally been a fair amount of agreement between Congress and the president on the roll call votes that comprised the presidential support score. Despite the 2 : 1 Democratic majority in the

House during most of President Gerald Ford's presidency, the House sided with the Republican president on more than half of the roll calls on which he took a position.[22] And unified party government did not guarantee that the president and Congress would always agree. Even with a 2 : 1 Democratic House majority in the 94th Congress, the House sided with President Carter only slightly more than 70 percent of the time. It would be inaccurate to describe the relationship between Ford and Congress as one of gridlock or between Carter and Congress as one of perfect harmony. Given a similar partisan division of the House with presidents of opposite parties, the scores are quite close. Seemingly, this adds support to Mayhew's position of minimal effects of divided versus unified party government.

But, as with the efforts to measure the impact of divided control on the passage of major new laws, it is necessary to ask whether the growing strength of parties has affected the level of agreement between Congress and the president. The reason presidents and Congress could reach agreement during periods of divided party control from the 1950s until the mid-1980s was that the parties in Congress were relatively weak and noncohesive. Members of Congress would regularly support positions taken by presidents of the opposite party. And during periods of unified control, members of Congress from the president's party would not always support him. With the development of strong parties, this changed. As I have documented elsewhere, the success rates in the House of Representatives for Ronald Reagan after 1982 and throughout George Bush's presidency were at an all-time low.[23] In five of the ten years, the House agreed with the president on 37 percent or less of the roll call votes. With strong governing parties and weak parties in the electorate, I argued that presidential-congressional agreement levels would fluctuate greatly depending on whether there was unified or divided party government. That was prior to the Clinton presidency and the 103rd Congress. The first two years of the Clinton administration have given us an opportunity to see what happens to the presidential-congressional agreement level with strong governing parties and unified government. In both 1993 and 1994, Congress agreed with President Clinton on 86.4 percent of the roll call votes on which he took a position.[24] (The rate for the House was 87.3 and 87.2 for the two years, respectively, and for the Senate it was 85.4 in both years.) That level was the highest since 1965. In that year, Congress supported the position taken by President Lyndon Johnson on 93.1 percent of the votes. But Johnson had the luxury of better than two-thirds Democratic majorities in both the House and the Senate. By comparison, for most of the 103rd Congress, Democrats comprised 56 percent of the Senate and 59 percent of the House.

To illustrate better the effect of divided versus unified party control on presidential-congressional agreement during an era of strong governing parties, I ranked the House and Senate members in order of their level of agreement with the president on roll call votes on which he took a position for each of the first two years of the five presidential terms beginning with the Carter presidency. I then asked what was the support level of the 218th House member and the 51st senator, the ones who would be needed to construct majorities in each chamber. This data is presented in Table 8. The effect is especially noticeable in the House. In a time of relatively weak parties (1977–1982), there is little effect from unified and divided party control. Despite the fact that Carter was dealing with a House of Representatives with 292 Democratic members in the 95th Congress and Reagan was faced with a House with only 192 Republicans in the 97th Congress, the difference in Presidential Support Score of the 218th member is not as large as one might expect and is, in fact, the same for Carter in 1978 as it is for Reagan in 1981. However, as the governing parties became stronger, the contrast between unified and divided governing situations became more marked. The Presidential Support Score of the 218th House member in the 103rd Congress is over thirty points higher than during the 99th and 101st Congresses. To put together House majorities for their positions, Reagan, during his second term, and Bush had to rely on members who supported them less than half of the time and, in some years, only slightly more than a third of the time. With unified party government in 1993 and 1994, Clinton could build a majority with members who supported his position over 70 percent of the time.

The conclusion from the data in Table 8 is clear. In an era of weak governing parties, the state of party control (unified versus divided) had only a modest effect on presidential-congressional agreement. With strong parties, the state of party control has had a major effect on the level of presidential-congressional agreement. The data suggest that when governing parties are weak, divided control of government may result in slightly lower levels of presidential-congressional agreement but not in gridlock or stalemate. When governing parties are strong, divided control makes it difficult to produce presidential-congressional agreement.

The 1995 session of the 104th Congress again demonstrated the volatility that exists in presidential-congressional agreement when the governing parties are strong. Exact figures are not available at this writing, but it seems that with the return to divided control, the levels of agreement between President Clinton and the Congress may drop to the levels of the last ten years of the Reagan and Bush presidencies. And if the governing parties continue to strengthen, the level in the entire 104th Congress may be even lower than in the decade from 1983 to 1992.[25]

Table 8

Presidential Support Score of 218th House Member and 51st Senator

President	Year	House	Senate
Jimmy Carter	1977	65	74
	1978	60	74
Ronald Reagan	1981	60	72
	1982	54	66
Ronald Reagan	1985	44	58
	1986	34	66
George Bush	1989	49	68
	1990	36	55
Bill Clinton	1993	72	80
	1994	72	81

Will the Governing Parties Remain Strong?

Relatively strong governing parties have been the exception, not the rule, in the history of U.S. politics. Prior to the current experience with them, one must go back to the early years of the New Deal to find anything that even approaches the current level of cohesion. And that occurred only after a major economic depression and a major alteration in voters' attachments to their political parties. By 1937, congressional Democrats were seriously split and a faction was developing in the Republican ranks that was not inalterably opposed to the New Deal. The diversity of the country, the limited influence that the national parties have over the selection of congressional candidates, the public distrust of strong political parties, and the umbrella nature of U.S. political parties have made it difficult to maintain episodes of strong, cohesive governing parties. The existence of strong governing parties in the House of Representatives since 1983, and somewhat less strong in the Senate more recently, is an unusually long deviation from the U.S. norm of weak governing parties. Indeed, there are no indications that the governing parties are about to become weaker and less cohesive. If that were the case, one might have expected a reduction in the cohesion of congressional Democrats in 1994, as those representing more conservative constituencies might distance themselves from the national party and its unpopular president. That did not occur. Instead, the failure to pass Clinton administration programs resulted from the unified opposition of Republicans, especially in the Senate where a minority still has the capacity to block legislation.

Moreover, the development of relatively strong governing parties occurred without a prior or simultaneous strengthening of voters attachment to the parties. Since the early 1970s, the United States has been in an era of dealignment. Fewer voters are strong party identifiers. More voters describe themselves as independents. The levels of split-ticket voting have been high. Yet one normally conceptualizes a linkage between the state of the party in the electorate and the state of the governing parties. When the party in the electorate is weak, candidates are believed to run independent, rather than party-oriented, campaigns. They appeal to voters on the basis of constituency concerns, as opposed to national party positions and ties. And upon winning office, these candidates will tend to side with constituency preferences on issues when there is conflict with party positions. The result is that governing parties are not cohesive. And in the past, the periods of strong congressional parties have normally occurred when party ties among voters have also been strong—the late 1890s and the 1930s.

Thus, the increased cohesion of the congressional parties appears independent of what has been occurring to party ties among voters. I can offer some reasoned speculation on why this is the case. It largely reflects the fact that politics in the United States has become nationalized. The late Speaker Tip O'Neill's adage that all politics is local in the United States is either no longer correct or the diversity of localism is far less than once was the case. The mobility of the population is such that, unlike previous generations, Americans are no longer born, raised, employed, and interred in the same place. The coverage of political news and policy issues is now national in scope. The media are increasingly nationalized not just in terms of television and radio but with newspapers as well. One can now watch Cable News Network (CNN) as well as buy *USA Today,* the *New York Times,* and the *Wall Street Journal* on the day of publication in most areas of the country. And despite the efforts to move the decisions of government back to state and local levels, the issues of major concern to voters—the economy, crime, drugs, and health care—are not just of concern to given states or localities. Is it any wonder that the political parties are also more national in nature?

Although the involvement of the national parties in the recruitment and selection of House and Senate candidates may have only increased to a modest level, the general election campaigns are becoming more nationalized. The national parties are actively engaged in training candidates; in suggesting appropriate campaign managers, consultants, media advisers, pollsters, and advertising firms; in providing issue themes and speech materials; and, most importantly, in raising and distributing funds to candidates directly and indirectly.[26] Increasingly, House and Senate candidates of the same party are working from the same script, emphasizing the same issues, running similar campaign ads, and receiving their financing from the same national sources. The nationalization of politics makes this possible and, in turn, contributes to an increase in nationalization. Upon arriving in Washington, those elected tend to have goals in common with others in their party, regardless of the locality from which they hail.

Thus, unlike previous episodes of strong governing parties in the United States, the current one will last far longer. Because they result from major changes in the political environment that have increasingly nationalized U.S. politics and not from more temporary cohesion of diverse party elements that result from a given overriding issue(s), the stronger governing parties may well be relatively permanent.

If the analysis presented above is correct, then elections will matter more than in the past. Unified party government will mean that policy initiatives will be more easily enacted and previous enactments more easily repealed. Divided government will result in frequent stalemates on major issues unless both parties favor moving in the same direction. (The Tax Reform Act of 1986 offers a good example.) Resolution of differences will not be impossible, but it will be time consuming and difficult. Moreover, the important, yet routine, work of government will take longer to complete.

Whether the United States continues to experience frequent periods of divided government, as has been the case for much of the time in the past fifty years, depends a good deal on voters' decisions. It might reasonably be argued that the imbalance between the strengths of the party in the electorate and of the party in government is unlikely to continue. If the governing parties remain relatively strong, then at some point voters may comprehend this condition and attach themselves more firmly to the parties than is currently the case. There should be a decline in independent identifiers and an increase in strong identifiers. Split-ticket voting should decrease and straight-ticket voting increase. Most importantly, we should enter a period when unified party government is the rule, not the exception. Strong governing parties will eventually lead to strong parties in the electorate. Rather than the party in electorate driving the party in the government, the reverse will occur.

Notes

1. David R. Mayhew, *Divided We Govern* (New Haven: Yale University Press, 1991).

2. Morris P. Fiorina, *Divided Government* (New York: Macmillan, 1992), and Sean Q. Kelly, "Divided We Govern? A Reassessment," *Polity* 25 (1993): 473–484.

3. Richard Neustadt, "Presidency and Legislation," *American Political Science Review* 49 (December 1955): 980–1021.

4. David R. Mayhew, *Party Loyalty Among Congressmen: The Difference Between Democrats and Republicans, 1947–62* (Cambridge: Harvard University Press, 1966).

5. Gary Orfield, *Congressional Power: Congress and Social Change* (New York: Harcourt Brace Jovanovich, 1975), and James L. Sundquist, *Politics and Policy* (Washington, D.C.: Brookings Institution, 1968).

6. James MacGregor Burns, *The Deadlock of Democracy: Four Party Politics in America* (Englewood Cliffs, N.J.: Prentice-Hall, 1963).

7. Norman H. Nie, Sidney Verba, and John R. Petrocik, *The Changing American Voter* (Cambridge: Harvard University Press, 1976).

8. The reason for including data only since 1971 is because the number of roll call votes increased markedly at that time. In the House, this resulted first from the use of recorded teller votes and second, and more noticeably, from the institution of electronic voting. Prior to 1971, recorded votes in the House were largely on final passage of bills, motions to recommit, and on important procedural matters. Most amendments were not subject to recorded votes. This makes comparisons of the pre- and post-1971 periods problematic. Although the Senate did not switch to electronic voting, it also experienced a large increase in the number of recorded votes at the same time.

9. Party votes were 66 and 67 percent of all roll calls in the House and Senate, respectively, in 1993. In 1994, the levels declined to 62 and 52 percent. These contrast most markedly with the levels in 1972, when only 27 percent of House roll calls and 36 percent of Senate roll calls were party votes. It is misleading to compare the levels of party voting in Congress since 1970 with previous ones because the frequency of roll call voting, especially in the House, increased dramatically after 1970. Prior to that time, roll calls were largely limited to votes on recommittal of legislation and on final passage.

10. It is worth noting that during the Clinton administration the party unity scores of Republicans have increased by more than five points over previous high levels.

11. David W. Rohde, *Parties and Leaders in the Postreform House* (Chicago: University of Chicago Press, 1991); Lawrence C. Dodd and Bruce I. Oppenheimer, "The New Congress: Fluidity and Oscillation," in *Congress Reconsidered,* 4th ed., ed. Lawrence C. Dodd and Bruce I. Oppenheimer (Washington, D.C.: CQ Press, 1989), pp. 443–449; and Paul Herrnson, *Party Campaigning in the 1980s* (Cambridge: Harvard University Press, 1988).

12. In *Divided We Govern,* Mayhew does include a second measure of governing: the number of highly publicized investigations, as a means of comparing periods of divided and unified party control.

13. Mayhew, *Divided We Govern,* p. 43.

14. Because this work was completed in February 1995, it was impossible to employ Mayhew's "second sweep" approach that relies on "long-term perspectives of policy specialists." (Ibid., p. 44.)

15. Ibid., p. 37.

16. If anything, during the Clinton administration, legislation is even more omnibus in nature. For example, the Budget-Reconciliation Bill of 1993 included both spending cuts and tax law changes in a single piece of legislation. In contrast, the 1981 economic package of the Reagan administration had the spending cuts and tax provisions in separate pieces of legislation. They count for two major new laws in Mayhew's calculations.

17. Originally there were two budget resolutions. The first, designed to set targets, was to be adopted by May 15. The second, designed to set ceiling, was to be adopted shortly after Labor Day (First Monday in September). With changes in the Budget Act that moved the reconciliation process up in the timetable, the second resolution became meaningless and was subsequently abandoned. For the purpose of this analysis, the

budget resolution refers to the first budget resolution in those years in which there were two.

18. These differences were eventually folded into the work of the 1990 Budget Summit.

19. An area of conflict between the Appropriations Committee and the authorizing committees in both the House and the Senate is legislating, providing, or defining authority within appropriations bills.

20. The argument presented in this section was drafted well before the 1995 budget shutdown. What occurred, however, is supportive of the point of view taken in this article.

21. See George C. Edwards III, *Presidential Influence in Congress* (San Francisco: W. H. Freeman, 1980); Mark A. Peterson, *Legislating Together* (Cambridge: Harvard University Press, 1990); and Jon Bond and Richard Fleischer, *The President in the Legislative Arena* (Chicago: University of Chicago Press, 1990).

22. Norman J. Ornstein, Thomas E. Mann, and Michael J. Malbin, *Vital Statistics on Congress, 1993–1994* (Washington, D.C.: CQ Press, 1994), p. 195.

23. Bruce I. Oppenheimer, "Declining Presidential Success with Congress," in *The Presidency Reconsidered,* ed. Richard W. Waterman (Itasca, Ill.: F. E. Peacock, 1993), pp. 75–92.

24. *Congressional Quarterly Weekly Report,* December 31, 1994, p. 3620.

25. As with the discussion of appropriations bills, the argument presented here was constructed long before evidence from the 104th Congress became available.

26. Paul Herrnson, "The Revitalization of National Party Organizations," in *The Parties Respond,* 2nd ed., ed. L. Sandy Maisel (Boulder, Colo.: Westview Press, 1994), pp. 45–68.

3

IDEOLOGY AND ELECTIONS

One of the most famous books in social science published in the long era following the end of World War II was titled *The End of Ideology*. In important respects, the book mirrored a widespread belief in the West as it was locked in bitter battle with communism. In the West, the argument went, the prewar ideological differences between communism, fascism, social democracy, and free enterprise capitalism had been resolved in favor of a new kind of social economy combining private ownership of most industry with problem solving and regulatory supervision by government. No longer would there be ideological divisions about what type of socioeconomic system would best serve the public. That issue was settled; technical expertise, not ideology, would solve problems.

It is difficult to locate an exact time that "the end of ideology" ended. As the extraordinary confidence generated by the immediate postwar boom evaporated in the face of persistent problems that refused to go away, such as poverty and racial division, ideology crept back in. Certainly, the rise of the New Left in the United States and Western Europe contributed to the reemergence of ideological divisions. Clearly, the bitter divisions created by the seemingly endless Vietnam War was a factor. Economic slowdowns and energy crises also played roles. And we can point to much more that challenged the previous orthodoxy that ideology in the West was dead. The selection of Margaret Thatcher as British prime minister in 1979 made it official. Ideology was very much alive and would divide political parties as well as factions within parties.

Modern ideological currents are different from those that shaped political discourse in the first half of the twentieth century. In that period, the most important issue was how to organize the economy. But an affluence undreamed of in the 1930s and important cultural changes have dramatically reshaped the issues raised by ideology in more recent times. Today, amenities, such as environmental concerns, are paramount in some ideologies. Cultural issues, such as the appropriate role of religion in public life, shape other ideologies, while racial and sexual issues have generated still additional ones. Yet, at the same time, economic differences have revived ideologies based on that traditional set of issues.

For political parties, the fragmentation and diversity of ideologies raise acutely the problem of coalition building. How can political parties draw some ideologies into their nets without deeply offending others? How can a party push prospective ideological disputes under the table to avoid disruption? And so on.

The essays in this section look closely at the important ramifications of ideology on elections and politics.

3.1

Candidate Appeals and the Meaning of Elections

Richard Joslyn

Introduction

Because of the centrality of concepts such as representation, citizen choice, popular influence, and implied consent in the U.S. form of government, and the importance of electoral systems for each of these concepts, political scientists are naturally concerned with the "meaning" of elections. As a result, a good deal of intellectual energy has been expended in an attempt to understand what is communicated and what is made more likely in a programmatic sense by the outcomes of elections.

Unfortunately, our understanding of the meaning of elections in the United States has come primarily from the analysis of the attitudes and behavior of the citizenry. An impressive amount of data concerning citizens' electoral behavior has been carefully collected over the past five decades, and a voluminous literature has appeared concerning the attitude-formation process and the electoral participation of both individuals and groups.

Focusing exclusively, or even primarily, on the behavior of the voter, however, risks the development of a limited and misleading view of elections. Voters, after all, do not behave in an environmental vacuum but respond to, and interact with, the behavior of other electoral participants. Research that fails to recognize this may incorrectly infer that citizen behavior observed in one context represents some inherent tendency or capability of citizens, and it may obscure the broader, systemic consequences of elections for democratic systems. As Benjamin Page has argued, "Electoral politics do not take place entirely inside voters' heads; what choices are made depend largely upon what choices are offered."[1]

In an attempt to contribute to a more complete understanding of U.S. elections, this chapter explores the rhetorical behavior of political candidates during election campaigns. Candidate behavior is clearly significant since candidates contribute much to the meaning of election campaigns, and their behavior represents a constraint upon how citizens and other actors, such as journalists, respond. An accurate understanding of elections requires a synthesis of what we know about the behavior of both the candidates and the citizens with whom they communicate.

This chapter is limited to one aspect of candidate behavior: the verbal appeals made by candidates to potential voters during election campaigns.[2] This approach assumes that one may look at election campaigns as communication events, that candidate communication is important because citizens are exposed to it directly and journalists are constrained by it, that the nature of the communication influences the extent to which elections contribute to political understanding, and that the types of communication candidates engage in reveal much about the meaning of elections more generally. Although candidates do many things, one of the most important is to tell us why we ought to vote for them. When they are telling us that, they are also telling us what the nature of the electoral choice is and what kind of message can be sent with one's vote. In Philip Converse's terms, we must understand not only the electoral "message-as-sent" and "message-as-received," but also the "message-as-shaped-by-candidates."[3] Although it is common to presume that the meaning of elections is that they provide an opportunity for citizens to control public policy decisions, the communication of candidates may actually deflect the attention of citizens away from such concerns. If so, the meaning of elections must lie elsewhere.

Perspectives on Elections and Campaign Communication

Before turning to an empirical analysis of the appeals used by candidates, it will be helpful to contrast several different approaches to elections and campaign communication. Although there are relatively few extensive, systematic studies of the communication of candidates, several different perspectives toward elections in general have been utilized by electoral scholars. Most scholarly comment on candidate communication has been critical of the quality of campaign rhetoric; that is nothing new. But scholars differ about the types of shortcomings they perceive, the reasons for these shortcomings, and their implications for the meaning of elections.

The brief review of the perspectives that follows is not meant to be exhaustive; rather, it is meant to illustrate the diversity of approaches to election campaigns and to assist in analyzing the significance of campaign communication. The perspectives to be contrasted may be labeled the *prospective policy-choice* approach, the *retrospective policy-satisfaction* approach, the *benevolent-leader* approach, and the *ritualistic* approach.[4]

The Prospective Policy-Choice Approach

Much of the post-1960 research on elections and voting behavior has shared a prospective policy-choice approach toward candidate communication. Although very little of this research has focused specifically or systematically on the rhetoric of candidates, the implicit assumptions of the research have been that elections are an opportunity for voters to contrast the opposing policy intentions of candidates and to choose the candidate with policy preferences most similar to their own. According to this approach, electoral choices center on the evaluation of policy positions, and election outcomes may be considered "mandates" for the policy promises of victorious candidates.

This policy-choice approach may be seen in a number of different areas of the literature on public opinion and voting behavior. One such area is the post-1964 literature on the belief systems of U.S. citizens. A number of researchers have attempted to demonstrate that the consistency, constraint, and ideological character of mass belief systems have undergone a quantum jump in the last two decades. Although there is considerable debate over the accuracy of these observations, for our purpose the most significant aspect of this line of inquiry is that the increase in ideology is often attributed to a more specific, consistent, and ideological discussion of public policy issues by political candidates in the post-1960 presidential elections. In the 1964 election, for example, the candidates are thought to have provided "sharply contrasting philosophies of government," with Barry Goldwater in particular providing "an ideological stimulus" and a "meaningful test of liberal-conservative sentiment."[5] The 1968 election included the third-party candidate George Wallace, whose "candidacy was reacted to by the public as an *issue* candidacy."[6] The 1972 election was one in which candidate "issue positions were unusually sharply defined,"[7] and it marked the end-point of a twelve-year process during which there was an "upgrading in the quality of political rhetoric and debate" and an "increased articulation of the ideological differences between the parties."[8] Norman Nie, Sidney Verba, and John Petrocik summarized much of this line of argument in their analysis of public opinion since the 1950s when they argued that candidates had shown an increased willingness to present voters with "meaningful bundles of issues," with positions "on the liberal-conservative continuum that [are] both unambiguous and fairly far from the center," with "issue choices," and with "a coherent set of issue positions."[9]

A second body of literature has argued that candidate policy-oriented rhetoric not only has had an effect on the structure of citizen belief systems but has also significantly altered the nature of the process by which citizens make a candidate choice, and the meaning that may be attached to a particular electoral outcome. The policy-oriented rhetoric of candidates and the increased tendency of citizens to perceive policy-oriented differences between the parties and to have constrained policy positions themselves were thought by some to permit electoral outcomes to be interpreted as policy referenda, policy mandates, and "popular control of public policy."[10] For example, Gerald Pomper has argued that party victories in elections "can now reasonably be interpreted as related to the mass choice of one set of issue positions over another,"[11] and Richard Boyd has asserted that there are at least some issues on which "the public severely limits the options of leaders at the time policy is made."[12] Although this literature has become concerned more recently with the thorny theoretical and methodological issues associated with measuring precisely the prevalence of "policy" or "issue" voting, the assumption of this modern emphasis is that the rhetoric of candidates has some capacity to allow, if not encourage, citizens to consider public policy controversies when making candidate choices. In fact, one of the most sophisticated contributions to this literature has concluded that in the 1976 presidential election, "the policy differences consensually perceived to exist between the candidates, coupled with prior differences in voter positions on these issues, had a noteworthy effect on voters' comparative assessments of the candidates, and through these invidious assessments, the policy terms ultimately left their mark on final voting decisions."[13]

A third body of research that reflects this policy-choice approach to candidate communication is the developing literature on the effects of campaign communication on citizen perceptions. Much of this research has focused on the ability of campaign communication to increase the accuracy of citizen perceptions of the prospective policy positions of candidates and has studied the policy-related impact of presidential debates and televised spot advertisements. For example, the Patterson and McClure study of the 1972 spot ads of presidential candidates focused on the ability of ads to alter the policy preferences and perceptions of voters. Although the authors found that there are two sides to political advertising—an illusory and symbolic side as well as a substantive and reasonable side—it was the latter that they found to be both more prevalent and more influential. In their judgment, "presidential candidates do make heavy use of hard issue information in their advertising appeals" and "people do come to understand better where the candidates stand on election issues from watching televised political commercials."[14] Similarly, Charles Atkin and Garry Heald explored the relationship between radio and television advertising exposure and the accuracy of perceptions about the policy preferences of two congressional candidates in 1974,[15] and others have explored the possibility that exposure to presidential debates leads to more accurate perceptions of candidate policy positions.[16] Two of these authors have stated categorically that "the 1976 presidential debates produced a better informed electorate than would have been the case without them."[17]

In short, the literature just cited shares the assumption that elections have meaning because they provide the electorate with a measure of popular influence—or perhaps even of popular control—over future public policy decisions. Although there may be some variation in the clarity and distinctiveness of candidate policy positions and in the accuracy of the electorate's perceptions of those positions, many observers of U.S. elections believe that elections permit the populace to make programmatic choices in advance of their enactment. In fact, this is probably the dominant approach to elections and campaign communication among political scientists.

The Retrospective Policy-Satisfaction Approach

A second approach to elections asserts that elections give citizens a periodic opportunity to evaluate recent programmatic decisions made by incumbents and the social conditions extant at any given time so that they can decide whether the incumbent candidate or party has performed satisfactorily. The message that is sent by the electorate, according to this view, is one of general preference for either continuity or change, as indicated by whether or not the electorate "throws the rascals out."

Support for this approach comes from observations of candidate rhetoric focusing on placing blame and claiming credit for previous policy decisions and existing social conditions.[18] This discourse often fails to reveal what the candidate's future policy intentions or preferences are, preferring instead to focus on the recent past. Also, the discourse is often not careful about holding public officials responsible only for policy decisions or consequences over which they had some control or could have had some influence. Nonetheless, a good deal of campaign communication centers on whether incumbent officeholders have been unduly inattentive to or unsuccessful in dealing with some set of social, economic, or political conditions. Incumbents, of course, are intent on persuading voters that conditions are improving and problems are being solved; challengers delight in pointing out policy failures and unsolved problems.

From this perspective, the main contribution of news coverage of public affairs to electoral decision making comes between campaign periods, as a result of daily surveillance by the press of policy decisions and social conditions. This coverage is thought to contribute, in a pervasive yet subtle way, to general feelings of malaise or optimism, worry or satisfaction. This information base may then be used by the public, not to compare the future policy promises or intentions of competing candidates, but rather to evaluate the conflicting attempts by candidates to take credit and place blame for policy successes and failures.

Retrospective policy-satisfaction judgments are much less demanding of voters than are prospective policy-choice judgments. Rather than trying to measure the distance between candidate and voter policy preferences, the retrospective satisfaction view requires only that voters reach a general conclusion about their level of satisfaction with recently made political decisions and currently experienced political conditions. Once this general conclusion has been reached, the voter's decision rule is a relatively simple one: If conditions are acceptable, reward the incumbents by returning them to office; if conditions are unacceptable, punish the incumbents by removing them from office.

This approach represents, then, a referendum of sorts on the behavior of incumbents and incumbent administrations, rather than an indication of future policy preferences. Any "mandate" conferred by a particular electoral outcome, therefore, is simply a general statement of preference for the status quo or for change, rather than a more specific mandate for particular policy initiatives. Through the exercising of these retrospective judgments by the electorate, a measure of democratic control may be preserved. This control, or influence, comes not from a basis of specific public policies but from the creation of an incentive among decision makers to anticipate the preferences of citizens and to accomplish desirable policy outcomes, through whatever means they select. Just how much popular influence is possible through such a process is uncertain, however, given the possibilities of citizen misperceptions; the ability of incumbents to engineer short-term, preelection benefits; and the difficulty of assigning responsibility for policy performance to any one candidate or institution.[19]

The Benevolent-Leader Approach

Both of the approaches to elections considered so far focus on the public policy content and consequences of campaigns and elections. Yet it is clear that elections also involve nonprogrammatic competition between two or more human beings. This nonprogrammatic competition involves attempts to convince the populace that the personal attributes of a candidate make him or her a "fit leader."

When elections are seen as an exercise in leadership rather than policy selection, our attention is directed toward the nonpolicy aspects of electoral communication. This perspective requires us to consider the desirable leadership attributes in cultures like our own and to study the ways in which these attributes are presented, contrasted, and emphasized.

Obviously, a fair amount of the campaign communication of both candidates and journalists focuses on the nonprogrammatic personal characteristics of candidates for public office. Candidates represent not only past and future policy decisions but also personalities and characters to which other people respond. Verbal and nonverbal communication regarding these personal characteristics is prevalent both before and during an election campaign. In fact, even communication involving policy alternatives may really be concerned with the creation of impressions about a candidate's personality; hence, public policies sometimes are one of many vehicles through which such impressions are created.

This approach also assumes that citizens are willing and able to form perceptions concerning the character traits of candidates. This is partly because information regarding these characteristics is so readily available and partly because judging the character of another human being is something we do frequently and know something about. The perceptions that citizens form in this way may not be particularly rich or accurate—we often speak of a citizen's *image* or *impression* of a candidate, for example—but they are thought to be part of the natural process of responding to human communication and choosing between prospective leaders. Since this approach holds that the evaluation of the character traits or personalities of candidates is an important determinant of the citizen's candidate choice and vote, candidates capable of creating the most positive personal impression are more likely to achieve electoral success.

If this is an accurate description of U.S. election campaigns, then the meaning of elections is not to be found in any programmatic preferences (either past or future) indicated by the citizenry but rather in the conferral of approval on an officeholder who begins his or her tenure with a measure of support and legitimacy. The victorious candidate is more likely to embody culturally desirable leadership traits and to have been the most successful at creating a reassuring or comforting personal impression than to represent any sort of aggregate preference or mandate for specific policy choices. In fact, in this view, an electoral victory grants to the benevolent leader considerable policy latitude within which to maneuver, experiment, and bargain. In other words, this perspective does not view elections as a process by which the citizenry controls or influences public policy, except in the most inadvertent or indirect way. It is, however, a process by which human societies select an attractive, comforting focus of attention possessing, initially, a measure of legitimacy and support.

There is considerable evidence in support of this benevolent-leader approach to election campaigns. At the presidential level, both campaign news coverage and candidate communication contain abundant information about candidate personas. Furthermore, insiders' accounts of presidential campaign decision making indicate the care with which impressions of personas of candidates are constructed, preserved, and demolished.[20]

At the congressional level, incumbent members of the U.S. House of Representatives present themselves to their constituents in such a way as to leave favorable personal impressions. Richard Fenno, in his analysis of the "home styles" of members of Congress, finds that representatives believe their prospects for reelection depend more on how they are perceived as persons than on the public policy positions they have taken. Toward this end, legislators attempt "to convey their qualifications, their sense of identification and their sense of empathy" to their districts. This communication is seldom rich with policy discussions or proposals, although policy issues may be used as a vehicle for creating positive personal impressions. So, for example, one congressman (B) focuses almost exclusively on one issue (national defense) about which there is considerable consensus, while attempting to convey an impression of popularity, humor, and trustworthiness. Another congressman (C) is conversant on a variety of issues but is more concerned with remaining visible to his constituents and leaving the impression of being concerned about them. Even the most issue-oriented congressman (D) uses bold, outspoken, rational, policy-focused forms of communication to demonstrate verbal agility and mental quickness and to attempt to create feelings of empathy between his constituents' cynicism and his "antipolitician" criticism of government. Issue-related debates, then, are not used by incumbents to permit citizens to exert some measure of influence over policy decisions, but to convey their "trustworthiness" to "prospective constituents."[21]

The benevolent-leader approach to elections differs from the two policy-oriented approaches in at least three significant ways. First, the benevolent-leader approach holds that taking positions on public policy questions is not the most significant or prevalent type of candidate campaign appeal. At the presidential level, for example, Page finds little evidence in candidate rhetoric for "issue candidacies," "meaningful policy alternatives," "coherent bundles of policy preferences," or "issue-oriented party realignments." Instead, policy-related appeals are more notable for their ambiguity, vagueness, and invisibility. At the congressional level, Fenno finds considerable issue-related rhetoric, but much of it focuses on consensually held values and is used to depict the personal qualities of the incumbent.

A second way in which this approach differs from the first two policy-oriented approaches is in the amount and type of learning that is apt to take place during an election campaign. Given the paucity, ambiguity, and intent of policy choice and satisfaction appeals at both the presidential and congressional levels, it is difficult to see how campaign rhetoric could contribute much to the policy-related understanding of citizens. Instead, the learning that is apt to occur concerns the personal characteristics (such as competence, empathy, and leadership qualities) of the candidates.

Third, the benevolent-leader approach differs from the policy-oriented approaches in that the primary meaning of elections is something other than the popular-influence-over-public-policy model posited by policy-oriented researchers. Instead, presidential elections provide the voter with the opportunity to select candidates with attractive personal characteristics. This represents a much more indirect avenue for popular influence, so much so that Page is uncomfortable with treating it as a democratic phenomenon. In fact, he concludes that

> even if . . . the electoral process casts up a paragon of benevolent leadership every time, we would still have to ask whether it is not a debasement of language to call this democracy. It has about it a flavor of citizen abdication, of giving up on instrumental benefits of government and settling for the symbolism of a father figure or a dignified elected monarch.[22]

At the congressional level, Fenno argues that one implication of incumbent rhetoric is that our notion of representation must be altered to allow for behavior other than achieving congruence between the policy preferences of constituents and the policy decisions of legislators. Constituents may want things other than policy agreement from their representatives—such as assurances of access and trustworthiness—and incumbent rhetoric reflects this understanding. Although Fenno is not as distressed as Page is that elections and representation may not be as policy-oriented as some maintain, it is clear that Fenno's approach represents a significant departure from the policy-oriented approaches.[23]

The Ritualistic Approach

A fourth perspective on candidate communication, and one that probably represents a minority view among political scientists, maintains that elections have nowhere near the policy- or leadership-choice significance found by others. In fact, the ritualists, represented best by Murray Edelman and W. Lance Bennett, hold that the most significant features of candidate communication and elections are their irrationality, symbolism, and articulation of consensual values. In this view, elite communication consists largely of myths and cultural ideals (such as "free enterprise, honesty, industry, bravery, tolerance, perseverance, and individualism") and lacks substance concerning public policies.[24] These myths strike a responsive, but noncognitive, chord in the mass citizenry and are capable of stimulating political controversy as individuals differ over which myth to apply to which circumstance. Communication containing these myths tends to be dramatic and filled with imagery or symbols, and its imprecision permits multiple interpretations on the part of the citizenry. The myths themselves are selected from a fairly rigid cultural consensus concerning the limits of acceptable debate and rhetoric, and they stimulate recognition and response from the deepest levels of our consciousness.[25]

Election campaigns, in this view, are a ritual in which mythical representations are transmitted to and reinforced among the populace. "Rituals use dramatic themes and actions to attract attention, simplify problems, emphasize particular principles, and structure the responses of participants."[26] The meaning of elections, then, is not to be found in the populace's controlling policy decisions, except in the most trivial of senses. The populace might reject the policy proposals of a candidate (e.g., George McGovern's guaranteed minimum income plan) due to the confusion stimulated by the unfamiliar mythical context in which it is placed, rather than out of a cognitive understanding of what the policy entails. Elections, then, serve mainly to establish the dominance of authorities, to perpetuate the submissiveness of the powerless, and to act as a conserving and stabilizing force. As Edelman has observed, "most campaign speeches consist of the exchange of clichés among people who agree with each other. The talk, therefore, serves to dull the critical faculties rather than to arouse them."[27]

Political observers have criticized the emptiness of candidate communication for some time. The ritualists, however, view this emptiness as a fundamental aspect of candidate communication; hence, it is not reformable. Bennett, in particular, is critical of researchers (usually policy-oriented ones) who criticize candidate communication and then suggest ways in which elections could be reformed to increase the substance, rationality, or clarity of these appeals. These reformist sentiments, according to Bennett, ignore the inevitability of the political communication of any ritual and, ironically, reflect and contribute to the mythical view of the policy-making capabilities of elections by suggesting that they can be reformed. Instead, he says, one ought to recognize the limited policy-making meaning of elections and realize that their significance is to be found in their ability to "limit the possibilities for political change, broad interest representation, or effective political action ... while organizing support for the government and reinforcing particular images of policy and society."[28]

To the ritualists, then, it is not the policy-oriented communication of candidates per se that is significant, or even the discussions of past performances or personal qualities. Rather, it is the articulation of culturally agreed upon values or worldviews. Furthermore, the ritualists consider the variations in candidate appeals that are typically studied to be epiphenomena. Instead, it is the similarity of the myths and symbols used by all candidates that is of most consequence.

The ritualists also do not consider election campaigns to be opportunities for public education or enlightenment. Instead, they believe campaigns "dull the critical faculties" and serve to reinforce prevailing worldviews and general principles.

Finally, to the ritualists, elections do not represent opportunities for popular control or even popular influence, for that is only a part of the mythology of elections. Instead, it is primarily elites who benefit from elections through the legitimation of their positions and the delimiting of popular influence. Nonelites primarily benefit only from the symbolic reassurance that elections provide: "In short, the standard view of elections as policy processes ignores the functions of campaign practices in the context of the election ritual. As a result, it is easy to overlook the possibility that the public opinion expressed in response to campaign issues has less to do with making policy than with reducing social tensions and reinforcing enduring images of the political order."[29]

Having distinguished between these four approaches to U.S. election campaigns, we can now use the approaches to analyze more profitably the content of campaign rhetoric. While there is undoubtedly an element of empirical accuracy to each of the approaches, it is also likely that one or more of the approaches are more accurate descriptions of election campaigns than the others are. In the remainder of this chapter, I will attempt to determine which of the four perspectives are the most consistent with the campaign appeals made by candidates and, thereby, get a handle on the most likely meaning of electoral outcomes.

The Content of Candidate Appeals

In the paragraphs that follow, I will analyze the candidate appeals made in over eight hundred televised spot ads and in the two 1988 televised presidential debates. Political commercials and debates are two forms of campaign communication through which candidates make unfiltered appeals and to which a large proportion of the citizenry is exposed; thus, these forms are especially important for the definition of an election and for citizen responses to that definition. The appeals made by candidates have been divided into four categories, which match up with the approaches to elections discussed above. After the content of the appeals made in these formats is analyzed, an evaluation of the four approaches and of the meaning of elections will be possible.

Examples of candidate appeals consistent with the prospective policy-choice approach to elections are shown in Figure 1. The first example from a 1964 Barry Goldwater commercial reveals a specific policy preference regarding an all-volunteer army. The second example, a Paul Sarbanes commercial, contains a less specific position regarding Social Security benefits, but it could probably be safely inferred from the ad that the candidate would oppose attempts to diminish the benefits of those on Social Security. The examples from the 1988 presidential debates also reveal fairly specific issue positions: Michael Dukakis's opposition to the death penalty and George Bush's preference for curtailing the growth in government spending.

In general, this type of candidate appeal gives the populace enough information with which to locate a candidate in some "issue space" and to make an informed guess about the candidate's programmatic behavior once in office. As a result, this rhetoric enhances the possibility of issue voting and the conferring of policy "mandates" by the voters.

Candidate appeals consistent with the retrospective policy-satisfaction approach typically place blame or claim credit for policy decisions and political conditions. In the process, such rhetoric asks voters whether they (or others) are better or worse off than they were before, and it encourages voters to reward or punish incumbent parties and candidates. Retrospective-satisfaction appeals also sometimes simply raise an issue or social condition without indicating either who is responsible for it or what the candidate would do about it.

Figure 2 contains examples of retrospective policy-satisfaction appeals. In the first two political advertisements, Richard Nixon and Lyndon Johnson attempt to take credit for economic prosperity and peace. In the next two ads, gubernatorial candidates blame their opponents for past policy decisions and worsening social conditions. In the final two ads, Jimmy Carter and Phil Hart attempt to arouse retrospective assessments by drawing attention to a variety of unsolved problems.

In the televised debate examples, Dukakis raises a number of unsolved social and economic problems without indicating what he would do about them, and Bush attempts to claim credit for the performance of the U.S. economy and the passage of a statute involving medical care.

Appeals about the personal attributes of candidates are consistent with the benevolent-leader approach to elections. In Figure 3, we can see several

Figure 1. **Prospective Policy-Choice Appeals**

Televised Commercials

Goldwater:	I want to end the draft altogether and as soon as possible. In order to keep this nation strong and keep the peace, our military services need trained volunteers. We must attract men and women who will dedicate their careers to the military services. And we'll attract them with good pay, good career opportunities, and real security for their families. The present draft system is dangerously outmoded, it's wasteful, and it's unfair to our young people. What we need is a good professional corps, which has real pride in its service to the cause of peace and freedom.
Sarbanes:	Franklin Roosevelt wanted to provide security for older people in their retirement years. Is that a fundamental objective of this society? Is that what a decent society oughtta be all about? I think it is. And if someone comes along to me and says, "Well, we're gonna cut the old people and their retirement in order to give a big tax break to the very rich." I mean my response to that is, well, what kind of sense of priorities is that?

Televised Debates

Dukakis:	. . . I think you know that I've opposed the death penalty during all of my life. I don't see any evidence that it's a deterrent and I think there are better and more effective ways to deal with violent crime.
Bush:	. . . the way you kill expansions is to raise taxes. And I don't want to do that and I won't do that. And what I have proposed is something much better . . . and that is what I call a flexible freeze that allows growth— about 4 percent or the rate of inflation—but does not permit the Congress just to add on spending.

Figure 2. **Retrospective Policy-Satisfaction Appeals**

Televised Commercials

Nixon:	Americans are working at better jobs for more pay than ever before. And we must continue this sound growth to stay strong and to keep the peace.
Narrator:	Vote for Nixon and Lodge November 8th. They understand what peace demands.
Narrator:	When you're in the voting booth on November 3rd, keep this in mind. America is stronger and more prosperous than ever before and we're at peace. Vote for President Johnson November 3rd. The stakes are too high for you to stay home.
Narrator:	Pete Flaherty wants you to believe he cut taxes while he was mayor of Pittsburgh. The truth is that after he was elected mayor, Flaherty rammed through the Pittsburgh city council a 20 percent increase in property taxes, and a 40 percent increase in his own salary. He took Pittsburgh so far into debt that the city's credit rating has dropped twice since he left office. So the question is this: Can the man who drove Pittsburgh to its knees put Pennsylvania back on its feet? The one man who can is Dick Thornburgh.
Narrator:	For twelve years, during the lifetime of most of our children, New York State has been governed by one man. In twelve years, we've increased the air pollution in our cities by 60 percent. After twelve years, two thirds of our population lives near polluted water. The Hudson has become a sewer, the Niagara River a drain for a poisonous mercury. Every twelve months we've spent a half a billion dollars on highways, while transit fares increased 20 to 50 percent each year. In twelve years we've turned our back on reality. In twelve years we've become the victims of political neglect. Do we need four more? Vote for Goldberg, Patterson.

(continued)

Carter:	The Republican TV commercials assure us the economy's healthy, inflation's controlled, our leadership is great. But when I look around I see every trip to the supermarket a shock, cities collapsing, suburbs scared, policemen cut, welfare skyrocketing. That's reality. The Republicans won't face up to it, but we can change it. Americans have done it before and we'll do it again. It's a long, tough job; it's time we got started.
Hart:	You don't have to be a young revolutionary to say something's wrong. We think that we're the healthiest people in the world—best medical system. Truth is, we're eighteenth among twenty-three of all the developed nations. We can do better than that.
Narrator:	Phil Hart, the senior Senator from Michigan.

Televised Debates

Dukakis:	Our opponents say things are o.k.; don't rock the boat; not to worry. They say we should be satisfied. But I don't think we can be satisfied when we're spending $150 billion a year in interest alone on the national debt, much of it going to foreign bankers. Or when 25% of our high school students are dropping out of school or when we have 2 1/2 million of our fellow citizens, 1/3 of them veterans, who are homeless, living on streets and in doorways in this country. . . .
Bush:	I want to keep this economic recovery going. More Americans at work today than at any time in history; a greater percentage of the workforce . . . I am proud to have been part of an administration that passed the first catastrophic health bill and in that there are some provisions that will be very helpful to the kind of people we're talking about here.

Figure 3. **Benevolent-Leader Appeals**

Televised Commercials

Kennedy: This is Senator Edward Kennedy of Massachusetts. When I came to the United States Senate some six years ago the man I looked to for real leadership in that body was your own Warren Magnuson. He's a man of great power in that body, but he uses his power compassionately, humanely, and for the interests of the people not only of this state but of the nation. I hope you'll send him back to the United States Senate where he belongs.

Narrator: Jimmy Carter knows what it's like to work for a living. Until he became governor he put in twelve hours a day in his shirt-sleeves during harvest at his farm. Can you imagine any of the other candidates for president working in the August sun? That's why Jimmy Carter has a special understanding of the problems facing everyone who works for a living. America needs someone like this as president. Vote for Jimmy Carter in your Democratic primary.

Johnston: Some politicians think they can fool all the people, all the time. The position they took yesterday is changed today and forgotten tomorrow. They'll tell you whatever they think you want to hear. Well, that kind of politics is a thing of the past. The people of this state want straight talk, not false promises; honesty, not arm waving. Integrity and hard work—that's what we need in the United States Senate.

Narrator: The Constitution does not tell us what kind of man a president must be. It says he must be thirty-five years old and a natural-born citizen. It leaves the rest to the wisdom of the voters. Our presidents have been reasonable men; they have listened. They have thought clearly and spoken carefully. They have cared
                                                            (continued)

about people, for the pieces of paper on which they sign their names change people's lives. Most of all, in the final loneliness of this room, they have been prudent. They have known that the decisions they make there can change the course of history or end history altogether. In crisis and tragedy, we have found men worthy of this office. We have been fortunate. Vote for President Johnson on November 3rd. The stakes are too high for you to stay home.

Televised Debates

Dukakis: The Vice President made that pledge (not to raise taxes). He's broken it three times in the past year already. So it isn't worth the paper it's printed on.

Bush: . . . I want to be the one to banish chemical and biological weapons from the face of the earth. But you have to have a little bit of experience to know where to start and I think I've had that.

---

examples of such appeals. The commercials attempt to convey the compassion of Warren Magnuson, the empathy and vigor of Jimmy Carter, the integrity of Bennett Johnston, and the prudence of Lyndon Johnson. The debate excerpts speak to the integrity and experience of George Bush. What these appeals have in common is their focus on the character traits or personalities of candidates for public office.

The final approach to elections—the ritualistic perspective—is illustrated with the candidate appeals in Figure 4. There we see television commercials that evoke the electorate's fear of communism and affection for the flag, the space program, and the Statue of Liberty. The debate excerpts show candidates articulating consensual values—such as economic growth, deficit reduction, work, and "investing" in children—in a manner that is so vague and ambiguous as to represent no risk to or revelation by the candidates. Such rhetoric is typically of no help in predicting the policy intentions of candidates, although it may comfort and reassure the electorate that the candidate shares a regard for the values and icons of U.S. society.

When the appeals made by candidates in a sample of over eight hundred spot ads are categorized into the four types illustrated above, the distribu-

Figure 4. Ritualistic Appeals

Televised Commercials

Teacher:	Hand over your heart, ready, begin. (Scenes of young children reciting the pledge juxtaposed with Khrushchev's belligerent threats against the United States.)
Goldwater:	I want American kids to grow up as Americans. And they will if we have the guts to make our intentions clear, so clear they don't need translation or interpretation, just respect for a country prepared as no country in all history ever was.
Narrator:	In your heart, you know he's right. Vote for Barry Goldwater.
Narrator:	Once, in an hour of strife and danger, a young Marylander strained for a glimpse of a flag. The answer greeted him from these ramparts. A century and a half later, another Marylander pauses, reflecting on those events. His name is Glenn Beall. His roots are deep in Maryland. What has much of the strife this flag has seen been all about? Glenn Beall thinks it's been a struggle by a people who demand the right to choose who will govern for them, not over them, men who will represent them. Glenn Beall knows how Marylanders feel about their flag, their state, about the kind of country they want this to be. That's why Maryland needs Glenn Beall in the United States Senate.
Narrator:	Have we lost the spirit that put man on the moon? The spirit that enabled us to solve the toughest problems and meet the greatest challenges? Or do you believe that spirit is still in us, that we have the greatest resources, technology, and minds of any country in the world, and that with strong leadership we can put those to work and let that spirit . . . Ted Kennedy, because we've got to do better.
Kennedy:	This is the country that put mankind's footprints in the valley of the moon, and I say that we can meet our challenges in the 1980s.

(continued)

Narrator:	Labor Day, 1980. Governor Reagan speaks to the people of the nation.
Reagan:	Beside that torch that many times before in our nation's history has cast a golden light in times of gloom, I pledge to you I'll bring new hope to America. This country needs a new administration with a renewed dedication to the dream of an America, an administration that will give that dream new life, and make America great again. I want more than anything I've ever wanted to have an administration that will, through its actions at home and in the international arena, let millions of people know that Miss Liberty still lifts her lamp beside the golden door.

Televised Debates

Dukakis:	We've got to invest in economic growth in this country, in every part of this country. Building that kind of growth expands revenues and helps to bring down that deficit . . . we have to bring interest rates down and we will as we come up with a good solid plan with the Congress for bringing that deficit down. . . . We can help people to live better lives and, at the same time, save money by helping hundreds of thousands of families on welfare to get off of welfare and to become productive citizens again.
Bush:	I want to hold the line on taxes and keep this, the longest expansion in modern history, going until everybody in America benefits. I want to invest in our children because I mean it when I say I want a kinder and gentler nation. . . .

tion shown in Table 1 results. Clearly, the candidate rhetoric of political commercials is most consistent with the retrospective policy-satisfaction and benevolent-leader approaches to elections. The ritualistic approach comes in a distant third, and the prospective policy-choice approach receives little support in these data.[30] The prevalence of benevolent-leader appeals is a conservative estimate since it ignores all of the nonverbal persona cues made in televised advertising.

Table 1

Content of Televised Political Spot Advertisements (in percent) (n = 803[a])

Type of candidate appeal

Prospective policy choice	17[b]
Retrospective policy satisfaction	62
Benevolent leader	64
Ritualistic	38

[a]The 803 ads represent the advertising campaigns of over two hundred candidates for public office. They cover campaigns from 1960 to 1984 for a variety of offices (e.g., there are 281 senatorial ads, 231 presidential ads, and 170 House ads). Most (688) of the ads are from general election campaigns and from victorious candidates (524); a majority of the ads were used by Democrats (504) and by incumbents (379). Most (62 percent) of the candidates have 1 or 2 ads included in this sample; eleven candidates account for 239 (30 percent) of the ads. Removing those 239 ads from the sample, however, does not change appreciably the distribution of candidate appeals in this table.

[b]The percentages in this column do not sum to one hundred because an ad may be consistent with more than one approach.

Table 2

Content of Televised Presidential Debates (in percent)

Type of Candidate Appeal	First Debate	Second Debate
Prospective policy choice	33	24
Retrospective policy satisfaction	28	19
Benevolent leader	15	10
Ritualistic	23	47
Total	99	100

In contrast, the rhetorical content of the 1988 televised presidential debates was quite different (see Table 2). In the first debate, the most prevalent type of appeal was the prospective policy-choice appeal, even though it only represented about one-third of the debate content. Retrospective and ritualistic appeals were also common, whereas explicit benevolent-leader appeals were relatively rare. In the second debate, ritualistic appeals dominated, followed by the much less prevalent prospective policy-choice and retrospective policy-satisfaction appeals. Explicit benevolent-leader appeals were again fairly uncommon.

Obviously, there are some significant differences in the appeals made by candidates in spot advertising and in face-to-face televised debates. While advertising transmits primarily retrospective and benevolent-leader appeals, debates contain mainly ritualistic appeals and, to a lesser extent, prospective policy-choice and retrospective policy-satisfaction appeals. The benevolent-leader approach to elections receives little support from the rhetoric of debates, at least as far as *what the candidates actually say* is important.

Previous studies have found that presidential debates typically center around a discussion of policy issues. In fact, one analysis of the 1960 debates found that the majority of candidate statements contained specific policy positions, the reasoning behind the policy positions, or the use of evidence to support the policy positions taken by candidates; an analysis of the 1976 debates found that candidates responded with issue-related comments about 80 percent of the time.[31] The analysis conducted here reveals that a good deal of those policy-related appeals either ask voters to make retrospective policy-satisfaction judgments or discuss policies in ways that allow candidates to demonstrate their belief in vague, consensual values. Hence, the discussion of policies in presidential debates is just as apt to represent ritualistic rhetoric as it is to allow voters to make prospective policy-choice decisions.

Conclusion

This look at the appeals made by candidates in two of the most visible campaign formats has found a different level of support for each of the four approaches to elections. Candidate appeals are perhaps the most consistent with the retrospective policy-satisfaction and ritualistic approaches, since those appeals are a significant portion of both advertising and debate content. The evidence is somewhat weaker for the benevolent-leader approach, since appeals of that type prevail in advertising but are relatively uncommon in debates. Finally, this analysis is the least supportive of the prospective policy-choice approach. Although that type of appeal emerges in televised debates, it is rare in advertising and represents a minority of the rhetoric even in debates. This finding takes on theoretical significance because it forces us to reevaluate the meaning that is commonly attributed to elections and electoral outcomes. I will conclude by discussing three implications of this pattern of candidate communication for the meaning of electoral choices and of elections more generally.

First, candidate appeals make unlikely the kind of intended, prospective policy choices that are usually valued by electoral scholars. Candidates make it difficult for voters to know what their future intentions are beyond the support for consensually held values and policy goals. There may be certain circumstances—"critical election" periods and whenever there is an "insurgent" candidate, for example—where more specific, future-oriented policy positions of candidates become known to the citizenry and are used to guide electoral choices. In more normal times, however, it would be surprising if voters were making prospective policy choices based on what the candidates tell them.

Second, this lack of intended, prospective policy meaning does not mean that elections have no policy significance at all. In fact, a number of other policy-related meanings to elections are possible and are more plausible in light of candidate communication.[32] For example, elections may have an intended, retrospective policy meaning consistent with the prevalence of such appeals by candidates. If candidate appeals help voters decide whether or not to "toss the rascals out," based on a global evaluation of policy satisfaction, it may create in officeholders a greater incentive for virtuous programmatic behavior. It is, however, a much more blunt, indirect, and problematical method of influencing the contours of public policy.

It is also entirely possible that electoral choices have prospective but *unintended* policy consequences. That is, we may select a public official for nonpolicy reasons and, in the process, get an officeholder with certain policy preferences (previously unknown to us) different from his/her opponent's. If electoral winners misinterpret their victory as a mandate for their policies (as victors are wont to do), they may even be encouraged to be more assertive about those same policy preferences. Candidate rhetoric encourages this type of result by deflecting the attention of the citizenry away from these hidden policy positions. Although this possibility preserves a policy significance for elections, it is some considerable distance from the idea of democratic influence or control over public policy.

Third, although we may be tempted to bemoan the possibility that elections usually do not have a direct, intended, prospective policy consequence, and that what policy significance there is to elections is more likely to be indirect, retrospective, and unintended, this does not begin to exhaust the range of other interesting possibilities. Apart from their prospective policy meanings, elections may also help shape the political agenda, reinforce cultural myths and values, insulate officeholders from accountability, channel popular participation away from more violent and disruptive forms, and allow for the construction of the modern liberal state. In fact, as one of the editors of this volume has argued elsewhere, it may be that the fact that elections are held is more important than their particular outcomes.[33] If that is true, candidate appeals would still be important since, presumably, for elections to have these other consequences, citizens would still have to be convinced that electoral choices have some significance.

We need to think more carefully, then, about the difference that having elections makes and to construct a view of elections that takes account of the behavior not only of citizens and voters but of candidates and other relevant actors as well. Candidate rhetoric does not provide a fertile basis for analyzing elections in the prospective policy-choice manner with which much of the voting behavior literature is concerned. Yet, candidate rhetoric is real, patterned, and important. A complete and accurate view of elections must synthesize this behavior with that of voters and take account of how candidates spend their time and money to persuade us that we ought to behave in a particular manner. It is hoped that this analysis has made a contribution toward this shift in focus and toward the development of a more plausible and comprehensive approach to elections.

Notes

1. Benjamin Page, *Choices and Echoes in Presidential Elections* (Chicago: University of Chicago Press, 1978), p. 4. V. O. Key, Jr., has made a similar point: "Voters respond to what they see and hear; the nature of their response depends upon what they see and hear (which, in turn, is conditioned by what is in their heads to begin with). Points of political leadership and of communication of political intelligence, by influencing what people see and hear, fix the range of voter response (within the limits of the situation as shaped by the irrepressible flow of events) as they transmit information to the electorate." V. O. Key, Jr., *The Responsible Electorate: Rationality in Presidential Voting, 1936–60* (Cambridge: Harvard University Press, 1966), pp. 110–111.

2. Verbal communication is not, of course, the only way in which candidates communicate with citizens. Masters has argued that the nonverbal gestures of candidates are also a revealing aspect of elite/nonelite interaction. Roger D. Masters, "The Impact of Ethology on Political Science" (paper presented at the International Political Science Association Colloquium on Biopolitics, Paris, 1975).

3. Philip E. Converse, "Public Opinion and Voting Behavior," in *Handbook of Political Science, Nongovernmental Politics,* vol. 4, ed. Fred I. Greenstein and Nelson W. Polsby (Reading, Mass.: Addison-Wesley, 1975).

4. These perspectives are described in more detail in Richard Joslyn, *Mass Media and Elections* (New York: Random House, 1984); and Richard Joslyn, "Political Advertising and the Meaning of Elections," in *New Perspectives on Political Advertising,* ed. Lynda Lee Kaid, Dan D. Nimmo, and Keith R. Sanders (Carbondale: Southern Illinois University Press, 1986).

5. John Osgood Field and Ronald E. Anderson, "Ideology in the Public's Conceptualization of the 1964 Presidential Election," *Public Opinion Quarterly* 33 (1969): 380, and John C. Pierce, "Party Identification and the Changing Role of Ideology in American Politics," *Midwest Journal of Political Science* 14 (1979): 33.

6. Philip E. Converse, Warren E. Miller, Jerrold G. Rusk, and Arthur C. Wolfe, "Continuity and Change in American Politics: Parties and Issues in the 1968 Election," *American Political Science Review* 63 (1969): 1097.

7. James A. Stimson, "Belief Systems: Constraint, Complexity, and the 1972 Election," *American Journal of Political Science* 19 (1975): 141.

8. Arthur H. Miller, Warren E. Miller, Alden S. Raine, and Thad A. Brown, "A Majority in Disarray: Policy Polarization in the 1972 Election," *American Political Science Review* 70 (1976): 754.

9. Norman H. Nie, Sidney Verba, and John R. Petrocik, *The Changing American Voter* (Cambridge: Harvard University Press, 1976), pp. 151, 163, 173, and 192.

10. Richard W. Boyd, "Popular Control of Public Policy: A Normal Vote Analysis of the 1968 Election," *American Political Science Review* 66 (June 1972): 429.

11. Gerald M. Pomper, "From Confusion to Clarity: Issues and American Voters, 1956–1968," *American Political Science Review* 66 (June 1972): 426.

12. Boyd, "Popular Control of Public Policy," p. 429.

13. Gregory B. Markus and Philip E. Converse, "A Dynamic Simultaneous Equation Model of Electoral Choice," *American Political Science Review* 73 (December 1979): 1068. An interesting attempt to analyze the parameters of "issue voting" may be found in George Rabinowitz and Stuart Elaine Macdonald, "A Directional Theory of Issue Voting," *American Political Science Review* 83 (March 1989): 93–121. See also Milton Lodge, Kathleen M. McGraw, and Patrick Stroh, "An Impression-Driven Model of Candidate Evaluation," *American Political Science Review* 83 (June 1989): 399–419, for an attempt to determine how voters link their perceptions of candidate policy stands with their evaluations of candidates.

14. Thomas E. Patterson and Robert D. McClure, *The Unseeing Eye* (New York: Putnam, 1976), p. 23.

15. Charles Atkin and Garry Heald, "Effects of Political Advertising," *Public Opinion Quarterly* 40 (1976): 216–228.

16. George F. Bishop, Robert W. Oldendick, and Alfred J. Tuchfarber, "The Presidential Debates as a Device for Increasing the 'Rationality' of Electoral Behavior," in *The Presidential Debates,* ed. George F. Bishop, Robert G. Meadow, and Marilyn Jackson-Beeck (New York: Praeger, 1978), and Arthur H. Miller and Michael Mackuen, "Learning about the Candidates: The 1976 Presidential Debates," *Public Opinion Quarterly* 43 (Fall 1979): 326–346.

17. Miller and Mackuen, "Learning about the Candidates," p. 344, and Joseph Wagner, "Media Do Make a Difference: The Differential Impact of Mass Media in the 1976 Presidential Race," *American Journal of Political Science* 27 (August 1983): 407–430. Wagner has shown that newspaper readers are better able than others to distinguish between the policy preferences of presidential candidates, even after controlling for a number of other factors. In his words, "Differences between the candidates' positions on the issues is the stuff of politics. It is, and ought to be, an important focus of concern, interest, and debate in a democracy."

18. See, for example, Morris P. Fiorino, *Retrospective Voting in American National Elections* (New Haven and London: Yale University Press, 1981); David R. Mayhew, *Congress: The Electoral Connection* (New Haven: Yale University Press, 1974); and Key, *Responsible Electorate.* A good example of an analysis that uses the retrospective satisfaction approach to understand the 1984 presidential election is Donald R. Kinder, Gordon S. Adams, and Paul W. Gronke, "Economics and Politics in the 1984 American Presidential Election," *American Journal of Political Science* 33 (May 1989): 491–515.

19. Edward Tufte, *Political Control of the Economy* (Princeton, N.J.: Princeton University Press, 1978).

20. Robert Macneil, *The People Machine* (New York: Harper and Row, 1968); Dan Nimmo, *The Political Persuaders* (Englewood Cliffs, N.J.: Prentice-Hall, 1970); Gene Wykoff, *The Image Candidates* (New York: Macmillan, 1968); Joe McGinniss, *The Selling of the President, 1968* (New York: Trident, 1969); and Dan Nimmo and Robert L. Savage, *Candidates and Their Images* (Pacific Palisades, Calif.: Goodyear, 1976).

21. Richard F. Fenno, Jr., *Home Style: House Members in Their Districts* (Boston: Little, Brown, and Co., 1978).

22. Page, *Choices and Echoes,* pp. 152–153.

23. Fenno, *Home Style.*

24. W. Lance Bennett, "Culture, Communication, and Political Control" (paper presented to the American Political Science Association, Washington, D.C., 1980), p. 3.

25. Another example of this perspective may be found in Dan Nimmo and James E. Combs, *Subliminal Politics: Myths and Mythmakers in America* (Englewood Cliffs, N.J.: Prentice-Hall, 1980). They argue that candidate communication is primarily mythical in nature, filled with images, illusions, fantasies, and "pseudo-realities."

26. W. Lance Bennett, *Public Opinion in American Politics* (New York: Harcourt Brace Jovanovich, 1980), p. 386.

27. Murray Edelman, *The Symbolic Uses of Politics* (Urbana: University of Illinois Press, 1964), pp. 17–18.

28. Bennett, "Culture, Communication, and Political Control."

29. Bennett, *Public Opinion in American Politics,* p. 390.

30. This raises the possibility that Patterson and McClure happened to pick an unusually policy-oriented series of spot ads for their analysis. The paucity of specific policy appeals in spot ads is corroborated in Larry J. Sabato, *The Rise of the Political Consultants* (New York: Basic Books, 1981), p. 129. Sabato viewed more than eleven hundred spot ads and reports that U.S. spot ads contain few specific policy appeals, much fewer than ads shown in Great Britain.

31. John W. Ellsworth, "Rationality and Campaigning: A Content Analysis of the 1960 Presidential Campaign Debates," *Western Political Quarterly* 18 (December 1965): 794–802, and David O. Sears and Steven H. Chaffee, "Uses and Effects of the 1976 Debates: An Overview of Empirical Studies," in *The Great Debates, 1976: Ford v. Carter,* ed. Sidney Kraus (Bloomington: Indiana University Press, 1979).

32. Robert Weissberg, *Public Opinion and Popular Government* (Englewood Cliffs, N.J.: Prentice-Hall, 1976), pp. 22–24.

33. Benjamin Ginsberg, *The Consequences of Consent* (Reading, Mass.: Addison-Wesley, 1982), p. 5.

3.2

Does Ideology Matter?

Kathleen Knight and Carolyn V. Lewis

Over the last three decades, there have been continual debates over the impact of ideology in U.S. presidential elections. The general pattern of the argument was outlined in *The American Voter*.[1] The publication of Philip Converse's classic "The Nature of Belief Systems in Mass Publics" in 1964, coinciding as it did with the campaign of Barry Goldwater, accelerated the controversy.[2] Over the course of the debates, just about every aspect of the definition and measurement of ideology has been explored.[3] But, the question of whether ideology really matters in voters' decision making remains unsettled.

Political commentators often describe voters' behavior as if it is impelled by ideological forces, and politicians interpret electoral returns as mandates for ideological programs. Analysts of aggregate public opinion dynamics are also prone to describe the public in terms of ideological direction, or "mood."[4] At the same time, empirical research on individuals' decisions about how to vote generally fails to uncover much ideologically based motivation on the part of the mass electorate. The dominant finding at the "micro" (individual) level is succinctly summarized in the statement that the mass public is "innocent" of ideology.[5]

In this chapter, we focus on two conceptual definitions of ideology that are frequently treated in isolation from each other: sophistication and sentiment. We produce a model of ideological influences on the presidential vote that takes into account both conceptions of ideology. By limiting our model to measures of partisan and ideological sentiment and ideological sophistication, we are able to analyze all of the presidential elections from 1964 to 1992 using identically constructed variables. Our data on ideological sentiment will also allow us to address this aspect of congressional elections through 1994, but in less detail. The results of the cross-time analysis should help to settle some fundamental questions about ideology. Most prominent among these are whether ideology is a relatively stable influence on the electorate, whether its influence is dependent upon the nature of the campaign, and whether the influence of ideological feeling in the U.S. electorate has grown across time.

Two Faces of Ideology

The debate over ideological influences in presidential elections has involved two distinct theoretical approaches to the conceptualization of ideology. These can be most concisely summarized under the headings of *sophistication* and *sentiment*.[6] Ideological sophistication can be defined as "thinking ideologically," or evaluating political objects with reference to an underlying liberal-conservative continuum. Ideological sentiment has to do with direction and intensity of feelings—whether one is more favorably disposed toward liberals and "liberalism" than toward conservatives, or vice versa.

The former can be regarded as the "traditional" approach to ideology. In some of these characterizations, ideological sophistication is taken to be *necessary* for meaningful ideological evaluation.[7] In some other work, the expression of ideological "affect" (or "identification") is taken as *sufficient* to indicate an ideological influence in the voting decision.[8]

These formulations can be viewed as the opposite extremes of the debate. Somewhere in between are more complicated formulations that propose a *conditional* relationship between ideological "activation," or the possession of an "ideological schema," and the impact of ideological sentiment.[9] Finally, there is the *environmental* formulation, which proposes that the impact of ideology is dependent on the nature of the election campaign.[10] A further alternative posits a more holistic environment where political knowledge is transmitted through the broad range of social interactions between activists and less attentive segments of the electorate.[11] From this perspective, it is possible to suggest that the impact of ideological influences in the electorate may evolve over time through social mechanisms and mediated cognitions.

Ideological Sophistication

The American Voter's original analysis of the potential influences of ideology on the vote was in part motivated by journalistic accounts of the election of Dwight Eisenhower in 1952, "which picture[d] an electorate seeking respite from continued 'leftist' pressure toward social and political change."[12] The more comprehensive debate of the era centered (as it does today) on whether the United States was undergoing a partisan realignment—a change in the balance of power between the parties in government reflected in an enduring change in the partisan predispositions of the mass public.[13] One of the most frequently hypothesized engines of partisan realignment remains ideology.[14]

Angus Campbell and his colleagues examined the assumptions underlying such ideologically based interpretations and identified a set of minimal conditions that individual voters would need to meet in order for the voting decision to be said to be motivated by ideological considerations.[15] They paid particular attention to the policy concerns central to journalistic accounts of the 1952 and 1956 presidential campaigns—privatization of federal utility projects, national health insurance, government aid to education, integration, and cutting taxes. But their data-collecting endeavor focused scant attention on the "hot button" campaign issues of the day—Communism, Korea, and corruption.

The *American Voter* surveys of the 1950s period also did not contain any direct reference to the terms "liberal" and "conservative" in the interview schedule. In assessing whether citizens could behave as if impelled by ideological forces, Campbell and his colleagues looked at knowledge of party positions on issues, constraint across issue opinions, "level of conceptualization," and an early variant of the conservatism scale developed by Herbert McClosky.[16] They concluded: "The forces not based on party loyalty that influence the decisions of the American electorate appear almost wholly free of ideological coloration."[17]

The "levels of conceptualization" is a judgmental coding of verbal responses evaluating the presidential candidates and political parties originally employed in *The American Voter* to assess the "structure of thought" that individuals apply to politics.[18] In asking citizens to articulate what they liked and disliked about the candidates and parties, the authors of *The American Voter* were attempting a brief version of the type of studies of political thinking best exemplified by a group of scholars who employed intensive verbal interviewing techniques (sometimes over more than one session) with small samples of respondents.[19] From a technical standpoint, they were asking a representative sample of the U.S. public to provide verbal *rationalizations* of their current evaluations of the presidential candidates and parties. Verbal responses for the so-called *likes/dislikes* questions have been collected in every presidential election year since 1952.

Although the original level of conceptualization coding process made further distinctions, the theoretical core of the scheme classifies each respondent into one of four categories based on the breadth and depth of their rationalizations ascertained from reading the entire protocol of "likes/dislikes" responses. The authors of *The American Voter* reasoned that answers displaying a broad range of considerations about groups and issues in politics would be "capped" by analytic concepts representing a relatively high order of abstraction like the liberal/conservative continuum. The terms "liberal" and "conservative" were described as a kind of political "shorthand" that allowed a large volume of information to be stored and communicated in a concise and efficient fashion. Individuals who evaluated the candidates and parties with respect to an underlying abstract continuum were designated *ideologues*.

Two other significant modes of political evaluation were identified by Campbell and his colleagues.[20] These were *group benefits*, or what has become in more modern parlance "group heuristics,"[21] and *nature of the times*, which has received extensive attention elsewhere under the rubric of "retrospective voting."[22] A residual category, called *no issue content*, was also defined for people who offered little of substance to explain their evaluations, or who said nothing at all.

A number of attempts to replicate and update the levels of conceptualization took place over the years. In 1969, John Field and Ronald Anderson undertook an analysis based on the Survey Research Center's "Master Code" record of the verbal responses to the likes/dislikes questions in the 1964 presidential election study.[23] They were the first to forward an *environmental*, or *contextual*, explanation of the impact of ideology on vote choice. Field and Anderson argued that ideology mattered in the 1964 election because the campaign explicitly activated an ideological dimension of judgment. They found that the percentage of the U.S. public that could be classified as ideologues[24] had more than doubled from the 12 percent reported by *The American Voter* for 1956 to 27 percent in 1964. In 1970, John Pierce suggested that in a more ideologically charged context ideology might come to modify partisanship.[25]

In 1979, Norman Nie, Sidney Verba, and John Petrocik replicated the "Master Code" strategy for the entire period from 1952 to 1972.[26] They proposed that 1956 was the low point of ideological activation in the U.S. public and reported that their data showed a steady increase in the percentage of ideologues from 1956 through 1972. Their explanation also emphasized the political environment and campaign context, but additionally illuminated several trends that suggested that the public might be ripe for realignment with more explicit ideological content. These trends included: a fading of the traditional liberal/conservative issues of the New Deal through generational replacement, greater issue constraint presumably driven in part by cue giving by ideologically driven candidates, and an activation of anti-government sentiment on the part of both the political Left and Right.[27]

A number of other scholars following Pierce have endeavored to maintain the levels of conceptualization variable over time by coding the verbal transcripts of the National Election Study interviews.[28] These data take the series through 1988, but do not quite match the trend reported by Nie, Verba and Petrocik. In 1982, Pierce and Paul Hagner also detail an increase in ideological conceptualization between 1956 and 1964 but show a slight decline between 1968 and 1972, possibly attributable to the fact that the survey included the young cohort of new voters enfranchised by the Twenty-sixth Amendment.[29] Since 1972, the proportion of the public estimated to fall in the "ideologue" category has remained within sampling error of 20 percent.[30]

The fact that only about a fifth of the public spontaneously rationalized political evaluations in terms of an underlying liberalism/conservatism over the course of the "Reagan revolution" is suggestive of a threshold or "cognitive barrier," such as that first articulated by Converse in 1964, which limits the absorption of ideological signals from the larger political environment. From this perspective one would argue that ideology does matter, but only to a minority of what might be called, in the parlance of the political cognition research, "ideology specialists."[31] This position is consistent with Kathleen Knight's analysis of the 1980 presidential election.[32]

Ideological Sentiment

In emphasizing above that the levels of conceptualization were based on the verbal rationalizations that people offer for their political evaluations, we wish to draw attention to a frequently overlooked aspect of ideology. Evaluations assume an affective direction (like/dislike) and a greater or lesser intensity of feeling. The tendency to ignore, or discount, the influence of ideological sentiment has deep roots in political science.

Measures of identification with the labels liberal and conservative, or likelihood of voting for a party designated by each of the labels, were occasionally obtained from mass samples as far back as the 1930s and increasingly in the 1960s. However, because policy issues were assumed to be the primary stuff of true (rationalistic) ideological thinking, self-identification tended to be dismissed when it contradicted results obtained from aggregate investigations of issue opinions. Thus, as early as 1968, Lloyd Free and Hadley Cantril observed that the public seemed to be "ideologically conservative" but "operationally liberal," when considered in terms of public policy.[33] They treated an index of issue opinions as the superior instrument for measuring general ideological sentiment at the individual level.

In describing self-identification, or self-placement on a liberal/conservative continuum, as "ideological," Free and Cantril were following a convention common in the 1950s of treating the part of ideology that might be purely affective as suspect. This was not simply because, at the individual level of analysis, most of the public failed to live up to the assumptions underlying political commentators' descriptions of aggregate election results as representing policy mandates, but also because sentiment itself was suspect. An artificial dichotomy existed between rationalistic ideology, which tended to be treated as an organizing principle beneficial in its effect on political discourse, and sentiment, which could be summarized in ideological terms as potentially dangerous.

The authors of *The American Voter* were not alone in identifying the 1950s as a period of ideological quiescence. However, other authors who heralded the "end" of ideology were writing of a much more malevolent force.[34] Ideology, in the dominant view of the late 1950s, evoked images of the Nazi conquest of Europe, totalitarian communism in Eastern Europe and China, or even of the excesses of the more fervent U.S. anticommunism of the early 1950s. This is made particularly clear in Edward Shils's contrast of ideology with "civility."[35] Ideology, in this view, is not the benign "organizing device" that aids in the retention of political information, but a set of blinders—a barrier to reason. Empirical findings emphasizing the ideological innocence of the U.S. public tended to reinforce impressionistic ones and were packaged with findings from psychology and sociology in the scholarly reassuring metaphor of an "elite defense of democracy."[36]

Although the authors of *The American Voter* viewed political evaluations as a mixture of both cognitive and affective elements, this balanced perspective did not entirely carry over into their view of ideology.[37] In their search for ideological influences in electoral decision making, the authors of *The American Voter* relied upon an early version of the McClosky scale and upon the rationalistic notion of ideology as an abstract organizing device in which the "sense of a continuum" was as important as the use of ideological terminology. They explicitly "set aside" considerations of intensity or enthusiasm in classifying respondents with respect to the levels of conceptualization. By contrast, in considering party identification, sentiment was primary and benign, even *beneficial*. Affective attachments to the parties were established early in life and served to motivate "greater psychological involvement in public affairs."[38] The party identification index attempted to capture variations in the intensity of attachment to the party labels. The ubiquity of the party labels on the ballot insured that partisan sentiment was translated into the individual's vote.

It is important to remember that the authors of *The American Voter* never claimed that ideology was nonexistent among the public; rather, they claimed that ideological influences were relatively circumscribed. They found that when ideological thinking was evident it operated to reinforce or undergird psychological forces like partisanship. Thus, ideology in the 1950s had little independent influence on the vote. Based on the data of the 1960s and 1970s, Warren Miller, one of the authors of *The American Voter,* revised his position to propose that the "non-ideological use of ideological labels," evident in the simple concept of "ideological identification," could exhibit such an independent influence.[39]

The cumbersome notion of "nonideological" ideology referred to ideological sentiment that was not necessarily consistent with party identification and did not necessarily operate to constrain issue positions along an underlying liberal/conservative continuum, but nonetheless functioned to distinguish between the presidential contenders. In this view, which must be categorized with the revisionists, ideological sentiment requires no greater cognitive capacity than partisan sentiment. In order for either to have a measurable impact on the vote, citizens must possess some differential degree of favorability toward the political objects represented by the labels. In such circumstances, cleavages that are explicitly phrased in ideological terms may crosscut partisan divisions and create the potential for realignment.[40]

Both the classical definition of party identification and Levitan and Miller's conception of ideological identification anticipated the reemergence of an interest in sentiment or emotion on the part of political science researchers.[41] The fundamental insight of this new generation of researchers is that emotions require research, rather than assumption. For these researchers, emotion is not necessarily irrational. Feelings might interfere with reason, but then again, feelings and reason might work in concert. More importantly, from the standpoint of the research we present below, feelings, or sentiment, might exist in the absence of all but the most minimal cognition. (The minimal degree of cognition required is mere recognition of the object that engendered the feeling.) From this perspective, it is simply not necessary to determine whether likes and dislikes are undergirded by rationalizations that employ ideological language. In the words of one of the premier researchers in this area: "Preferences need no inferences."[42]

Questions intended to ascertain the general sentiment of each respondent toward liberals and conservatives were included in the National Election Study surveys beginning in 1964 using an instrument called the "feeling thermometer." In the analysis that follows, we have created an index of net ideological sentiment by subtracting each individual's rating of "liberals" on the feeling thermometer from his or her rating of "conservatives." It is worth noting that, while only about 20–25 percent of the public rationalizes evaluations of the parties and candidates using some sense of a liberal/conservative

Figure 1. **Liberal and Conservative Sentiment**

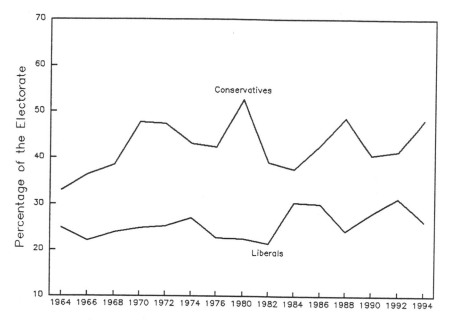

Source: American National Election Studies, 1952–1992 Cumulative Data File, and American National Election Studies, 1994.

Notes: Percentages were calculated using a trichotomized version of the "conservative-liberal" feeling thermometer difference. Those persons who felt more warmly toward conservatives than liberals were classified as conservatives. Those persons who felt more warmly toward liberals than conservatives were classified as liberals. Those persons who gave identical ratings to both groups were classified as moderates. For clarity, the percentage of moderates over time is not shown. The data for 1978 are not available.

continuum, a much greater percentage of the public is willing to rate the ideological groups. The percentage of respondents expressing differential (i.e., nonzero net) liberal/conservative sentiment in the American National Elections Studies ranged from a low of 57 percent in 1964 to a high of 75 percent in 1980. Figure 1 plots net liberal/conservative sentiment in the national public from 1964 to 1994. For simplicity of presentation, we have collapsed net feeling thermometer sentiment into two categories. Respondents who rated liberals more favorably than conservatives are called liberals, while respondents who rated conservatives more warmly than liberals are termed conservatives. Respondents who had zero net affect (i.e., those who rated liberals and conservatives at the same point) or who did not rate both ideological groups were excluded. Figure 1 displays the percentages of the public falling in each of these two categories.

Figure 1 suggests that ideological sentiment has been a factor in national presidential elections at least since Goldwater. The percentage of conservatives has exceeded the percentage of liberals in every survey for which we have data. The rise of conservative sentiment in the public proceeded relatively slowly from 1964 and suffered some obvious setbacks at the time of Watergate and the end of the Vietnam War. In 1980, conservative sentiment rose to its highest point—the only point at which conservatives represented an absolute majority among the public (53 percent). The vicissitudes of governing seemed to have taken their toll on conservative sentiment during Reagan's first term but it then rebounded to 49 percent in 1988. Both the congressional election year of 1990 and the presidential campaign of 1992 seemed to have had a mild detrimental effect on conservative sentiment. But the 1994 election saw conservative sentiment rise again to a near majority (48 percent).

Liberal sentiment, in contrast, was quite flat until after Ronald Reagan assumed office, hovering between 21 and 26 percent from 1964 to 1982. The Walter Mondale/Geraldine Ferraro campaign of 1984, however, was accompanied by a reawakening of liberal sentiment. This decayed during the 1988 election, then rose slowly to its peak (31 percent) in 1992. By the 1994 congressional election, liberal sentiment had declined but, at 26 percent, remained higher than its average for the 1960s and 1970s.

This graph of simple ideological sentiment suggests that ideology matters more than it did three decades ago, and that it has become more polarized. Barely two-thirds of the public expressed differential evaluations of liberals and conservatives in 1964. By 1980, this figure had risen to closer to three-fourths of the public and, by 1994, was still near this peak.

Does Ideology Matter?

What kind of expectations should be held about the relative influence of ideology in presidential elections over time? In the traditional view, the direction of ideological sentiment should influence the vote only among respondents who tend to organize their political perceptions along liberal and conservative lines. This will generally be a minority of the public. Since the ability to organize political objects along abstract dimensions requires some cognitive capacity, the extent of ideological sophistication is expected to be fairly stable over time.[43] The revisionist view holds the effects of ideological sentiment to be much more pervasive. In addition, the revisionist view would argue that the effects of ideology operate at an emotional level, and are therefore somewhat malleable—capable of being influenced by the efforts of the political campaigns, and other social interaction processes.[44]

Much political journalism of the last several decades has focused on a liberal/conservative cleavage in the electorate. In brief, the story can be laid out as follows: The 1950s represented a period of ideological somnolency. The previous high point of ideologically based terminology in election campaigns had occurred in 1932 when Franklin Roosevelt and Herbert Hoover had explicitly contested over the question of who represented the "true liberal" position.[45] The Goldwater election activated an ideological dimension of evaluation by popularizing the conservative label as the opposite of the liberal one. A residue of this activation carried over into the 1968 election, but was diluted by issues of race and the war in Vietnam. In 1972, the Republican campaign organizations succeeded in associating the liberal label with a number of negatively regarded political groups and issues summarized in Phyllis Schaffley's felicitous slogan "amnesty, acid, and abortion." This might have carried over into the 1976 election, however, Watergate and the pardon of Richard Nixon saw a reassertion of partisanship.

The stage was set for the Reagan campaigns of the 1980s. While the depth of the policy mandate can be debated, there is little doubt that Reagan was swept into office on a tide of pro-conservative sentiment.[46] In 1988, seeking to capitalize on the momentum of the Reagan years, the campaign of George Bush attempted to mobilize antiliberal sentiment and to attach the liberal label firmly to Michael Dukakis. While this strategy worked well enough in 1988, it was not sufficient to withstand the combined assault of a popular Democratic candidate and the perceptions of a sluggish economy in 1992.

Method

The analysis presented here considers both ideological sophistication and ideological sentiment in a simplified model of the vote decision. The model is simplified in order to allow direct comparisons of the coefficients across years, as well as comparison of the relative contribution of ideology within election years. It is a probit model in which the probability of voting for the Republican candidate in a particular presidential election is a function of both relative partisan sentiment and relative ideological sentiment. Each of these variables is measured as the difference in evaluation on a hundred-point "feeling thermometer" scale of two objects that are assumed to be opposites.[47] All of these variables are available in the same format starting in 1964. The feeling thermometer difference measures have attractive properties beyond simply being available across nearly thirty years. Both measures have a real zero point where partisan and ideological sentiment are evenly balanced. Also, since partisan and ideological sentiment are measured in the same scale, the raw coefficients can be directly compared, both within and across years.[48]

To allow the influence of ideological sophistication to be considered, the model also includes a dummy (0 or 1) term for having been classified as an "ideologue" in the levels of conceptualization and interactive terms for the influence of ideological sophistication on partisan and ideological sentiment (the main effects). In simple terms, the full model can be written as follows:

$$Z = b_1 + b_2 (FTR - FTD) + b_3 (FTC - FTL) + b_4 (I) + b_5 [(FTR - FTD)*I]$$
$$+ b_6 [(FTC - FTL)*I] + e$$

where:

> Z is an index that determines the probability of voting for the Republican candidate for president,
>
> $(FTR - FTD)$ is the difference in feeling thermometer evaluations of the Republican and Democratic Parties,
>
> $(FTC - FTL)$ is the difference in feeling thermometer evaluations of conservatives and liberals, and
>
> I is a dummy term equal to 1 when the respondent is classified as an Ideologue and 0 otherwise.[49]

Since this is a probit model, the dependent variable—the binary vote for either one candidate or the other—is transformed into a probability distribution that is roughly "s" shaped. The probit models are estimated separately for each presidential election year.

Findings

The progress of ideological sentiment in the electorate has already been illuminated by considering the balance of sentiment toward liberals and conservatives for the entire period in Figure 1. The percentages of conservatives and liberals are not mirror images, in part because of the volatility of the neutral category. Conservative sentiment grew during the 1960s and, after the Watergate setback, surged to 53 percent in 1980. In 1982 and 1984, perhaps surprisingly, pro-conservative sentiment declined to the level of the late sixties, only to climb again to 49 percent in 1988. Conservative sentiment quieted down in the early 1990s but resumed its near majority status with the congressional election of 1994. Liberal sentiment fluctuated within a much narrower range between 1964 and 1982 (24 ± 3 percent). In 1984 and 1986, there was a rise of pro-liberal sentiment that was effectively quashed by the 1988 campaign, only to rise quickly through 1992. Clinton's election may have seen the high water mark of liberal sentiment. By the Republican "revolution" of 1994, the extent of liberal sentiment was essentially the same as it had been in the Lyndon Johnson landslide of 1964.

Sophistication and Sentiment

In the final part of this paper, we investigate the role of ideology in the voting decision in more detail. Ideology is certainly not the only factor affecting the voting decision. The "strict traditionalist" school would argue that in a properly specified model the impact of ideology will be quite limited, or nil. A more broadly held position is that the impact of ideology depends on the electoral context.[50] Testifying to the large number of scholars who believe ideology *might* have some influence are numerous models that control for ideology, generally by including the liberal/conservative scale as an independent variable. Finally, there are those studies that find an impact of ideology in detailed models of particular elections.[51]

Here the desire for cross-time comparability limits the detail with which the model can be specified. Still, the crucial influences of partisanship can be controlled and the magnitude of partisan sentiment can be directly compared with liberal/conservative sentiment. This means that certain considerations in the voting decision, most notably issues, are left out. If ideological sentiment was a pure summary of issue positions, for example, to include issues would diminish, or remove, the direct effect of ideological sentiment. Given the degree to which issues change from election to election, and the variations in the way they have been measured, however, to include issues would restrict comparisons across time.

Our model seeks to test the influences of party and ideology in a manner that allows the raw coefficients to be directly compared across years. Partisan and ideological sentiments are each measured as a difference in feeling thermometer evaluations on a scale that has a theoretical range of -100 to $+100$. We conceptualize ideology in two ways: (1) as relative sentiment toward liberals and conservatives (the feeling thermometer difference), and (2) as "sophistication," or the spontaneous use of the liberal/conservative continuum in rationalizing evaluations of the candidates and parties. Ideological sophistication is measured as a binary dummy variable defined as "1" for respondents classified as "ideologues" in the levels of conceptualization coding scheme and "0" for nonideologues. The dummy interaction terms have the effect of reducing the probit equation to the main effects $(b_1 + b_2 + b_3) + e$ for nonideologues. The interaction terms yield the differences in the coefficients for the constant and the partisan and ideological sentiment variables due to classification as an ideologue. They must be added to (or subtracted from, if negative) the corresponding main effects to yield the size of the coefficients for ideologues.

Due to the deletion of cases containing missing data on any variable, we would expect that the sample used in the analysis would be somewhat more sophisticated and Republican, than the sample as a whole. The model *ns* for 1968, 1980, and 1992 were reduced by the exclusion of third-party voters. In 1972, the *n* for the full model was reduced because level of conceptualization was obtained in a split-half survey design.

If the traditional view of ideology is correct (i.e., if sophistication is necessary before ideological sentiment has an impact), then the effect of ideological sentiment should be carried predominantly by the interactive term for liberal/conservative sentiment. The dummy term (increment to the constant due to classification as an ideologue) would not be expected to be significant, since this would suggest a predisposition to vote one way or the other simply because one thinks ideologically. Nonetheless, it is required if the equation is to be specified correctly. Support for the various revisionist views will be found in significant main effects of ideological sentiment on the vote.

The main effect for partisan sentiment should be significant in all years and can be expected, a priori, to be larger than any direct effect of ideology. Significant partisan interactive effects would indicate that thinking ideologically (i.e., evaluating candidates and parties with reference to a liberal/conservative continuum in the open-ended responses) influences partisan evaluations. This effect would not be expected. The findings for each of the presidential elections are presented in Table 1.

1964: In 1964, the landslide Johnson-Goldwater election is reflected in the significant negative constant. This means that even when the effects of partisan and ideological sentiment were zero, there was a less than fifty-fifty chance that the respondent would vote Republican. For nonideologues, the influence of partisan sentiment is roughly five times that of ideological sentiment, even though both coefficients are significant at the .01 level or better. The significant positive coefficient for the ideologue main effect means that individuals who rationalized their evaluations with reference to overarching abstractions like the liberal/conservative continuum had a significantly greater probability of voting for Goldwater than the rest of the sample, even when their partisan and ideological sentiments are assumed to be zero. The ideological sophistication interaction with partisanship is not significant, as expected. The ideological sophistication interaction with ideological sentiment is, however, significant and more than doubles the predicted effect of ideological sentiment on presidential vote. The coeffi-

Table 1
Probit Models of Presidential Vote**

Variable	Probit Coefficients (t statistics)							
	1964	1968	1972	1976	1980	1984	1988	1992
Constant	−.540*	.277*	.495*	.034	.260*	.404*	−.008	−.198*
	(−8.31)	(2.85)	(6.44)	(0.57)	(3.22)	(6.72)	(−.12)	(−3.15)
Party	.033*	.057*	.042*	.057*	.034*	.042*	.041*	.047*
	(11.99)	(10.43)	(9.14)	(11.97)	(10.01)	(14.62)	(14.03)	(14.42)
Cons–Lib	.006*	.002	.016*	.011*	.012*	.016*	.016*	.021*
	(2.30)	(0.57)	(4.94)	(3.67)	(3.90)	(5.46)	(5.51)	(6.63)
Party x Ideologue	.000	−.001	−.003	−.003	−.001	.011	−.004	−.004
	(0.03)	(−.05)	(−.25)	(−.34)	(−.13)	(1.34)	(−.61)	(−.52)
Cons–Lib x Ideologue	.009*	.014*	.018*	−.001	.021*	.007	.011	−.003
	(2.01)	(2.31)	(2.55)	(−.25)	(2.60)	(0.93)	(1.56)	(−.44)
Ideologue	.366*	.083	.093	.323*	−.095	.245	−.129	.048
	(3.09)	(0.59)	(0.54)	(2.78)	(−.53)	(1.59)	(−.82)	(0.32)
N	1078	622	676	1114	714	1189	1085	1260
Pseudo R–Sq	.72	.71	.74	.75	.78	.83	.82	.85

Source: American National Election Studies, 1964, 1968, 1972, 1976, 1980, 1984, 1988, and 1992.

*$p < .05$

**Probit coefficients and McKelvey Psuedo R–Squared calculations were obtained from Microcrunch, version 2.1. "Party" refers to the party feeling thermometer difference, "Cons–Lib" refers to the ideological feeling thermometer difference, and "Ideologue" refers to the dummy term for classification as an ideologue. The interaction terms are designated by the variable name times the ideologue dummy variable.

cient for ideological sentiment among ideologues is .015 ($b_3 + b_6$), but only .006 for nonideologues. Thus, it appears that in 1964, when Goldwater hoisted the conservative banner, the effects of ideological sentiment were largely limited to those who possessed some facility with the terms.

1968: In 1968, relative partisan sentiment had a significant influence on the two-party vote, but the impact of ideological sentiment operated entirely through the ideological sophistication interaction. Ideological sentiment had a significant effect on vote choice only among "ideologues," but among ideologues its impact was marginally greater than it was in 1964. The 1968 results illustrate two effects: (1) there seems a clear demonstration of the theory offered in *The American Voter* that ideological sentiment affects the vote only when citizens are able to "think ideologically," and (2) once ideological sentiment is activated among ideologues, it remains a potent force even in a presidential campaign not generally colored by traditional liberal/conservative appeals.

1972: In 1972, both partisan and ideological sentiments had significant impacts on the vote, but the impact of partisanship was about two and a half times greater than that of ideological sentiment among nonideologues. The effect of ideological sentiment among ideologues was still more than twice as large as for nonideologues in 1972. In fact, ideological sentiment had as much impact on the vote among nonideologues in 1972 as it did among ideologues in 1964 and 1968.

1976: The closeness of the Jimmy Carter/Gerald Ford contest is reflected in the constant for the probit equation for 1976. The partisan and ideological sentiment main effects are both significant, but the impact of partisan sentiment was five times that of ideological sentiment among nonideologues. This finding does not seem at all unreasonable for a nonideological election that featured the most conservative Democratic candidate since FDR's first campaign running against the man who pardoned Richard Nixon. The nonsignificant coefficient for the interaction of ideological sophistication and ideological sentiment suggests that what muted ideological influences there were in the 1976 election penetrated the general public relatively evenly. People who rationalized their political evaluations in terms of a liberal/conservative continuum were no more likely to be influenced by ideological sentiment than those who did not. However, ideologues were significantly more disposed to vote for the Republican candidate when partisan and ideological sentiments were otherwise evenly balanced.

1980: The probit equation for the 1980 election indicates ideological sentiment returned with even more force in the first Reagan campaign. As in 1972, the influence of partisan sentiment was somewhat reduced—outweighing that of ideological sentiment by about two and a half to one. Ideological sentiment was three times more important among ideologues in 1980 than among nonideologues. In fact, among those who rationalized evaluations with reference to a liberal/conservative continuum in 1980, the coefficient for ideological sentiment ($b_3 + b_6 = .033$) is *equal* to that for partisan sentiment ($b_2 + b_4 = .033$).

1984: In 1984, ideological sentiment had a slightly stronger impact on the vote than it had in 1980. The coefficient for partisan sentiment also increased in 1984, but the relative size of the two influences remained at about 2.5 : 1. In 1984, however, those who articulated their evaluations with respect to a liberal/conservative continuum were no more influenced by ideological sentiment than those who did not. The ideological implications of the Mondale/Ferraro campaign, the Rainbow Coalition, and the "San

Francisco Democrat Party" required no special familiarity with abstractions like the liberal/conservative continuum to be translated into meaningful sentiment.

1988: The George Bush/Dan Quayle campaign of 1988 sought to mobilize negative sentiment toward the "L-word" and attach the liberal label securely to Dukakis. Despite more overt efforts to appeal to ideological sentiment, vote choice was no more ideological in 1988 than it was in 1984. Also, as in 1984, the impact of ideological sentiment on the vote choice was no greater for those who rationalized their political evaluations in liberal/conservative terms than for those who did not explicitly use such abstractions.

1992: The 1992 election witnessed the increased influence of both partisan and ideological sentiments in the public as a whole, but the relative influences of the two remained roughly the same as in 1984 and 1988. For a third consecutive time, the influence of ideological sentiment penetrated fairly evenly into the voting public and required no special demonstration of familiarity with a liberal/conservative continuum. Unlike the 1960s and 1970s, neither the ideologue interaction terms nor the ideologue main effect dummy term are significant.

The results of the probit equations across time suggest that ideological sentiment has come to play an increasing role in presidential elections. Ideology does not matter as much as partisan sentiment does, but it does matter more than it did thirty years ago. In the 1960s and 1970s, ideological sentiment had a relatively modest effect on the voting decision *unless* such sentiment was undergirded by a sophisticated tendency to rationalize evaluations in ideological terms. In the 1980s, ideological sentiment began to have an increasingly powerful effect on vote choice. After the revolution of Reagan's first term, the increasing influence of ideological sentiment penetrated more evenly into the electorate as a whole. Thus, ideology not only mattered more but it also mattered to more people.

Discussion

On the whole, the results of this analysis are more consistent with the "revisionist" than with the "traditionalist" conception of ideology. Our analysis cannot speak to the 1950s because comparable data are not available, but by the time Goldwater made the first explicit linkage between the conservative label and the Republican Party, ideological sentiment had already penetrated into the public at large. However, while the public was not entirely "innocent" of ideological influences, ideological sentiment played a much larger part in the voting decisions of citizens who had a certain ready familiarity with ideological terminology. The 1964 findings might be viewed as support for a mixed model of ideological influences where both environmental and conditional effects are present.

Goldwater's activation of ideological sentiment among the voting public did not carry over into the 1968 election. Ideological sentiment was confined to the "ideology specialists"—people who were sufficiently familiar with the political abstractions to use them spontaneously in evaluating the candidates and parties. The findings of 1968 most closely approximate the traditionalist perspective. The voting public is found innocent of ideological influences.

The 1970s witnessed some increase in the influence of ideological sentiment, but ideological sophistication still conditioned its full impact, even in the 1980 election. As the 1980s gave way to the 1990s, however, the impact of ideological sentiment became more pervasive. It was no longer necessary to check whether the respondent articulated evaluations of political objects with respect to an underlying abstract continuum before ideological sentiment could be said to affect vote choice.

Yes, Ideology Matters

The answer to the question of whether ideology matters must be a solid "yes." Our ability to look across time allows us to say not only that ideological sentiment matters, but also that ideological sentiment matters more now than it did in the 1960s and 1970s. In making this assessment, we do not intend to say that the United States has become a "nation of ideologues." It appears, in fact, that individual U.S. voters are no more likely to rationalize their evaluations with references to the liberal/conservative continuum than they have been since the 1960s. We do mean to say that ideological sentiment penetrated into electoral choice to some extent in the earlier era and that its influence has become more pervasive over the last three decades.

The cross-time findings are suggestive of a process of gradual penetration of feelings about candidates and groups labeled liberal and conservative into electoral decision making. The public is by no means saturated with ideological sentiment. But, it is possible that ideological sentiment might have to take on a different character in order to capture the imagination of that quarter of the electorate who have expressed no difference in feeling about liberals and conservatives as of yet.

It is also worthwhile to consider that, while conservative sentiment predominates in the U.S. public, there is still a stable pool of liberal sentiment that appears capable of activation by explicitly liberal appeals. However, it may be the case that R. D. Rotunda's rendition of the rise and demise of "liberalism as word and symbol" (and that of the "progressive" label in an earlier era) is a better approximation of the underlying process.[52] He argues, in essence, that the popular label of an era becomes saddled with an excess baggage of predominantly detrimental meaning over time. Perhaps, liberals can take comfort in the eventual and inevitable decline in the popularity of the conservative label in its turn.

It may be, however, that Democrats and liberals are too quick to take comfort in the scholarly discourse, whether it be the "elite defense of democracy" or the inevitable decline of a popular label. Successive Republican presidential campaigns may have accelerated the demise of liberal sentiment by consciously linking negative associations with the "L-word." Evidence that the public generally did not think ideologically did not deter Republicans from appealing to more vaguely conservative sentiment over the long run. Nor did the Goldwater defeat cause more than a short-term retreat from the explicit use of the conservative label.

The story of Republican success in the 1994 congressional election appears to be a story of planning and effort by conservatives over the long haul. Looking back at the trend in conservative sentiment in Figure 1, it is worth noting that conservative sentiment in 1994 was the highest it had ever been in a congressional election year. While we have not undertaken analysis of individual level vote choice in congressional elections, we suspect that once we successfully controlled for other factors such as incumbency we would find that ideological sentiment penetrated the congressional electorate increasingly over time as well.

With respect to the question of realignment, this analysis suggests further hypotheses that need to be tested in a more refined analysis. In the absence of major economic crisis, it may be the case that partisan "adjustments" take place incrementally. The "nationalization of southern politics," begun in the 1960s, bore its fruit in the 1980s.[53] The nationalization of congressional politics, begun in the late seventies with integrated national negative advertising campaigns against the House leadership, seems to have achieved success in the 1994 election. It remains to be seen whether the conservative strategy will remain unified in 1996.

We conclude with a couple of important caveats. The first is methodological. In attempting to make comparisons across presidential elections over time, we have, of necessity, left out many additional factors relevant to vote choice during any particular campaign. The inclusion of these additional factors, like assessments of the economy or other campaign issues, could change the estimated effect of ideological sentiment in any given year. But, our interest here has been in comparisons across time.

The second caveat has to do with the study of sentiment or emotions more generally. The unfortunate bifurcation of attention in research on thinking and feeling is largely promoted by the false dichotomy between reason and passion. In urging the rebalancing of research attention in the direction of investigating sentiment, we do not wish to leave the impression that we think emotion is necessarily benign or beneficial. Emotions can be powerful motivators of political behavior, both for good and ill. Greater attention to the realm of political sentiment should also include renewed attention to the darker and more dangerous side of emotions in politics.

Notes

1. Angus Campbell, Philip E. Converse, Warren E. Miller, and Donald E. Stokes, *The American Voter* (New York: Wiley, 1960).

2. Philip E. Converse, "The Nature of Belief Systems in Mass Publics," in *Ideology and Discontent,* ed. David Apter (New York: Free Press of Glencoe, 1964).

3. See Donald R. Kinder, "Diversity and Complexity in Public Opinion," in *Political Science: The State of the Discipline,* ed. Ada R. Finifter (Washington, D.C.: APSA, 1983); Robert C. Luskin, "Measuring Political Sophistication," *American Journal of Political Science* 31 (1987): 856–899; and Kathleen Knight, "Ideology and Public Opinion," in *Research in Micropolitics,* vol. 3, ed. Samuel Long (Greenwich, Conn.: JAI Press, 1989), for reviews.

4. For example, Benjamin A. Page and Robert M. Shapiro, *The Rational Public* (Chicago: University of Chicago Press, 1990); James A. Stimson, *Public Opinion in America: Moods, Cycles, and Swings* (Boulder, Colo.: Westview Press, 1991); and Michael MacKuen, Robert S. Erikson, and James A. Stimson, "Peasants or Bankers: The American Electorate and the U.S. Economy," *American Political Science Review* 86 (1992): 597–611.

5. Kinder, "Diversity and Complexity," and Philip E. Converse, "Popular Representation and the Distribution of Information," in *Information and Democratic Processes,* ed. John A. Ferejohn and James H. Kuklinski (Urbana: University of Illinois Press, 1990).

6. Empirical researchers have tended to use the term "affect" to refer to feelings, emotions, or sentiments. This may stem from a desire to avoid the normative (antirational) implications sometimes ascribed to the latter terms (a point we develop in the text) or, perhaps, from a desire to sound more like psychologists, or both. We will generally use the term "sentiment" to refer to feelings, evaluations, or emotionally based responses to political objects. We generally use the term "affect" when speaking about other research efforts that have explicitly used that term.

7. For example, Campbell et al., *The American* Voter, and three works by Philip Converse: "The Nature of Belief Systems in Mass Publics"; "Public Opinion and Voting Behavior," in *The Handbook of Political Science,* vol. 4, ed. F. I. Greenstein, pp. 75–169 (Reading, Mass.: Addison-Wesley Press, 1975); and "Popular Representation and the Distribution of Information."

8. For example, Theresa E. Levitan and Warren E. Miller, "Ideological Interpretations of Presidential Elections," *American Political Science Review* 73 (1979): 751–771, and Pamela Johnston Conover and Stanley Feldman, "The Origins and Meaning of Liberal/Conservative Self-Identification," *American Journal of Political Science* 25 (1981): 617–645.

9. Ruth C. Hamill, M. Lodge, and F. Blake, "The Breadth, Depth and Utility of

Class, Partisan, and Ideological Schemata," *American Journal of Political Science* 29 (1985): 850–870; Kathleen Knight, "The Dimensionality of Partisan and Ideological Affect," *American Politics Quarterly* 12 (1984): 305–334, and "Ideology in the 1980 Election: Ideological Sophistication Does Matter," *Journal of Politics* 47 (1985): 828–853; and William G. Jacoby, "Levels of Conceptualization and Reliance on the Liberal-Conservative Continuum," *Journal of Politics* 48 (1986): 423–432.

10. John O. Field and Ronald Anderson, "Ideology in the Public's Conceptualization of the 1964 Election," *Public Opinion Quarterly* 33 (1969): 380–398; John C. Pierce, "Party Identification and the Changing Role of Ideology in American Politics," *Midwest Journal of Political Science* (1970): 25–42; and Norman R. Nie, Sidney Verba, and John R. Petrocik, *The Changing American Voter,* (Cambridge: Harvard University Press, 1979).

11. James A. Stimson, "A Macro Theory of Information Flow," in Ferejohn and Kuklinski (eds.), *Information and Democratic Processes.*

12. Campbell et al., *The American Voter,* p. 264.

13. V. O. Key, "A Theory of Critical Elections," *Journal of Politics* 17 (1955): 3–17, and V. O. Key, "Secular Realignment and the Party System," *Journal of Politics* 17 (1959): 3–18; E. E. Schattschneider, *The Semi-Sovereign People* (New York: Dryden Press, 1960); Walter Dean Burnham, *Critical Elections and the Mainsprings of American Democracy* (New York: Norton, 1971); Edward G. Carmines and James A. Stimson, *Issue Evolution: Race and the Transformation of American Politics* (Princeton, N.J.: Princeton University Press, 1989); and John R. Petrocik, "Realignment: New Party Coalitions and the Nationalization of the South," *Journal of Politics* 49 (1987): 347–375.

14. For example, Levitan and Miller, "Ideological Interpretations," and Warren E. Miller, "Party Identification, Realignment, and Party Voting: Back to Basics," *American Political Science Review* 85 (1991): 557–568.

15. Campbell et al., *The American Voter.*

16. Herbert McClosky, "Conservatism and Personality," *American Political Science Review* 52 (1958): 27–45.

17. Campbell et al., *The American Voter,* p. 550.

18. Ibid., p. 222.

19. M. Brewster Smith, Jarol S. Brunner, and R. W. White, *Opinions and Personality* (New York: Wiley, 1956); and Robert E. Lane, *Political Ideology* (New York: Free Press, 1962), and *Political Thinking and Consciousness* (Chicago: Markham, 1969).

20. Campbell et al., *The American Voter,* pp. 222–250.

21. Henry E. Brady and Paul M. Sniderman, "Attitude Attribution: A Group Basis for Political Reasoning," *American Political Science Review* 79 (1985): 1061–1078.

22. Morris P. Fiorina, *Retrospective Voting in American National Elections* (Cambridge: Harvard University Press, 1981).

23. John O. Field and Ronald Anderson, "Ideology in the Public's Conceptualization of the 1964 Election," *Public Opinion Quarterly* 33 (1969): 380–398.

24. We have followed the convention of collapsing the subcategory of "near ideologue" with that of "ideologue," as was done in part of the work reported by authors of *The American Voter* and much subsequent research.

25. Pierce, "Party Identification."

26. Nie, Verba, and Petrocik, *The Changing American Voter.*

27. *The Changing American Voter* engendered a flurry of controversy after its publication. A substantial amount of the increase in issue constraint they found was attributed to changes in the response format of the issue items (see George F. Bishop, A. J. Tuchfarber, and R. W. Oldendick, "Change in the Structure of American Political

Attitudes: The Nagging Question of Question Wording," *American Journal of Political Science* 72 [1978]). The levels of conceptualization have also been challenged (see, for example, Eric R.A.N. Smith, "The Levels of Conceptualization: False Measures of Ideological Sophistication," *American Political Science Review* 74 [1980]: 685–696, and Carol A. Cassel, "Issues in Measurement: The 'Levels of Conceptualization' Index of Ideological Sophistication," *American Journal of Political Science* 28 [1984]: 617–645).

28. Coders have so far included John Pierce, Paul Hagner, Pinky Wassenberg, Charleen White, and Kathleen Knight. The 1992 data are being coded by William Jacoby. All of the data are available from the Interuniversity Consortium for Political and Social Research.

29. John O. Pierce and Paul R. Hagner, "Research Update: Conceptualization and Party Identification, 1956–1976," *American Journal of Political Science* 26 (1982): 377–387.

30. Because coding for the 1992 levels of conceptualization was not complete at the time we undertook our analysis, we employed a surrogate obtained from the SRC Master Codes. Our surrogate, which counts all occurrences of the terms "liberal" and "conservative" in the Master Codes, tends to be somewhat less generous in assigning individuals to the "ideologues" category than that of Nie, Verba, and Petrocik (1979). Our surrogate figure for ideologues in 1992 is 23 percent. See Kathleen Knight and Carolyn Lewis, "Ideology and the American Electorate," in *Perspectives on American and Texas Politics,* ed. Kent L. Tedin, Donald S. Lutz, and Edward P. Fuchs (Dubuque, Iowa: Kendall/Hunt, 1992).

31. Susan Fiske and Shelley E. Taylor, *Social Cognition* (New York: Random House, 1984), and Richard D. Lau, "Political Schemata, Candidate Evaluation, and Voting Behavior," in *Political Cognitions,* ed. Richard D. Lau and David O. Sears (Hillsdale, N.J.: Lawrence Earlbaum, 1986).

32. Kathleen Knight, "Ideology in the 1980 Election: Ideological Sophistication Does Matter," *Journal of Politics* 47 (1985): 828–853.

33. Lloyd Free and Hadley Cantril, *The Political Beliefs of Americans* (New York: Simon, 1968).

34. Daniel Bell, ed., *The End of Ideology* (New York: Free Press, 1960), and David P. Apter, introduction to *Ideology and Discontent,* ed. David P. Apter (New York: Free Press of Glencoe, 1964).

35. Edward Shils, "Ideology and Civility," *Sewanee Review* 66 (1958): 450–480.

36. Adorno et al., *The Authoritarian Personality;* McClosky, "Conservatism and Personality"; Lane, *Political Ideology;* Seymour M. Lipset, *Political Man* (Garden City, N.Y.: Doubleday/Anchor, 1960).

37. Carolyn V. Lewis, *Affective Polarization in American Politics* (Ann Arbor, Mich.: University Microfilms, 1992), and "In the Shadow of Reason: The Use of Emotions in the American Vote" (Western Michigan University, 1995, manuscript).

38. Campbell et al., *The American Voter,* p. 143.

39. Levitan and Miller, "Ideological Interpretations."

40. Ibid.

41. For example, Robert P. Abelson, Donald R. Kinder, Mark D. Peters, and Susan T. Fiske, "Affective and Semantic Components in Political Person Perception," *Journal of Personality and Social Psychology* 42 (1982): 619–630; Pamela Johnston Conover and Stanley Feldman, "Emotional Reactions to the Economy: I'm Mad as Hell and I'm Not Going to Take It Anymore," *American Journal of Political Science* 30 (1986): 50–78; George E. Marcus, "The Structure of Emotional Response: 1984 Presidential Candidates," *American Political Science Review* 82 (1988): 735–761; Denis G. Sullivan and Roger D. Masters, "Happy Warriors: Leaders' Facial Displays, Viewers' Emotions,

and Political Support," *American Journal of Political Science* 32 (1988): 345–368; George E. Marcus and Wendy Rahn, "Emotions and Democratic Politics," in *Research in Micropolitics*, vol. 3, ed. Samuel Long (Greenwich, Conn.: JAI Press, 1990); James H. Kuklinski, Ellen Riggle, Victor Ottati, Norbert Schwarz, and Robert S. Wyer, "The Cognitive and Affective Bases of Political Tolerance Judgements," *American Journal of Political Science* 35 (1991): 1–27; and George E. Marcus and Michael MacKuen, "Anxiety, Enthusiasm, and the Vote: The Emotional Underpinnings of Learning and Involvement during Presidential Campaigns," *American Political Science Review* 87 (1993): 672–685.

42. Robert Zajonc, "Feeling and Thinking: Preferences Need No Inferences," *American Psychologist* 35 (1980): 151–175.

43. Philip E. Converse, "Public Opinion and Voting Behavior," in Greenstein (ed.), *The Handbook of Political Science*.

44. Field and Anderson, "Ideology in the Public's Conceptualization"; Pierce, "Party Identification"; Nie, Verba, and Petrocik, *The Changing American Voter;* and Stimson, *Public Opinion in America*.

45. Ronald D. Rotunda, *The Politics of Language* (Iowa City: University of Iowa Press, 1986).

46. Thomas Ferguson and J. Rogers, "The Myth of America's Turn to the Right," *Atlantic Monthly,* May 1986, 43–53.

47. Although there has been a good deal of discussion about the dimensionality of liberalism/conservatism [see Fred N. Kerlinger, *Liberalism and Conservatism* (New York: Lawrence Earlbaum Press, 1984); Conover and Feldman, "Origins and Meaning"; and Knight, "Dimensionality of Partisan"], we feel that the assumption that the terms are analytically treated as opposites is reasonable on both practical and theoretical grounds.

48. In 1964 and 1968, coding practices limited the range of the difference to –97 to +97, and there are differences in the overall variances across years, but neither of these problems is serious enough to affect our conclusions.

49. The surrogate for 1992 is created from a count of explicit mentions of the terms "liberal" or "conservative" in the Master Codes. A single mention is sufficient to be classified as an "ideologue" on the surrogate variable in 1992. Analysis was conducted on the 1984 and 1988 data using a similar surrogate and obtained results similar to the protocol coded variable for the same years.

50. Field and Anderson, "Ideology in the Public's Conceptualization," and Pierce, "Party Identification."

51. Warren E. Miller, Arthur H. Miller, Alden Raine, and Thad A. Brown, "A Majority Party in Disarray," *American Political Science Review* 70 (1976): 753–778; and Warren E. Miller and J. Merrill Shanks, "Policy Directions and Presidential Leadership," *British Journal of Political Science* 12 (1982): 299–356.

52. Rotunda, *Politics of Language.*

53. Schattschneider, *Semi-Sovereign People.*

3.3

State Legislative Elections: Choices or Echoes?

John Frendreis, Alan R. Gitelson, Gregory Flemming, and Anne Layzell

In his celebrated study of electoral behavior, V. O. Key observed that "as candidates and parties clamor for attention and vie for political support, the people's verdict can be no more than a selective reflection from among the alternatives and outlooks presented to them."[1] A fundamental assumption of Key, and that of most democratic theorists, is that if elections are to matter, they should offer policy choices in any given election. The same observation was made over forty years ago by E. E. Schattschneider and his colleagues as a necessary condition for electoral linkage between public opinion and policy output, in their exposition of a responsible parties model.[2]

Clearly, there is little evidence that we have evolved into responsible parties. In turn, the decline-of-party thesis, prevalent since the mid-1960s, has raised doubts among some scholars regarding the role that political parties and, more to the point, party labels play in distinguishing the issue positions of candidates for political office. Nevertheless, political scientists have made considerable efforts to better understand the link between issues and campaigns. Part of that effort has focused on what John Sullivan and Robert O'Connor regard as a central condition necessary for the popular control of public policy: "that opposing candidates for the same elective office must differ in their attitudes toward the issues ... an essential component of any realistic [democratic] linkage model."[3]

Scholarly work regarding this issue has focused, for the most part, on congressional and presidential electoral campaigns. Sullivan and O'Connor looked at U.S. House of Representative candidates in the 1966 election and found that the two parties' candidates did differ on the issues and that, in the aggregate, the electorate "was offered a substantively significant choice in the Congressional election."[4] If the linkage between public opinion and policy outputs is relatively weak, it is not, according to Sullivan and O'Connor, "a result of the party system's failure to provide choices"; rather, it is the result of the tendency of the electorate—in the aggregate—to select a Congress that is considerably more moderate than either the most liberal or most conservative alternatives possible given the available candidates.[5] While the outcome of the 1966 congressional election may not have had a significant impact on the aggregate issue alignments by members of Congress in the policy-making process, the opportunity for that election to affect public policy was clearly present in party competitive races where a significant majority of candidates held distinct and opposing issue positions.

Other studies have extended the research of Sullivan and O'Connor. Gerald Wright and Michael Berkman, in an analysis of the 1982 senatorial election, conclude that both candidates and voters take seriously the role of issues in the campaign process and that there are "clear patterns of policy effect on Senate election outcomes."[6] In their study on U.S. presidential elections, Edward Carmines and David Gopoian argue "that collective electoral response is a dual function of both preferences on policy issues and assessments of candidates," although they further suggest that a major link between public opinion and public policy "comes about through issue-based electoral coalitions that have their roots in the party system and are reinforced by the policy orientations of presidential administrations."[7] This strain of work, however, has not been expanded to include state legislative races.

In this chapter we begin to fill this void. Our focus is on understanding the extent to which the issue positions held by slates of state legislative candidates present choices to the voters in elections and to what extent the decisions made by voters between these choices lead to legislative bodies with particular ideological compositions. We thus address two related questions. The second one is the question posed in the title of this volume: Do elections matter? The first question, however, is perhaps even more basic: Can elections matter?

Issues, Ideology, and Partisanship

A fuller understanding of the linkage role of elections justifies a shift in research focus to lower-level offices for two reasons. First, lower-level offices, such as state legislative and county offices, are responsible for public policy that is substantively important and collectively represents hundreds of billions of dollars in annual expenditures. Second, what happens at these levels is relevant for electoral and partisan politics at higher levels. We would argue, for example, that the continued incomplete development of the Republican Party in many parts of the South is as much a function of what has or has not happened at the local level of the political system as it may be a function of national and statewide politics.[8]

Of course, the states have long been a research setting for the study of partisan competition.[9] In addition to the various efforts to develop indicators of interparty competition[10] or determine the antecedent conditions of interparty competition,[11] a sizable literature has sought to understand the linkage among partisan competition, other political and socioeconomic variables, and state public policy.[12] The latter research in particular represented an attempt to empirically evaluate Key's (1949) famous thesis linking a lack of party competition to "the development of issueless, faction-ridden, and often undemocratic state political systems."[13]

Given the centrality of issue-based politics to this matrix of party activity, issues, elections, and public policy, it is curious that the issue content of state electoral politics—especially of state legislative electoral politics—has largely been considered only indirectly or impressionistically. Indeed, the relationship between issue choices and state legislative electoral competition has never been examined at the level of the actual candidates for state legislative office. The first section of the research reported below addresses this concern, seeking an answer to an initial, basic question: Do state legislative elections present voters with slates of candidates whose views on significant policy issues differ? We approach this by addressing two related questions: First, do state legislative elections provide for state legislative slates that reflect different issue and/or ideological belief systems among the candidates? Second, are there broad partisan differences in individual state legislative contests? Together, these questions address the issue of whether candidate issue positions and candidate partisan identification represent a significant and identifiable choice—or merely an echo—in state legislative races. Following this, we turn to a second basic question about the 1992 state legislative elections: Did the elections matter?

Choices or Echoes: The 1992 State Legislative Elections

In the fall of 1992, we surveyed all Democratic and Republican general election candidates for the upper and lower state legislative houses in eight states: Arizona, Colorado, Florida, Illinois, Missouri, South Carolina, Washington, and Wisconsin.[14] These eight states were selected in order to provide representative coverage with respect to regions and to the degree of party strength and competitiveness within each state.[15] The states are also representative in terms of recent measures of state legislative competition. At least one state falls into each quintile of competitiveness, as measured by Joseph Aistrup, and at least one state falls into each quartile of competitiveness, as measured by Thomas Holbrook and Emily Van Dunk.[16]

A total of 1,657 candidates for state legislative office were surveyed. With valid responses from 997 state legislative candidates, the response rate was 60 percent of the population sampled. The response rates varied across the eight states, from 54 percent in Illinois and South Carolina to 74 percent in Washington; in all but two states the response rate did not vary by more than 9 percent.

To assess their issue positions, the candidates were asked a set of six Likert-type questions on their positions regarding a variety of issues: government efforts to stimulate employment, equal rights for women and minorities, trade protectionism, the need to cut government spending, and abortion. The questions were worded so that conservative responses required agreement in some cases and disagreement in others; in the analysis that follows, the responses have been recoded so that a one represents the most liberal response and a five represents the most conservative response. Depending on the hypothesis, the number of legislative candidates analyzed varies from all 997 to the 584 candidates running in races with two candidates for which responses from both candidates are available.

Could the Election Matter?

Our general assumption is that systematic issue differences between candidates will correspond to a general liberal-to-conservative continuum, with ideological positioning reflecting the contours identified in most discussions of contemporary partisan politics within the United States: Republicans will take more conservative positions than Democrats. Nested within this assumption is a second assumption that the issues examined cohere into a single identifiable dimension.

Of course, it is not necessary that issues correspond to a basic underlying dimension in order for the voters to be presented with choices in elections. However, it is necessary for issue positions to be related across issues relevant to the voters if the aggregate choices presented to the voters are to represent coherent governing options represented by the two party slates.

As a first step, then, we examined the interrelationship between the candidates' responses to the six-issue items. Factor analysis reveals that five of the six items load on an initial factor; the exception is the protectionism item.[17] To the extent that the latter is related to the general ideological dimension, the "conservative" response is to oppose protectionist action by the government. However, separate analyses within each party show that this is only true for Republican candidates. For Democratic candidates, the relationship was less clear; if anything, the "conservative" response for Democrats is to favor protectionist action.

The lack of correspondence between attitudes toward trade protectionism and the other issues is indicated further by a reliability analyses of summated scales based on all six and the remaining five items (the original six minus trade protectionism). The five-item scale is substantially more reliable than the six-item scale (standardized item α of .70 versus .51); the correlation of trade protectionism with each of these scales is quite low (e.g., .26 with the more reliable five-item scale). At the same time, the correlation between the five-item scale and the candidates' self-positioning on the standard seven-point NES ideology scale is quite high ($r=.72$). As a result, in the remaining analysis, we only consider the candidates' positions on the five-issue items that are related to the broader ideological dimension, as well as their scores for the summated five-item scale.

Our general research question is whether or not the candidates presented to the voters in state legislative elections provide the voters with choices regarding significant issues. We first consider this in the aggregate, that is, by examining whether the overall slates of candidates presented to the voters in each state differ with regard to the issues. We note at the outset that our data only examine the issue positions held by the candidates, rather than, for example, the voters' perceptions of these differences. While an analysis of the issue positions held by voters is relevant to a comprehensive overview of analysis of issue definition in state legislative campaigns, we suspect that the nature of the specific campaigns play an important role in determining to what extent differences between the candidates' are reflected in voters' perceptions of these differences.

Table 1 presents the mean differences between the slates of Republican and Democratic candidates running for state legislative seats in the 1992 election. To reiterate, candidates were asked their positions on five issues (listed in the appendix), with possible responses ranging from one (most liberal) to five (most conservative). The questions concerned the government's role in providing jobs and a good standard of living, equal rights for women, the government's role in securing racial minorities' rights, abortion rights, and whether government should provide fewer services in order to reduce government spending. An overall position score, a summated scale divided by five (to match the metric of the five items), was also created.

Table 1

Differences in Mean Issue Positions Between Democratic and Republican Candidates in 1992 State Legislative Elections

State	Good Jobs	Equal Rights for Women	Must Cut Government Services	Equal Rights for Minorities	Right to Abortion	Overall	N
Arizona	1.71*	.25	2.08*	1.90*	1.91*	1.54*	78
Colorado	1.85*	.47*	2.17*	1.04*	1.30*	1.40*	97
Florida	1.52*	.34*	1.81*	1.14*	1.47*	1.25*	124
Illinois	1.46*	.14	1.18*	.70*	1.06*	.91*	154
Missouri	1.35*	.59*	1.47*	.99*	1.78*	1.21*	166
South Carolina	1.57*	.43*	1.01*	1.11*	1.48*	1.09*	166
Washington	1.31*	.57*	1.47*	.78*	2.13*	1.26*	124
Wisconsin	1.54*	.33	1.32*	1.39*	2.05*	1.32*	106

Note: Entries equal the mean difference between Republican and Democratic candidates for the state legislature for the 1992 election. Entries equal the mean difference between aggregate party scores; scores on issue positions range from liberal (1) to conservative (5). Entries in the last column under the heading "Overall" are based on a composite score of candidates' positions on all five issues. Since the entries represent a difference between Republican scores and Democratic scores, the positive figures indicate that Republicans consistently took more conservative positions than Democrats. Entries denoted by an asterisk represent statistically different means ($p \leq .05$, two-tailed test).

The results in Table 1 show clear and consistent differences between the Republican and Democratic candidates, with the differences invariably in the expected direction—Republican candidates hold more conservative positions than Democrats. These differences are statistically significant in all states and for all issues, with the exception of women's rights in Arizona, Illinois, and Wisconsin. The party slates generally differed the most over abortion rights and the government's role in managing the economy, while they differed least with respect to women's rights. The first two issues appear to conform most closely with elite party views on abortion and government regulation in which the Republicans and Democrats take polarized policy positions. Women's rights, while a contentious issue between the two parties during the struggle over the Equal Rights amendment during the 1970s and 1980s, has not raised itself as a major debating point in state campaigns during the 1990s, a finding supported by our own analysis.

The differences in the overall scores indicate that Republicans and Democrats differed the most in Arizona and Colorado, while the two parties' candidates were closest in Illinois and South Carolina. Although we hope at a later time to examine more fully the bases and implications of these interstate differences, we would note at this point that there is essentially no relationship (Kendall's tau=-.07) between these state-level issue differences and the most recent level of state legislative electoral competition reported by Aistrup.[18] However, our small sample of states argues against attaching too much significance to the absence of any relationship between issue differences and electoral competition at this time.

The pattern of interparty differences is essentially the same when we shift our focus from aggregated slates of candidates to the specific choices presented to the voters—pairs of competing candidates. Table 2 shows the average differences in issue positions between the pairs of competing candidates, across the states and for each legislative house. The small numbers of complete races for the upper houses mean conclusions here must be tentative, but the general pattern is the same for both houses—with the overall differences reasonably close to the aggregated state differences. With two minor exceptions, the average voter in each state was presented a choice on each issue, with Democratic candidates taking more liberal positions and Republican candidates taking more conservative positions. As was true for the aggregated slates of candidates, the competing candidates differed least with respect to equal rights for women. Also as was true for the aggregated slates, the competing candidates differed most in Arizona and Colorado.

In individual races, of course, there are instances of Democrats taking more conservative positions than Republicans; depending on the issue, between 10 and 16 percent of the individual races display this pattern. Even

Table 2

Differences in Mean Issue Positions Between Democratic and Republican Opponents in State Legislative Races, by State

State	Good Jobs	Equal Rights for Women	Must Cut Government Services	Equal Rights for Minorities	Right to Abortion	Overall	N
Upper House							
Arizona	2.13*	.25	2.00*	2.38*	1.86*	1.66*	7
Colorado	1.83*	1.50	2.50*	.83	1.83*	1.70*	6
Florida	.50	-.25	1.38*	.25	1.25*	.63	8
Illinois	1.58*	.23	1.62*	1.42*	2.45*	1.36*	12
Missouri	1.33	.33	1.33	.50	2.50*	1.20*	6
South Carolina	.80	.60	1.00	.60	1.80*	.96*	5
Washington	1.13*	.63	1.86*	.63	1.63*	.94*	7
Wisconsin	1.50	0	1.50*	.75	2.00	1.15	4
Lower House							
Arizona	1.83*	.21	2.44*	2.21*	1.37*	1.58*	18
Colorado	1.81*	.52*	2.04*	1.46*	1.04*	1.47*	26
Florida	1.39*	.54*	1.91*	1.65*	1.78*	1.38*	23
Illinois	1.23*	.19	1.13*	.84*	.70*	.90*	31
Missouri	1.49*	.58*	1.54*	.88*	1.55*	1.21*	48
South Carolina	1.50*	.88*	.94*	1.00	1.59*	1.23*	16
Washington	1.12*	.38	1.48*	.54	2.32*	1.21*	24
Wisconsin	1.11*	.32	.96*	1.61*	2.36*	1.27*	28

Note: Entries equal the mean difference between Republican and Democratic opponents in contested legislative races. Republicans are expected to score higher than Democrats on each issue scale, with the result that the mean differences between Republican and Democratic opponents are expected to be positive. The number of cases presented equals the number of contested races (paired observations) in each state. Entries denoted by an asterisk represent statistically different means ($p \leq .05$, two-tailed test).

more common is the tendency for competing candidates to express the same position on these issues. This occurrence ranges from a low of 13 to 16 percent on the items relating to the need to cut services to balance the budget and the role of government in job creation (respectively) to a high of 48 percent on the item relating to equal rights for women. Even on the latter item, however, the number of cases in which liberal Democrats face conservative Republicans is four times as great as the reverse. Significantly, the ideological choices are sharper when all of the issues are considered together. For the overall issue scale, Democrats take more liberal positions than Republicans 89 percent of the time, while the reverse is true in only 6 percent of the races.

Contrary to the assumptions of Benjamin Page and Kenneth Shepsle, who argue that emphasizing specific policy stands is too costly for candidates, it would appear that the 1992 state legislative elections in these states presented the voters with a choice—at least in terms of the issue positions held by the competing candidates.[19] This is true whether we consider the individual races or the overall composition of the candidate slates presented by the Democratic and Republican Parties.

Did the Elections Matter?

Did the voters' choices in these elections make a difference in the ideological composition of the various legislative houses? Our data do not permit us to examine the intentions of the voters of these eight states, but we can examine the outcome. In their study of the 1966 congressional election, Sullivan and O'Connor estimated the ideological composition of the Congress that was elected and compared this to the Congress that would have been elected if the election results had been reversed—that is, if the losers had won and the winners (except for unopposed winners) had lost.[20]

We present a similar analysis in Table 3. The results are more mixed. In each case, the ideological composition of the legislature would have switched from being slightly liberal to slightly conservative (or vice versa). However, in only five of the sixteen legislative houses would the change have been as great as one point on the five-point scale. This reflects the fact that the voters did not uniformly pick liberals or conservatives as winners in these elections; rather, across each of the states, the voters elected mixed groups of candidates (in terms of party, which we have shown is related to issue positions). Thus, a reversal of the election would have produced a different legislature—more conservative in most states, since Democrats won most of the contested races across these eight states. However, the resulting legislatures would have differed in degree but not in their fundamental ideological composition.

Table 3

Differences in Mean Issue Positions Between Winning and Losing Candidates in State Legislative Elections

State	Mean Difference Between Winning and Losing Candidates	Mean Difference If Losers Had Won and Winners Had Lost	Ideological Swing	N
Upper House				
Arizona	.977*	-.849*	-1.826	21
Colorado	-.340	.687	+1.027	16
Florida	.011	-.040	-.051	30
Illinois	.432	-.542*	-.975	47
Missouri	-.224	.224	+.448	15
South Carolina	-.784*	.320	+1.104	31
Washington	-.325	.138	+.463	20
Wisconsin	-.596	.038	+.634	16
Lower House				
Arizona	.542	-.473	-1.015	57
Colorado	-.208	.223	+.431	81
Florida	-.180	.209	+.389	94
Illinois	-.095	.153	+.248	107
Missouri	-.256	.199	+.455	151
South Carolina	-.107	.143	+.250	93
Washington	-.520*	.499*	+1.019	52
Wisconsin	-.013	.076	+.089	90

Note: Entries equal the mean difference between the winning and losing groups of candidates in 1992 state legislative races. Entries are based on a composite score of candidates' positions on five issues (see text). The scores range from liberal (1) to conservative (5). Entries listed in the first column represent the difference between the winning and losing candidates. Entries listed in the second column represent the difference between the hypothetical "winning" and "losing" candidates if all losers and unopposed winners had won and all opposed winners had lost. Negative entries indicate that losers are more conservative than winners; positive entries indicate that losers are more liberal than winners. Entries denoted by an asterisk represent statistically different means ($p \le .05$, two-tailed test).

Of course, the swings would be much greater if the most conservative or most liberal candidates won in every race, which would be tantamount to overwhelming partisan landslides. However, such shifts are exceedingly rare in contemporary U.S. politics. Even in 1994, when Republicans held or improved their strength in all fifteen of the legislative chambers that held elections (in the eight states examined above), the average gain in seats across the eight chambers was 5 percent—probably enough to alter the average ideological composition, yet not nearly enough to shift the ideological center of gravity substantially rightward.

Nevertheless, decisions are made by legislative majorities, not by the average ideological positions of the complete legislature. Thus, our analysis of the aggregate choices offered to these voters only addresses a portion of the question, "Do elections matter?" A complete answer must extend beyond election day to an understanding of how the outcomes of elections are translated into policy decisions.

Conclusions

Our results at the state legislative campaign level support and extend the earlier research findings of Sullivan and O'Connor in their examination of congressional campaigns.[21] State legislative candidates systematically differed in the views they held on five important issue areas and, in the aggregate, the voters were offered a substantively significant choice in the elections for the upper and lower houses in the states under investigation. We also found that there were broad partisan issue differences in individual state legislative contests. In effect, the Democratic and Republican Parties offered the electorate candidates holding distinct and competing ideological and issue stances.

If the linkage between public opinion and policy outputs is relatively weak, it is not, according to our analysis, a result of the party system's failure to provide candidates with alternative policy positions on key issues. Together, our findings address the issue of whether candidate issue positions and candidate partisan identification represent a distinctive choice or merely an echo in state legislative races. The electorate is offered a choice, not an echo, regarding the issue and ideological orientations of the Democratic and Republican state legislative candidates. Our results also provide evidence that contradicts a common assumption that members of state legislatures are much less issue-oriented than their counterparts in Congress.

While our research focused on the self-declared issue positions of candidates, we did not examine or analyze the role that issues specifically played in the dynamics of the campaign process. While we can conclude that issue and ideological differences exist between competing party candidates, we cannot determine how issues were mediated during the campaign. We can only speculate at this time that policy differences between the candidates may be reflected in subsequent legislation supported by winning candidates. Future analysis must examine more closely the link between campaign strategy and issue debate and the specific observations of voters regarding their perceptions of candidate policy positions.

This issue is closely tied to a related matter that also needs to be addressed further: the examination of policy outcomes as measured by the voting patterns of successful candidates to the state legislature. Are personal issue positions correlated with legislative voting behavior? Put differently, if the voters select a particular legislature from an array of possible choices, will the subsequent behavior of this legislature reflect the ideological choices offered to the voters at the time of the election? Sullivan and O'Connor (1972) and Miller and Stokes (1963) found a strong correlation between candidates' personal beliefs and their congressional voting patterns, suggesting that the choices offered to the voters at the time of the election are relevant to subsequent policy choices by the candidates who are elected.[22]

The questions that we have addressed here are part of our broader research agenda, which seeks a clearer understanding not simply of what candidates think or do during the campaign process but of the complex interactions that exist in the election process between candidates, political parties, issues, voters, and policies. An important, and as yet unanswered, question concerns the relationship between candidate issues and electoral competition. For example, V. O. Key maintains that electoral competition breeds issue differences and that lack of competition leads to issueless policies. Yet it is just as likely, in examining the role of candidates and political parties in the campaign process, that the nature of the differences between competing candidates leads to greater or lesser competition between political parties.

Ultimately, it is a better understanding of this complex interaction of actors in the political system that presents the greatest challenge to our knowledge of, first, the link between candidate campaigns and voter choice and, second, the connection between public opinion and policy output. That knowledge is clearly linked to the various actors that influence election outcomes. A more comprehensive understanding must begin with a clearer perception of the opinions and desires that voters bring to the electoral environment and must follow the process through the actions of candidates, responses of voters, and subsequent behavior of elected officeholders, until the process begins anew at the next election. Only then will we have a clearer understanding as to whether—and precisely in what ways—elections do matter.

Appendix

The following questions from the State Legislative Candidate Survey sought to measure the self-reported ideological and issue orientations of Republican and Democratic candidates for the state legislature.

Ideological Orientation

Below is a scale on which the political views people might hold are listed. Where would you place yourself on this scale? (1 = very liberal; 2 = liberal; 3 = somewhat liberal; 4 = moderate, middle of the road; 5 = somewhat conservative; 6 = conservative; 7 = very conservative).

Issue Orientation

Please circle the number that best represents your position on the following issues. (1 = strongly agree; 2 = somewhat agree; 3 = neutral; 4 = somewhat disagree; 5 = strongly disagree):

- The role of the government is to see to it that every person has a job and a good standard of living;
- Women should have an equal role with men in running business, industry, and government;
- Government should provide fewer services, even in areas such as health and education, in order to reduce spending;
- The government should place new limits on foreign imports in order to protect American jobs;
- Equal opportunity for blacks and whites to succeed is very important, but it's not really the government's job to guarantee it;
- By law, a woman should always be able to obtain an abortion as a matter of personal choice.

Notes

This research was partially supported by a university research leave and by several Research Support Grants from the Office of Research Services of Loyola University Chicago.

1. V. O. Key, Jr., *The Responsible Electorate* (Cambridge: Harvard University Press, 1966), p. 2.

2. American Political Science Association, *Toward a More Responsible Two-Party System* (New York: Rinehart, 1950).

3. John L. Sullivan and Robert E. O'Connor, "Electoral Choice and Popular Control of Public Policy: The Case of the 1966 House Elections," *American Political Science Review* 66 (1972): 1257.

4. Ibid., p. 1264.

5. Ibid.

6. Gerald C. Wright, Jr., and Michael B. Berkman, "Candidates and Policy in United States Senate Elections," *American Political Science Review* 80 (1986): 567.

7. Edward G. Carmines and J. David Gopoian, "Issue Coalitions, Issueless Campaigns: The Paradox of Rationality in American Presidential Elections," *Journal of Politics* 43 (1981): 1189.

8. For example, see John R. Frendreis, James L. Gibson, and Laura L. Vertz, "The Electoral Relevance of Local Party Organizations," *American Political Science Review* 84 (1990): 231–232.

9. See, for example, Joseph A. Aistrup, "State Legislative Party Competition: A County-Level Measure," *Political Research Quarterly* 46 (1993): 433–446; Charles J. Barrilleaux, "A Dynamic Model of Partisan Competition in the American States," *American Journal of Political Science* 30 (1986): 822–840; Samuel C. Patterson and Gregory C. Caldeira, "The Etiology of Party Competition," *American Political Science Review* 78 (1984): 691–707; C. Anthony Broh and Mark S. Levine, "Patterns of Party Competition," *American Politics Quarterly* 6 (1976): 357–384; Austin Ranney, "Parties in State Politics," in *Politics in the American States,* 1st ed., ed. H. Jacob and K. Vines (Boston: Little, Brown and Co., 1965); and Joseph A. Schlesinger, "A Two-Dimensional Scheme for Classifying the States According to Degree of Interparty Competition," *American Political Science Review* 49 (1955): 1120–1128.

10. For example, Aistrup, "State Legislative Party Competition."

11. For example, Barrilleaux, "A Dynamic Model," and Patterson and Caldeira, "The Etiology of Party Competition."

12. For example, Richard Dawson and James Robinson, "Interparty Competition, Economic Variables, and Welfare Policies in the American States," *Journal of Politics* 25 (1963): 265–289; Brian R. Fry and Richard F. Winters, "The Politics of Redistribution," *American Political Science Review* 64 (1970): 508–522; and Michael Lewis-Beck, "The Relative Importance of Socioeconomic and Political Variables for Public Policy," *American Political Science Review* 71 (1977): 559–566. For a further review, see Barrilleaux, "A Dynamic Model."

13. V. O. Key, Jr., *Southern Politics in State and Nation* (New York: Knopf, 1949), and Barrilleaux, "A Dynamic Model," p. 822.

14. This research was part of a larger study, the Election Dynamics Project (EDP), that examined the perception of state legislative candidates and county party leaders on the local campaign process. The EDP study also involved the survey of all Democratic and Republican county chairs in the eight states in our sample. See John Frendreis, Alan R. Gitelson, Gregory Flemming, and Anne Layzell, "Local Political Parties and the 1992 Campaign for the State Legislature" (paper presented at the annual meeting of the American Political Science Association, Washington, D.C., September 2–5, 1993), and "Local Political Parties and Legislative Races in 1992," in *The State of the Parties: The Changing Role of Contemporary American Parties,* ed. D. Shea and J. Green, pp. 133–146 (Lanham, Md.: Rowman and Littlefield, 1994), and John Frendreis and Alan R. Gitelson, "Local Political Parties and Legislative Races" (paper presented at the Ray C. Bliss Institute "State of the Parties" conference, Akron, Ohio, September 23–24, 1993), and "Parties, Candidates, and State Electoral Politics" (paper presented at the

annual meeting of the American Political Science Association, Chicago, August 31–September 3, 1995).

15. Based on data reported in Cornelius P. Cotter, James L. Gibson, John F. Bibby, and Robert J. Huckshorn, *Party Organizations in American Politics* (New York: Praeger, 1984).

16. Aistrup, "State Legislative Party Competition," and Thomas M. Holbrook and Emily Van Dunk, "Electoral Competition in the American States," *American Political Science Review* 87 (1993): 955–962.

17. Separate factor analyses for each party's candidates show the items loading on different, but related, dimensions. For the Democrats, the items load on two factors, one related to issues regarding race and women and a second related to the size and role of government and the economy. For Republicans, three dimensions emerge: economic policy, noneconomic domestic policy, and women's issues (women's rights and abortion). What this shows is that while considered as a whole these issues divide the candidates according to a general ideological dimension, within each party there are different points of division, most notably a tendency for Republican candidates' attitudes toward abortion and women not to be as closely related to attitudes toward other policies as they are for Democratic candidates.

18. Aistrup, "State Legislative Party Competition."

19. Benjamin I. Page, "The Theory of Political Ambiguity," *American Political Science Review* 70 (1976): 742–752, and Kenneth A. Shepsle, "The Strategy of Ambiguity: Uncertainty and Electoral Competition," *American Political Science Review* 66 (1972): 555–568.

20. Sullivan and O'Connor, "Electoral Choice."

21. Ibid.

22. Ibid., and Warren E. Miller and Donald S. Stokes, "Constituency Influence in Congress," *American Political Science Review* 57 (1963): 45–56.

Fresh Troops and Hardened Veterans

Religious Activists and Party Realignment in the 1990s

James L. Guth, John C. Green, Corwin E. Smidt, and Lyman A. Kellstedt

The 1992 and 1994 elections were stunning and confusing to citizens and pundits alike. The dramatic results of the 1994 campaign scarcely need elaboration: the Republican capture of the U.S. House of Representatives for the first time in forty years, the simultaneous takeover of the U.S. Senate, and major gains in state and local offices. The outcome was a major setback to the Democrats and an embarrassment for President Bill Clinton who, ironically, had benefited from a similar, if less sweeping, tide in 1992, deposing a sitting Republican president in an unusual three-way race. If elections ever do matter, surely it would be those of 1992 and 1994.

But the meaning of these contests is far from clear. What exactly did the public want? The choice of Clinton after twelve years of Republican rule led many to believe that the country longed for an activist national government. And yet the GOP landslide in 1994 suggested just the reverse: that people were tired of "big government." It is entirely possible, of course, that Americans are simply confused. An equally plausible alternative is that the United States is experiencing a major political transformation, a once-in-a-generation realignment of major party coalitions, but one that is moving forward by fits and starts.

These elections did have one undisputed effect: each brought to power a new set of political elites—new officeholders and new configurations of party and interest group activists who led their parties to victory.[1] In fact, critical additions to each party's activist corps played a major role in both campaigns: Bill Clinton's "New Covenant" in 1992 was fostered by a fresh corps of supposedly centrist Democratic activists who wanted a "New Democrat" in the White House, while Newt Gingrich's "Contract with America" was trumpeted abroad by a reconstructed and boisterous coalition of conservatives committed to an aggressive Republican Congress.

This essay examines an important element in the party activist corps: the Christian activists who were widely regarded as new additions to the Republican and Democratic coalitions in the 1990s. Journalists and scholars alike have focused recently on the so-called "religious" or "Christian" Right. These conservative religious folks and their "divisive" rhetoric were widely blamed for George Bush's downfall in 1992, but have also been credited with the elevation of Newt Gingrich two years later.[2] But the "Christian Left" was also active, although less publicized because of its smaller size, lower profile, and longer involvement in politics. Indeed, President Clinton himself, Vice-President Al Gore, and especially Hillary Clinton could be counted as part of this movement, which worked hard—but futilely—for congressional Democrats in 1994.[3] Where did these religious activists come from, and why are they attracting so much attention?

Religion and Party Activists

Party activists are usually drawn from social and economic groups that identify with each of the major parties—or at least from their more privileged strata.[4] The dominance of the U.S. two-party system means that most activists are channeled toward the party most likely to advance their values and interests. At any point, this distribution of activists constitutes the partisan "alignment": the interests that dominate electoral campaigns and support the victors' governing efforts. Although U.S. party coalitions are highly diverse, they are relatively stable. Major realignments of elite elements in party coalitions are rare but extremely important; they often presage dramatic changes at the ballot box. In fact, even minor realignments among activists can lead to significant departures.[5]

Scholars have identified three processes by which realignment occurs among party activists. The first is by conversion, when new activists abandon other identifications or apolitical status to join the party. Although most people inherit their partisan identification (or lack of it), personal experiences or political events may lead them to reconsider that identity. Even during eras of political stability, some conversion takes place, but sometimes dramatic changes in social life or political events lead large groups of activists to realign their partisan identifications. Indeed, such changes constitute a defining element of periods of political instability.[6]

Partisan conversion has more impact if it is accompanied by two other processes, politicization and mobilization, which can affect standpat partisans as well. Politicization occurs when potential activists come to see a direct connection between their concerns and political activity. In this sense, activist alignments are the collective result of the myriad decisions by individuals about which party can best advance their interests on a particular issue. Politicization may be particularly noticeable among converts, but the process is conceptually distinct from conversion; even for standpat partisans, politicization links them to their party in a new way. A final step in incorporating activists into the party is mobilization: motivating politicized partisans to actually participate in campaign activities. Some activists essentially motivate themselves because of strong interest in politics and intense opinions, but others must be informed, educated, and prompted to participate.[7]

Religion has shaped partisan alignments since the beginning of the Republic and has been a fertile source of party activists. Ever since the days of the Federalists and Jeffersonian Republicans, U.S. political parties have divided along religious lines; because of the diversity and fluidity of U.S. religion, those alignments have also been complex and fluid. Repeatedly, the rise of new religious movements and the decline of old religious establishments have been linked to the conversion, politicization, and mobilization of party activists. In the 1840s, for example, the new Arminian evangelicalism fed the many reform movements that infiltrated the Whig Party and later consolidated as a vigorous element in the new Republican coalition of the Civil War era.[8]

The word "conversion" has a special meaning when used in connection with religious activists. Many U.S. religious groups assiduously seek new adherents by "conversion." In fact, entire religious movements are dedicated to both attracting the unchurched and nonreligious and to bringing members of other churches to a new and better religious life. The political implications of religious conversion, whether on an individual level or as part of a collective movement, are evident: changes in religious belief and behavior are a potential source of change in political identity as well. Just as technological change and social mobility may lead workers to reevaluate their partisan affiliations, so might changes in religious values lead people to new party homes. Of course, such changes are by no means certain; like new workers, new converts may not connect their new religious identity to politics, choosing instead to "privatize" their faith. Nevertheless, religious conversion may make individuals more susceptible to politicization and mobilization. In fact, these effects may occur all at once, particularly if the individual is joined by many others with similar experiences. Such groups may enter politics with the "zeal of the convert." Conversely, a shift away from traditional religiosity might also leave individuals open to new political ties by cutting their social and institutional links to existing alignments.[9]

At the collective level, there are two main models of religious change: sect movements and church movements. In the contemporary United States, sectarian movements lead people to more traditionalist and conservative theology; church movements lead people to more modernist and liberal theology.[10] Historically, sectarian orientations have made people more interested in maintenance of social order and regulation of individual morals in the interest of otherworldly rewards; church movements, in contrast, have made people more interested in social reform, realization of religious values in everyday life, and thus a greater concern with this-worldly rewards. The tension between these orientations has existed in the United States since at least the turn of the century, with religious traditionalists formulating the theological and social tenets of Protestant fundamentalism, while modernists have sought to make religious life and institutions relevant through the "Social Gospel." Comparable struggles have appeared among U.S. Catholics and Jews.[11]

For most believers, religious beliefs are not automatically politicized. Issues and actors from the outside political world intrude on their individual or corporate lives and demand response: the Supreme Court outlaws school prayer or legalizes abortion; local governments decree sex education in public schools or the teaching of evolution in biology classes; the president and Congress debate aid to religious institutions, such as schools, relief agencies, or day care centers; or, famine abroad or unemployment at home overwhelm the resources of the churches' charitable agencies. In responding to these and other stimuli, religious people often forge broader connections between their faith and political identities.

The faithful have assistance in this process. Both religious and political institutions strive to help them make the connections between their beliefs and affiliations and their political choices. Most religious people are enmeshed in crisscrossing networks of institutional ties. The vast array of denominational agencies, religious media, church workers, family, and co-parishioners all provide potential sources of political guidance. Politicians seeking to tap the votes of religious communities also shape their appeals to the concerns of the faithful. All are potential sources of important political cues—and of political change among the religious. And, of course, religious people are not immune to nonreligious influences either. Although their beliefs and intense institutional connections may insulate them somewhat from other forces, they are subject to most of the same social and economic experiences as other citizens. Their social characteristics may attach them to parties and policy positions that are unrelated to religious influences. Many analysts would argue, for example, that social class status and attendant economic concerns typically overwhelm cultural influences such as religion in shaping U.S. party alignments.[12] Although we reject this argument, we must always be careful to consider such factors in our analysis.

In this chapter, we explore partisan realignment among the growing legions of religious activists. We first examine the degree to which religious change has contributed to shifts in party coalitions among activists, and then explore the various forces and mechanisms that have produced those partisan migrations: religious beliefs, new issues and ideologies, activating institutions and networks, and changes in demographic location. In this way, we hope to cast additional light on a development of growing importance for the U.S. electoral system: the politicization of American religion.

Data and Methods

This analysis is based on our 1990–1991 Religious Activist Survey, which studied 5,002 members of eight prominent religious citizens organizations, ranging roughly from Left to Right: Bread for the World, JustLife, Evangelicals for Social Action, the National Association of Evangelicals, Prison Fellowship, Focus on the Family, Concerned Women for America, and Americans for the Republic (the predecessor of the Christian Coalition). Although we focused on the Evangelical Protestant community, an important actor in contemporary Republican politics, the sample also includes theologically liberal religious activists, such as members of Bread for the World, who are more typical of contemporary Mainline Protestant and Catholic churches and constitute a "religious Left." The questionnaire included over 250 items, providing one of the largest data sets available on contemporary religious activism.[13]

To address the phenomenon of partisan change among religious activists, we asked each activist two questions: "Overall, how would you describe your political party identification at present: Strong Democrat, Not Strong Democrat, Lean Democratic, Independent, Lean Republican, Not Strong Republican, Strong Republican?" and "How would you have answered the same question at age 21?" Thus, we have each individual's assessment of his or her partisan stability or movement since entering the electorate. Although such recall questions may have reliability problems, these should be minimized in this affluent, well-educated, and politically active sample.[14]

Cross-tabulating responses to the two party identification items reveals a good bit of partisan stability, as well as considerable movement. Given the

nature of the sample, it is not surprising that more respondents report growing sympathy for Republicans than for the Democrats. Even so, the proportions making the migration are striking; many more activists were
Democrats at age twenty-one than remain Democratic today. In fact, the
numbers of early-life Democrats who now report some kind of Republican
identity are substantial: 25 percent of earlier Strong Democrats, 36 percent
of Not Strong Democrats, 45 percent of those Leaning Democratic, and 43
percent of pure Independents. On the other side, there are some Democratic
converts, but they are much less numerous: 6 percent of early Strong Republicans, 12 percent of Not Strong Republicans, 14 percent of Leaning
Republican, and 16 percent of pure Independents. Of course, some early
partisans became stronger or weaker in existing attachments, or deserted the
parties altogether to become pure Independents.

To capture all these shifts, we calculated a party change score by subtracting each activist's current party identification on the seven-point scale
from his or her original identification. The resulting index runs from –6
(Strong Republican at twenty-one, Strong Democrat now) to +6 (Strong
Democrat at twenty-one, Strong Republican now), with standpat partisans
at the midpoint of 0. This index will be the dependent variable in the
subsequent analysis.

Religious Change and Partisan Realignment

How are partisan movements related to the much-publicized changes in
religious life that have influenced the United States in recent years? Many
scholars have noted that the celebrated voluntarism and fluidity of U.S.
religion have culminated in almost incessant movement of individuals
among churches, between religious traditions, and in and out of serious
engagement with religious life. Some experts see the most vital recent
change as the growth of the Evangelical Protestant tradition, as these
churches hold their own young and have some success at converting those
brought up in Mainline Protestant, Catholic, and other traditions. Other
scholars contend that the classic religious movement associated with social
mobility—the ascension of working-class conservative Protestants into
Mainline churches—is still a "conversion" of some importance. And, although most U.S. Catholics are loyal to their faith, others have joined Protestant America in recent years, replacing smaller numbers of Protestants
making the opposite pilgrimage, toward Rome (or at least the local Catholic
parish).[15]

Although we cannot examine such transformations at length, we suspect
they influence partisan change in two ways. On the one hand, "converts"

may join the historically "normative" political party of their new tradition (Republican for Mainline Protestants, Democratic for Catholics, and mostly Democratic for Evangelicals) or, perhaps, they will sort themselves out in line with the new religious order in U.S. politics, with religious liberals from all traditions and secular activists joining the Democrats and committed believers from those same traditions (but especially the Evangelical) becoming Republicans.[16] So, the first measure of religious change used here includes conversions from one religious tradition to another (Evangelical, Mainline Protestant, Catholic, and a residual "other" category).

Changing religious "brands" may not be the only, or even the most important, religious shift for these activists or other citizens. Religious conversion often entails an intensification of religious faith. We measured this variable by asking respondents how important religion was to them at various stages in their lives, producing an index on the magnitude of the differences, running from –6 (major decline in importance since early adulthood) to +6 (major increase in importance). As the sample is drawn from activists in religiously based organizations, respondents are disproportionately located toward the "more important" end, so for purposes of analysis we combined all those whose faith had *not* increased in importance. Despite the skewed responses, the link between religious intensification and partisan change is often striking. Table 1 reports the current party identification, as well as the index of partisan change, of activists with differing combinations of the two types of religious change: in affiliation and in intensity.

The data reveal both the resilience of historic ethnoreligious party alignments and the reality of the "new religious order." Overall, Evangelical activists are the most Republican, while Mainline Protestants straddle the partisan mean, and Catholics are still on the Democratic side of the party divide. Clearly, Evangelicals have marched a long way from their predominantly Democratic allegiances of the 1930s toward their staunch Republican identification today. Mainline Protestant activists, with their lower levels of religious commitment, seem to be slipping away from their traditional role as the core of the GOP ethnoreligious alliance, while Catholics have been moving in the opposite direction, wandering away from their traditional Democratic home. These patterns among religious activists also correspond well with voting trends in recent U.S. national elections.[17]

Party identification varies not only by tradition but by the religious origins of those in each tradition. Among Evangelicals, standpatters are actually the least Republican group (5.30), exceeded by former Catholics (5.86), former Mainliners (5.62), and even converts from a miscellany of other backgrounds or none at all (5.36). Thus, among Evangelicals, the considerable partisan zeal of the convert has bolstered Republican affiliation; the

Table 1

Changes in Religious Tradition, Religious Intensity, and Party Identification Among Religious Activists*

Religious Tradition and Change		1 Much More	2	3	4 Same or Less	All	N=
					My Faith Has Become More (Less) Important:		
Evangelicals	ID	5.81	5.54	5.40	5.24	5.45	2,521
	+/−	+1.66	+1.06	+.56	+.30	+.78	
Standpat	ID	5.61	5.33	5.31	5.19	5.30	1,383
	+/−	+1.80	+.76	+.35	+.25	+.52	
Former Mainline	ID	6.02	5.67	5.54	5.49	5.62	682
	+/—	+1.19	+1.00	+.67	+.19	+.79	
Former Catholics	ID	5.82	5.91	6.00	5.23	5.86	260
	+/−	+2.53	+2.09	+1.62	+1.62	+2.01	
Former Other	ID	5.67	5.53	4.92	5.10	5.36	196
	+/−	+1.45	+1.07	+.10	+.55	+.85	
Mainline Protestant	ID	4.49	4.40	3.88	3.82	4.03	871
	+/−	+.66	+.20	+.08	−.39	−.01	
Standpat	ID	4.84	4.39	4.01	3.89	4.12	545
	+/−	+.60	+.18	+.10	−.29	+.03	
Former Evangelical	ID	4.17	4.38	3.76	3.73	3.87	217
	+/−	+.02	−.22	−.10	−.51	−.28	
Former Catholic	ID	3.70	4.55	3.45	3.39	3.73	55
	+/−	+1.14	+.73	+.13	−.50	+.34	
Former Other	ID	4.74	4.31	3.46	3.98	4.11	55
	+/−	+1.17	+.83	+.54	−1.13	+.50	
Roman Catholic	ID	4.53	3.58	2.99	2.92	3.16	565
	+/−	+1.30	+.30	+.18	+.06	+.21	
Standpat	ID	4.42	3.56	2.91	2.95	3.12	508
	+/−	+1.28	+.32	+.23	+.06	+.22	
All Converts	ID	4.87	3.65	3.73	2.54	3.49	57
	+/−	+1.35	+.16	−.36	−.04	+.09	

*Entries on the first line are mean party identification scores ranging from 1 "strong Democrat" to 7 "strong Republican." The italicized entries represent the mean reported movement toward the Republican Party since age twenty-one in that same group. Negative entries represent movement toward the Democratic Party.

Evangelical community's proselytizing success produces, as a byproduct, enthusiastic new GOP activists.

Ironically, the pattern among Mainline Protestants—the historic core of the GOP's elite—is just the reverse: standpatters are the most Republican group (4.12), reflecting no doubt the ancient Mainline allegiance to the GOP, but they are barely ahead of converts from "other" traditions (4.11). Evangelical and Catholic defectors to Mainline churches actually fall on the Democratic side (3.87 and 3.73, respectively). Evangelical converts may be fleeing the theological and political conservatism of these now uncongenial churches, while Catholic converts may be carrying with them some of their ancestral Democratic identity. Standpat Catholics are by far the most Democratic of all subgroups with a mean of 3.16, while converts to Catholicism are somewhat less strongly attached to the Democrats (3.49), perhaps reflecting in part their points of origin in more Republican religious communities.

These patterns are modified considerably by changes in religious intensity. Those for whom religion has become increasingly important since early adulthood are *much more Republican* in all three religious traditions, but the effect varies somewhat by tradition of origin. Among Evangelicals, the Republicanizing impact of intensification appears among the large contingents of standpatters and Mainline converts, but is somewhat irregular among the smaller groups of Catholic and "other" converts, although even there activists in one or both of the two lowest intensification categories are by far the least Republican.

Among Mainline Protestants, standpatters also become more Republican with intensification, but those reporting no change or an actual loss in religious intensity are slightly to the Democratic side of the mean, as are the two lower intensity groups among Evangelical converts. The pattern is irregular among Catholic and other converts—not surprising, given the small numbers in each cell—but it still obtains. For the Catholics in this activist sample, dramatic increases in religious intensity are also associated with Republican identification, more so among the converts than among lifelong Catholics; it should be noted, however, that relatively fewer Catholics report dramatic changes in the salience of religion, an experience that may be more in tune with Protestant revivalism, especially its Evangelical variant.[18]

Activists' current partisanship reflects differing amounts of change from their early identity. Table 1 also reports the mean party change score for each group. We see significant movement: Evangelicals as a group have edged over three-fifths of a scale point toward the Republicans; Catholics, just a fifth of a point in the same direction. Mainline Protestants collectively have been quite stable, barely inching toward the Democrats. Once again, however, partisan change varies by religious subgroup: among Evangelicals, former Catholics have jumped over two full points toward the GOP. Obviously, religious conversion can have a major impact on political affiliations as well. Converts from "other" traditions exhibited the next largest movement, followed by Mainline defectors, and last, standpat Evangelicals, who have edged only half a point toward the GOP. In the Mainline tradition, Catholic and other converts show significant drift toward the Republican party, although the former remain slightly Democratic. Standpat Mainliners exhibit little partisan movement at all; only the Evangelical converts have become substantially more Democratic. Among both groups of Catholics, the movement has been toward the GOP end of the scale, but not by much.

The role of religious intensification is easy to summarize: the greater the intensification of religious faith, the stronger the movement toward the Republican Party in all three traditions. Even among the various subgroups of standpatters and converts, the relationships are almost invariant and the pro-Republican movement in the highest category of intensification across all three traditions is especially noticeable. A strong renewal of religious interest and concern has clearly shaped the experience of many members of the GOP's new religious constituency and may account for some of the much-noticed (or lamented) vitality and militancy of the "Christian" element in the party.[19] Of course, the reverse is also true; declines in religious intensity are linked to Democratic party affiliation, which may explain the virulent hostility of some Democrats to the "old time religion" in politics.

These data suggest that the changing internal composition of U.S. religion is closely related to partisan realignment among religious activists and, perhaps, in the electorate. The growth of the most vital sector of the U.S. Protestant tradition, the Evangelical community, is clearly fueled not only by retention of those within the tradition but also by considerable numbers from other traditions, especially Mainline deserters, former Catholics, and other converts as well. That these converts assume the characteristic (if relatively new) political identification of the Evangelical community with even more enthusiasm than the "native-born" provides an added boost to the GOP. Mainline activists as a whole have not moved much, but even in this community those who report greater religious intensity are shifting toward the GOP, as is the comparable group of Catholics, although converts from Evangelicalism are fleeing to a Democratic sanctuary, where they are lodged with an increasing number of secularists.

What factors lie behind these changes? In the following pages, we investigate the religious beliefs, political agendas, ideologies, mobilizing forces, and demographic factors associated with changes in party identification.

Careful scrutiny shows that, for the most part, "new" Republicans look very much like "old" Republicans; the same holds true for Democrats. In other words, the very factors that predict party identification among partisan "standpatters" also point to the reasons that others have changed identities.[20] From this point on, then, we confine our attention to the 54 percent of respondents who report at least some change in party identification. Nevertheless, we have confidence that we are analyzing the very forces that both produce new and sustain old partisan allegiances among religious activists.

Religious Variables and Partisan Change

We have seen that religious change clearly has a major impact on partisan change, at least among these activists. To investigate the influence of religious factors more fully, we correlated a variety of religious measures with our party change index.[21] Table 2 reports the results of this exercise, as well as the evidence from a multiple regression using all these measures, in addition to our tradition change and intensification scores.

Not surprisingly, the strongest theological factor predicting partisan change is an index of Protestant fundamentalism, which incorporates beliefs central to that century-old movement; indeed, each individual component also correlates strongly with partisan change: belief in the historicity of Adam and Eve ($r = .56$), the inerrancy of the Bible (.54), the "Rapture" of the Church during Jesus' Second Coming (.49), the necessity of Jesus for salvation (.48), opposition to the ordination of women (.48), and insistence on the current applicability of the Apostle Paul's admonitions about the role of women in the Church (.48). Similarly, an index of traditional Christian orthodoxy, consisting of questions such the Virgin Birth of Jesus (.38) and the historicity of the Resurrection (.32), is correlated with shifts toward the Republican end of the continuum, as is a question tapping whether the respondent was a "born-again" Christian and what that response meant. The data from the theological indices are buttressed by items on religious self-identification. Not surprisingly, those calling themselves fundamentalists have moved furthest toward the GOP, followed by self-identified evangelicals, charismatics, and Pentecostals. Those choosing "mainline," "ecumenical," or "liberal" labels, in contrast, have gravitated toward the Democrats.[22]

Religious practice, however, shows more moderate correlations with party change, perhaps because of the generally high religious observance in this sample. Nevertheless, an Evangelical Piety index, made up of items such as the frequency of praying outside church, reading the Bible, and attending special religious events, still demonstrates a fairly strong connection. An index of spiritual experiences, however, has only a modest associa-

Table 2

Religious Variables and Change in Party Identification Among Religious Activists

	Partial r = *	Beta = **
Religious Beliefs and Practices		
Fundamentalism	.66	.32
Christian Orthodoxy	.43	
Born-Again Christian	.41	
Religious Self-Identification		
Fundamentalist	.42	.09
Evangelical	.24	−.08
Charismatic	.19	.07
Pentecostal	.19	
Mainline	−.28	
Ecumenical	−.42	−.06
Liberal	−.49	−.11
Religious Practice and Experience		
Evangelical Piety	.32	
Spiritual Experience	.21	
Religious Involvement	.08	
Religious Change		
Religious Intensification	.29	.09
Religious Change		
Standpat Evangelical		−.04
Catholic to Evangelical		.09
Standpat Catholic		.11

R = .50
Adj. R^2 = .25

*Coefficients are partial correlations between the party identification change score and the variable, controlling for original identification.

**The betas are from a multiple regression incorporating all variables in the table. Only statistically significant entries (p < .05) are reported.

tion, and an index of church involvement (church attendance, church activity, numbers of friends in the church) has only a weak, if statistically significant, link with change toward the Republicans. Obviously, the theological differences that have divided Evangelical and Mainline Protestants for a hundred years are now the stuff of party divisions—at least for these activists. Fundamentalist belief and identification have become powerful predictors of Republican affiliation. Although these religious elites are no doubt somewhat in front of their co-parishioners, the same divisions are increasingly apparent in the mass electorate.

To sort out the relative influence of these religious factors on partisan change, we ran a multiple regression with all the variables included in Tables 1 and 2. As the column with the betas shows, fundamentalist belief and identification (as well as charismatic self-description) have a powerful influence on partisan movement toward the Republicans, while liberal, ecumenical, and (surprisingly) evangelical self-identification move activists toward the Democrats when everything is taken into account. Note that Christian orthodoxy, born-again status, and the various religious practice and experience measures have no independent effects once the other variables are accounted for. Thus, it is not the orthodoxy or the piety often associated with the conservative Protestant community that creates Republicans, but rather the specific religious beliefs, especially those associated with historic Protestant fundamentalism, which have influenced the realignment.

The impact of religious conversion among traditions largely washes out when the theological variables are accounted for, but religious intensification still moves activists significantly in a Republican direction, as does conversion from Catholic to Evangelical and remaining a Catholic. When all the other theological and religious variables are entered, standpat Evangelicals are actually a little more likely to move toward the Democrats. Location in none of the other religious change categories produces a significant movement, once fundamentalism and other factors are controlled. Among these activists then, the religious causes of partisan change are firmly lodged in the religious beliefs that they bring into the political world. Religious movement and intensification in large part are concomitants of adherence to traditionalist beliefs.

Social Theology, Christian Militance, and Political Relevance

Conservative activists do not join the GOP because the Republican platform embraces fundamentalist theology; nor does the Democratic charter require belief in liberal theology. Yet, each theological outlook has long been associated with what might be called a "social theology," a fundamental set of beliefs about the nature of the social and political world and how Christians ought to behave in it. The central question has long been that of how the church and Christians should seek to transform society. Evangelicals long ago adopted an individualistic theory of social change, which posits that evil springs from the depravity of the human heart and that society can be improved only by the religious conversion and reform of the individual, not by collective reform efforts by government. In contrast, U.S. Catholics have traditionally held a more communitarian social theology, and Mainline Protestants (or more accurately, their elites) have been influenced by the Social Gospel of the Progressive Era and developed a more optimistic view of human nature, one that admits the possibility of reforming society through the operation of institutions, especially government.[23]

As we have shown elsewhere, these fundamental perspectives are still characteristic of activists from the three largest Christian traditions in the United States, but they may be producing different political results than in earlier eras. Evangelical Protestants, whose theology once told them to shun politics and concentrate on soul-saving, have now decided to create either a "Christian America," or at least an America where Christians can be safe or even politically influential. In turn, their encroachments have been resisted by more liberal Christians, who see the function of the church as helping the less fortunate and avoiding any kind of religious triumphalism.[24]

We created three different measures that capture these various orientations toward religion's social and political role (Table 3). The most powerful is our index of individualistic social theology. Each item in this index also correlates strongly with movement toward the Republicans: belief that social problems are best addressed by changing hearts, not institutions; that the church should stress individual morality, not social justice; that poverty is usually due to personal failures, rather than social constraints; and that widespread conversions would solve social ills. We also find a strong association between gravitation toward the GOP and a belief that human nature is basically evil. Similarly, those who think of religious faith primarily in individual, rather than corporate, terms also report growing Republican sympathies (data not shown). These tenets of traditional Evangelical social theology have an obvious "elective affinity" for the individualistic elements in GOP ideology: Not only religious faith but also social and economic advancement are ultimately individual in nature and cannot be produced by collective action. What governmental institutions can do is maintain a religious and moral climate that fosters individual responsibility. These orientations help explain why Christian Right activists are actually quite conservative on a broad range of issues, not just the social and moral ones emphasized by the national press (see below). Those on the communitarian end of the scale are not as consistently liberal, but can find much to admire in Bill Clinton's "New Covenant."

This individualistic social theology, long an Evangelical fixture, is now accompanied, however, by a new political orientation that we have labeled "Christian militance." Where once fundamentalist theology dictated abstention from useless involvement in politics, contemporary conservative Protestants have a different perspective. As Table 3 shows, Christian militance is strongly associated with movement toward the GOP, as are the individual items in the index: belief that there is only one correct Christian view on most political issues, that the United States needs a Christian political party,

Table 3

Social Theology, Political Relevance, and Change in Party Identification Among Religious Activists

	Partial r = *	Beta = **
Social Theology: Individualism/Communalism		
Social problems solved by changing hearts, not institutions	.49	
Church should stress individual morality, not social justice	.46	
Poverty due to individual inadequacies, not environment	.43	
Human nature is basically evil	.43	
If people were brought to Christ, social ills would vanish	.39	
Index	.60	.25
Christian Militance		
Only one correct Christian view on most political issues	.46	
United States needs a Christian political party	.34	
Christians need not compromise principles to win in politics	.25	
Clergy can be vital influences over parishioners' politics	.24	
Index	.54	.26
Political Relevance		
The religion of the candidate is important to my vote	.48	
My own religious beliefs influence my political choices	.18	
Index	.44	.04

R = .48
Adj. R^2 = .23

*Coefficients are partial correlations between the party identification change score and the variable, controlling for original identification.

**The betas are from a multiple regression incorporating all variables in the table. Only statistically significant entries are reported.

that Christians need not compromise principles to be effective in politics, and that clergy can be a major influence in the political lives of their parishioners. Our measure of political relevance adds to this pattern. Activists who say that the religious beliefs of candidates for public office are important to their vote choice, as well as those whose faith strongly influences their own political choices, are likely to have shifted partisan allegiances toward the GOP. Although many new Democrats see their own faith relevant to political decisions, they blanch at using a candidate's religious views as a basis for choice.[25] The multiple regression shows that both individualism and Christian militance are strong predictors of movement toward the GOP, with political relevance providing some additional help. These three indices alone explain almost one-quarter of the variance in the party change index. Thus, religious activists who have adopted the view that Christian values have clear implications for action, and who support political mechanisms and activities to implement those values, are exactly those who have come to make the GOP their home.

Political Agenda, Ideology, and Partisan Change

The party alignments of any era are defined in large part by salient issues of the time.[26] Recruitment of new activists and party elites, as well as conversion of those from another party or activation of longtime but quiescent party identifiers, are usually the result of such defining issues. Although a particularly powerful set of issues may continue to structure party alignments long after their supposed disappearance, old definitions are constantly being tested and challenged by new issues and attitudes.

Much ink has been spilt on the way the "moral and social agenda" of the conservative Christian community has encouraged activism and facilitated conversion from older allegiances. Abortion, gay rights, prayer in schools, parental rights, and a variety of other "cultural" issues have often been cited in explaining the appearance of the Christian Right. Has the eruption of these issues also prompted religious activists to reconsider their partisanship? In Table 4, we report the correlations of party change with two questions tapping issue salience and three indices of political ideology. In the first section of the Table, we use responses to a Gallup question on "the two or three most important problems confronting the United States." As the correlations show, activists who cited spiritual or religious problems were most prone to move toward the GOP, followed by those listing social issues such as abortion and gay rights. Mention of problems with the political process had only a very weak correlation with partisan movement; responses on the economy, none at all, even at the bivariate level. Those who said the nation's greatest problems were social welfare needs or maintenance of international peace and justice had become warmer toward the Democrats.

We also took a different approach to political agendas by asking activists a question modified from Ronald Inglehart's "postmaterial values" battery. Inglehart has argued that the fundamental values of Western publics are

Table 4

Political Agenda, Ideology, and Change in Party Identification Among Religious Activists*

	Partial r = *	Beta = **
Most Important National Problems		
Spiritual and Religious Failures	.37	
Social Issues	.16	
Political Process Problems	.08	
Economic Difficulties		
Public Order	−.05	
Defense Spending and International	−.19	
Social Welfare Needs	−.33	
Priorities for Government		
Raising Moral Standards	.39	
Maintaining Order in the Nation	.33	
Protecting Freedom of Speech	.11	
Giving People More Say	.11	
Maintaining High Economic Growth	−.11	
Protecting the Environment	−.54	
Political Attitudes and Ideology		
General Conservatism	.76	.18
Moralism	.63	
Ideological Change	.61	.59

R = .71
Adj. R^2 = .50

*Coefficients are partial correlations between the party identification change score and the variable, controlling for original identification.

**The betas are from a multiple regression incorporating all variables in the table. Only statistically significant entries (p . < 05) are reported.

shifting toward "postmaterialism," a concern with the quality of life, the environment, freedom of speech, and personal autonomy, rather than material well-being.[27] Unfortunately, Inglehart did not offer an option on maintaining traditional moral standards, so important to religious people, so we added such an item. As the second section of Table 4 illustrates, activists' choice of goals for the country are tied to partisan change; raising moral standards is correlated with pro-GOP movement, as is maintaining public order. Protecting freedom of speech and giving people more say are mildly associated with such change, perhaps reflecting the Christian Right's sense of exclusion from the political process, while maintaining high economic growth moves activists toward the Democrats. Those who see environmental protection as the nation's greatest challenge are strikingly more Democratic.[28]

Obviously, the issues of the 1980s and 1990s are associated with partisan change in the expected direction. Salience of spiritual, moral, and public order concerns have prompted the migration of former Democrats toward the GOP; "Christian Left" preoccupations with the environment, international peace and justice, and social welfare needs have moved others toward the Democrats. Each set of concerns reflects the traditional social theologies of the Evangelical movement, on the one hand, and Mainline Protestant and Catholic churches, on the other. These findings are confirmed by other evidence. In a battery of questions asking respondents which party does a better job with various policies, those who see the Republicans excelling at maintaining traditional moral standards and protecting family values are much more likely to have moved toward the GOP than activists preferring the Republicans on other issues (data not shown).

What about attitudes on the issues themselves? Although journalists have prattled on about the "social conservatism" of the Christian Right, this often obscures an important fact: It is very difficult to find any substantial area of public policy on which Christian Right activists are not conservative. A principal components factor analysis of over thirty questions on specific contemporary issues in our survey produces one large factor, which explains almost half the variance, and a number of smaller factors, which explain much less, alone or in combination. As the last section of Table 4 shows, this general conservatism factor has a massive correlation with the partisan change index, demonstrating that conservatives have moved toward the GOP and liberals toward the Democrats, paralleling changes over the past three decades among other activists and, to a lesser extent, in the mass public.

Breaking the general conservatism index into its component parts illustrates the universality of the ideological divide. Many social and "family values" attitudes correlate strongly with pro-Republican movement. Support for the death penalty (.61), opposition to the Equal Rights amendment (.60), prohibition of gays as public school teachers (.58), opposition to birth control information in public schools (.52), and antagonism to affirmative action programs (.52) had the largest correlations. But opinions on economic and social welfare issues were also strongly related to partisan change: the belief that free enterprise is the only economic system compatible with Christianity (.56), opposition to tax increases to help the needy at home (.57) or to assist the hungry abroad (.53), and rejection of a national health care system (.52). The sentiment that despite changes in the former Soviet Union we must still be cautious in relations with Russia is also tied to pro-Republican movement (.56), a finding reminiscent of the past popularity of Cold War attitudes among conservative Protestants.[29]

We also calculated a moral conservatism score, which taps support for traditional social mores and opposition to unconventional moral innovations. Those who agree that a diversity of morality is not healthy, that there is only one correct moral philosophy, that society should not tolerate deviant moral views, that the traditional family should be stressed, that one should not modify moral standards to fit the times, and that new lifestyles break down U.S. society are also demonstrably more likely to have moved toward the GOP, while those on the other side of these issues have become more Democratic.[30] All this evidence shows that conservative and liberal views in almost every policy domain have helped to sort out religious activists into competing partisan camps.

Does this partisan exchange reflect the movement of already conservative or liberal activists toward the "proper" party? Or, is it the final step in an ideological conversion, in which former liberals become more conservative, and thus more Republican, while former conservatives make the trip in the opposite direction? To address this issue, we produced an index of ideological change to parallel our partisan change score. As Table 4 shows, ideological change also correlates very strongly with partisan change. Thus, not only are former Democrats moving toward the GOP and former Republicans in the opposite direction, but they are doing so because of basic ideological transformations. As the multiple regression shows, ideological change overwhelms all other variables in predicting partisan movement, with general conservatism retaining some influence. In the multivariate analysis, the agenda items all drop out, as their explanatory power is absorbed by the powerful impact of ideological conversion. The ideological variables together explain fully half of the variance in the party change index. Thus, partisan change is fueled by strong political beliefs on the issues of the day, beliefs that for many activists represent a fundamental reordering of personal ideologies.

Political Mobilization and Party Change

New political agendas and emerging ideological changes do draw activists into the political arena and often transform their identities, but the mechanisms of mobilization vary from era to era. In contemporary religious politics, a great deal of analysis has been devoted to the role of the religious media, especially television, and to mobilization by clergy. In addition, many new activist groups, both liberal and conservative, have relied on the technology of direct mail to reach their clientele. While such mechanisms may be especially useful for reaching and activating potential sympathizers, there may well be an added effect of prolonged exposure to these messages: reordering of party ties.[31]

We asked respondents several questions about their sources of political information. As we have discussed in detail elsewhere, conservative religious activists depend on religious TV and religious radio, as well as direct mail, while liberals look to "secular" sources, such as newspapers, radio, and commercial TV. Do these habits relate to partisan change? Table 5 shows that reliance on religious radio is a major correlate of party change; this certainly supports the contention of some recent analysts that local religious radio is really at the cutting edge of the Christian Right movement today, rather than the national televangelism of the 1980s exemplified by Jerry Falwell and Pat Robertson.[32] Reliance on religious TV is still important, however, followed by direct mail. In contrast, use of commercial and secular news sources produces movement in the Democratic direction.

Clergy mobilization might have similar effects. Analysts in the 1960s and 1970s heralded the appearance of the "prophetic clergy," Mainline Protestant ministers who agitated on the Vietnam war, civil rights, hunger and poverty, and the nuclear arms race—all on the liberal side. More recently, a new "prophetic Right" has appeared among theologically conservative clergy, fighting the "culture wars" of the 1990s.[33] We asked our respondents a series of questions concerning issues raised by their clergy in various settings and found that liberal and conservative pastors do still speak politically, but on different issues. Liberals stress peace and justice, hunger and homelessness, and sanctuary for refugees; conservatives focus on school prayer, pornography, sexual morality, abortion, and, to a lesser but important extent, candidates for public office. We produced two indices from these responses: conservative issue mobilization and liberal issue mobilization. As Table 5 shows, respondents who hear more frequently from the pulpit about conservative issues report moving toward the GOP, while those listening to topical sermons favored by liberals have shifted toward the Democrats.

The most effective of these forces seem to be religious radio and TV, along with the clergy. As the multiple regression shows, reliance on religious radio is the single best predictor of partisan change, followed by religious TV. Pastoral involvement on either side of public issues is also a good predictor, moving activists in the expected direction. Direct mail use inclines activists toward the GOP, while reliance on secular sources abets change toward the Democrats. Nevertheless, the impact of all the variables combined is modest, explaining only 15 percent of the variance in the party change index. We suspect that much of the cue-giving here is "preaching to the converted," as Republicans and Democrats, whether standpat or converted, seek out congenial information sources.

We should also note that political leaders, both secular and religious,

Table 5

Political Mobilization and Change in Party Identification Among Religious Activists

	Partial *r* = *	Beta = **
Sources of Political Information		
Religious Radio	.50	.22
Religious Television	.40	.19
Direct Mail	.21	.07
Religious Periodicals	.09	
Opinion Magazines	−.12	
Work Associates	−.15	
Secular TV, Radio, Newspapers	−.24	−.07
Clergy Mobilization Focused On:		
Conservative Issues	.27	.10
Liberal Issues	−.29	−.13

$$R = .39$$
$$\text{Adj. } R^2 = .15$$

*Coefficients are partial correlations between the party identification change score and the variable, controlling for original identification.

**The betas are from a multiple regression incorporating all variables in the table. Only statistically significant entries ($p . < 05$) are reported.

have an important role in producing partisan change. Although the correlations are no doubt inflated by an admixture of ideological influences, we found that felt proximity to former President Reagan (r = .74), Pat Robertson (r = .60), Focus on the Family founder James Dobson (.58), the National Right to Life Committee (.50), and Concerned Women for America (.46) is strongly correlated with partisan change in a Republican direction, while similar proximity to the Catholic Church (−.37), the National Council of Churches (−.54), Jimmy Carter (−.59), and Jesse Jackson (−.63) is associated with growing Democratic allegiance. That the correlations are highest with the most vocally "political" religious leaders, rather than more centrist or cautionary Evangelical leaders like Billy Graham (.32) or Chuck Colson (.35), suggests that strong political cues from politicians or religious leaders may be required to influence alignments.

Demographic Variables and Partisan Change

Before we draw any conclusions about the nature of partisan change among religious activists, we need to address one more set of hypotheses about

Table 6

Demographic Factors and Change in Party Identification Among Religious Activists

	Partial r = *	Beta = **
Demographic Factors		
Education	−.34	−.23
Social Class	−.18	.07
Gender (Male)	−.15	−.08
Upward Mobility	−.04	.07
Income	.04	
Rural Residence	.07	
Rural Birth	.09	
Children in Religious Schools	.13	.09
Number of Children	.14	

$R = .30$
Adj. R^2 = .09

*Coefficients are partial correlations between the party identification change score and the variable, controlling for original identification.

**The betas are from a multiple regression incorporating all variables in the table. Only statistically significant entries ($p < .05$) are reported.

the sources of that change. Many authors have noted that the social mobility of many traditionally Democratic religious groups has brought them "naturally" to the GOP. Certainly, social advancement has prompted growing numbers of Catholics to identify with the GOP. In the same vein, the upward mobility of Evangelical Protestants—traditionally rural, working-class, and poorly educated—should also produce greater Republicanism. We must keep in mind, of course, that these activists are mostly middle-class in education and income, but many did come from much more modest backgrounds, so we may still be able to see some important trends.[34] Table 6 reports the correlations of various demographic characteristics with partisan change.

Surprisingly, most of the data actually works in the direction opposite of that predicted by the social mobility hypothesis. Among activists, the best educated more often report movement toward the Democrats, while those with some college education or less are most likely to have gone in the opposite direction. At the bivariate level, it is also those in skilled labor and clerical jobs who have moved most toward the GOP, not business and professional classes. Similarly, an index of upward mobility, measuring the improvement in class status of the activists compared to their parents, shows a small but *negative* association with increased Republicanism, but this effect reverses in the multivariate analysis when all other factors are accounted for. Women have likewise moved toward the Republicans, as have those with larger families—especially if the children are in religious schools. Rural upbringing has a very modest correlation with movement toward the GOP, as does current rural residence. Higher income has only a very modest association with change.

In the multivariate analysis, education overwhelms all the other variables, with additional years of education beyond the junior college level producing stronger Democratic tendencies. Thus, among these activists, at least, the economic factors that are often thought to differentiate party constituencies have only a modest and sometimes counterintuitive impact. Clearly, religious motivations and associated issue concerns have brought some members of "natural" Democratic economic constituencies toward the GOP and its agenda, while the "cosmopolitanizing" effects of graduate education and, perhaps, professional occupations, have moved others toward the Democrats.

Conclusions

Although a formal demonstration of the relative importance of all these factors in producing partisan change would take more space than we have, we can summarize the findings quite easily: partisan movement among these religious activists has as its proximate cause the powerful ideological conversions occurring among them. Ideological conservatives, new and old, identify with the Republican Party, while their liberal counterparts have stuck with—or moved toward—the Democrats. At the same time, we stress that both ideological change and partisan conversion have vital religious antecedents. Fundamentalist Protestant theology, individualistic social theology, Christian militance, and a new sense of the political relevance of religious beliefs have moved many religious people toward the Republicans. Both the new theology and the new politics have been transmitted, inculcated, and illustrated by a wide variety of actors and institutions: politicians such as Ronald Reagan and Jimmy Carter, who made religion a special concern; religious leaders who have entered politics, such as the Reverends Pat Robertson and Jesse Jackson; independent organizational entrepreneurs, such as James Dobson of Focus on the Family and Beverly LaHaye of Concerned Women for America; established religious institutions, such as the Catholic Church and National Council of Churches; and thousands of local clergy, religious talk show hosts—and the activists themselves.

Does all this really matter? We must note that the "Christian Right" has by all accounts become a major player in Republican politics, but do the trends detected among religious activists extend further? In fact, the evidence accumulates that the new religious divisions extend to all sorts of elite groups, both religious and political. Scholars have discovered similar, if sometimes piecemeal, evidence for religious change among national party convention delegates, major contributors to party committees, state and local party activists, religious professionals, and the voting public.[35]

The new religious order in U.S. party politics means several things. First, conflict over social issues will obviously intensify. Although Republicans may suffer the most visible struggles over abortion, gay rights, and other "family values" issues, Democrats will not be untouched; indeed, the portending GOP battles reflect the growing presence of formerly Democratic "social issue" conservatives among Republicans. Beyond this, however, the religious divide will have a broader cultural impact. The religious individualism of devout Evangelicals and some Mainline Protestants and Catholics finds clear echoes in the new economic conservatism of Newt Gingrich, while the strong communitarian emphases of official Mainline Protestantism and Catholicism struggle to find a voice in an increasingly secularist Democratic Party. Few issues—whether economic or international—are immune to the absorptive power of these respective social theologies. Thus, ideological colors of U.S. parties are likely to become even more distinct, enhancing political conflict at all levels, but certainly offering voters a clear choice.

Despite wildly different outcomes, then, both the 1992 and 1994 elections advanced religious realignment in U.S. politics. Increasingly, the two parties are not characterized by the old ethnoreligious alignments, with Evangelical Protestants, African American Protestants, and Catholics providing the Democrats their political base and Mainline Protestants girding the GOP. Instead, we find activists with strong religious commitments in all major Christian traditions moving in a more conservative and Republican direction, while those with a modernist religious bent, or none at all, are shifting to the Democrats.[36] This process has not yet reached its culmination and will influence U.S. party politics for many years to come.

Notes

The authors wish to acknowledge major financial support from the Pew Charitable Trusts, which made this study possible. Additional assistance was provided by the Institute for the Study of American Evangelicals at Wheaton College, the Research and Professional Growth Committee of Furman University, the Ray C. Bliss Institute for Applied Politics at the University of Akron, and the Calvin Center for Christian Scholarship.

1. For one of the best studies of party elites and activists, see Warren E. Miller and M. Kent Jennings, *Parties in Transition: A Longitudinal Study of Party Elites and Party*

Supporters (New York: Russell Sage, 1986). A comparison of party activists and other contemporary interest group activists is found in John C. Green and James L. Guth, "Big Bucks and Petty Cash: Party and Interest Group Activists in American Politics," in *Interest Group Politics,* 2nd ed., ed. Allan J. Cigler and Burdett A. Loomis (Washington, D.C.: CQ Press, 1986).

2. For evaluation of the evidence on the 1992 campaign, see John C. Green, James L. Guth, Lyman A. Kellstedt, and Corwin Smidt, "Murphy Brown Revisited: The Social Issues in the 1992 Election," in *Disciples and Democracy: Religious Conservatives and the Future of American Politics,* ed. Michael Cromartie (Grand Rapids, Mich.: Eerdmans), pp. 43–64.

3. Michael Kelly, "Saint Hillary," *New York Times Magazine,* May 23, 1993, 22–25, 63–66.

4. Miller and Jennings, *Parties in Transition,* pp. 75–78.

5. On the crucial role of elites in party realignments, see Edward G. Carmines and James A. Stimson, "On the Structure and Sequence of Issue Evolution," *American Political Science Review* 80 (September 1986): 901–920. Also see their *Issue Evolution* (Princeton, N.J.: Princeton University Press 1989), and Byron E. Shafer, "The Notion of an Electoral Order: The Structure of Electoral Politics at the Accession of George Bush," in *The End of Realignment? Interpreting American Electoral Eras,* ed. Byron Shafer (Madison: University of Wisconsin Press, 1991), pp. 37–84.

6. On changes in party activists, see John C. Green and James L. Guth, "The Transformation of Southern Political Elites," in *The Disappearing South?* ed. Robert P. Steed, Laurence W. Moreland, and Tod A. Baker (Tuscaloosa: University of Alabama Press, 1990), pp. 34–53, and the literature cited therein.

7. Consider the analysis in Steven J. Rosenstone and John Mark Hansen, *Mobilization, Participation, and Democracy in America* (New York: Macmillan, 1993).

8. A masterful discussion of this era is Richard J. Carwardine, *Evangelicals and Politics in Antebellum America* (New Haven: Yale University Press, 1993).

9. See Lynn D. Nelson and David G. Bromley, "Another Look at Conversion and Defection in Conservative Churches," and Lynn D. Nelson, "Disaffiliation, Desacralization, and Political Values," both in *Falling from Grace: The Causes and Consequences of Religious Apostasy,* ed. David G. Bromley (Beverly Hills, Calif.: Sage Publications, 1988), pp. 47–61 and 122–139, respectively.

10. A provocative analysis of sectarian and churchly movements is found in Roger Finke and Rodney Stark, *The Churching of America, 1776–1990: Winners and Losers in Our Religious Economy* (New Brunswick, N.J.: Rutgers University Press, 1992).

11. For a massive study of traditionalist movements all over the world, including U.S. fundamentalism, see the articles in Martin E. Marty and R. Scott Appleby, eds., *Fundamentalisms Observed* (Chicago: University of Chicago Press, 1991), especially chapters 1–3.

12. David C. Leege, Joel A. Lieske, and Kenneth D. Wald, "Toward Cultural Theories of American Political Behavior: Religion, Ethnicity, Race, and Class Outlook," in *Political Science: Toward the Future,* vol. 3, ed. William C. Crotty (Evanston, Ill.: Northwestern University Press, 1991), pp. 193–238.

13. For more detailed information about the survey, see James L. Guth, Corwin E. Smidt, Lyman A. Kellstedt, and John C. Green, "The Sources of Antiabortion Attitudes: The Case of Religious Political Activists," *American Politics Quarterly* 21 (January 1993): 65–80.

14. Some sensible comments on the reliability of recall data from political activists are found in Dorothy Nesbit, "Changing Partisanship Among Southern Party Activists," *Journal of Politics* 50 (May 1988): 322–24.

15. For a thorough discussion of how denominational change may influence political alignments in the mass public, see John C. Green and James L. Guth, "From Lambs to Sheep: Denominational Change and Political Behavior," in *Rediscovering the Religious Factor in American Politics,* ed. David C. Leege and Lyman A. Kellstedt (Armonk, N.Y.: M. E. Sharpe, 1993), pp. 100–117.

16. For a speculative essay on the transformation of U.S. religious politics in recent years, see Lyman A. Kellstedt, John C. Green, James L. Guth, and Corwin E. Smidt, "It's the Culture, Stupid! 1992 and Our Political Future," *First Things: A Journal of Religion and Public Life* 42 (April 1994): 28–33.

17. Lyman A. Kellstedt, John C. Green, James L. Guth, and Corwin E. Smidt, "Religious Voting Blocs in the 1992 Election: The Year of the Evangelical?" *Sociology of Religion* 55 (fall 1994): 307–326. See also David C. Leege, "The Decomposition of the Religious Vote" (paper presented at the annual meeting of the American Political Science Association, Washington, D.C., September 2–5, 1993).

18. For the importance of revivalism for politics in the Evangelical tradition, the classic work is still Timothy Smith, *Revivalism and Social Reform: American Protestantism on the Eve of the Civil War* (Nashville, Tenn.: Abingdon, 1957). U.S. Catholics did have a parallel tradition of revivalism, but one that never had quite the same defining impact on the church. See Jay P. Dolan, *The American Catholic Experience: A History from Colonial Times to the Present* (South Bend, Ind.: University of Notre Dame Press, 1992), pp. 224–228.

19. James L. Guth, John C. Green, Lyman A. Kellstedt, and Corwin E. Smidt, "Uncivil Challenges? Support for Civil Liberties Among Religious Activists," *Journal of Political Science* 22 (1994): 29–45.

20. Cf. V. O. Key's classic analysis of the way issues shape the behavior of "standpatters" and "switchers" in *The Responsible Electorate: Rationality in Presidential Voting, 1936–60* (Cambridge: Harvard University Press, 1966).

21. For the derivation of these measures, see Guth et al., "The Sources of Antiabortion Attitudes," p. 77.

22. For a discussion of the uses and pitfalls of measures of theological self-identification, consult Clyde Wilcox, Ted G. Jelen, and David C. Leege, "Religious Group Identifications: Toward a Cognitive Theory of Religious Mobilization," in Leege and Kellstedt (ed.), *Rediscovering the Religious Factor,* pp. 72–99.

23. David C. Leege and Lyman A. Kellstedt, "Religious Worldviews and Political Philosophies," in Leege and Kellstedt (ed.), *Rediscovering the Religious Factor,* pp. 216–231; James L. Guth, John C. Green, Lyman A. Kellstedt, and Corwin E. Smidt, "Onward Christian Soldiers: Religious Activist Groups in American Politics," in *Interest Group Politics,* 4th ed., ed. Allan J. Cigler and Burdett A. Loomis (Washington, D.C.: CQ Press, 1995), esp. pp. 63–66. In many ways, the contemporary Evangelical individualism is simply a legacy from the nineteenth century; see George M. Thomas, *Revivalism and Cultural Change* (Chicago: University of Chicago Press, 1989).

24. George Marsden discusses "the Great Reversal" by which conservative Protestants withdrew from politics in the early 1900s, in his *Fundamentalism and American Culture* (New York: Oxford University Press, 1980), pp. 85–93. For a good account of the "reversal of the Great Reversal," see Robert Wuthnow, *The Restructuring of American Religion* (Princeton, N.J.: Princeton University Press, 1988).

25. For a discussion of the perceived political relevance of religion, see James L. Guth, John C. Green, Lyman A. Kellstedt, and Corwin E. Smidt, "The Political Relevance of Religion: Correlates of Mobilization" (paper presented at the annual meeting of the Midwest Political Science Association, Chicago, April 14–16, 1994).

26. For the best defense of this argument, see James L. Sundquist, *Dynamics of the Party System,* rev. ed. (Washington, D.C.: Brookings Institution, 1983).

27. Ronald Inglehart, *Culture Shift* (Princeton, N.J.: Princeton University Press, 1990).

28. For more on these activists' response to the Ingelhart items, see Guth et al., "Onward Christian Soldiers," pp. 66–67.

29. Ted G. Jelen, "Religion and Foreign Policy Attitudes: Exploring the Effects of Denomination and Doctrine," *American Politics Quarterly* 22 (July 1994): 382–400.

30. For a discussion of many of these items on moralism, see Pamela Johnston Conover and Stanley Feldman, "Religion, Morality, and Politics: Moral Traditionalism in the 1980s" (paper presented at the annual meeting of the American Political Science Association, Washington, D.C., 1986).

31. Ted G. Jelen and Clyde Wilcox, "Preaching to the Converted: The Causes and Consequences of Viewing Religious Television," and Michael R. Welch, David C. Leege, Kenneth D. Wald, and Lyman A. Kellstedt, "Are the Sheep Hearing the Shepherds?" in Leege and Kellstedt (ed.), *Rediscovering the Religious Factor,* pp. 235–269. On direct mail, see R. Kenneth Godwin, *One Billion Dollars of Influence* (Chatham, N.J.: Chatham House, 1988).

32. Erling Jorstad, *Popular Religion in America: The Evangelical Voice* (Westport, Conn.: Greenwood Press), pp. 125–133.

33. On the clergy activism of the 1960s and 1970s, see Jeffrey Hadden, *The Gathering Storm in the Churches* (Garden City, N.Y.: Doubleday, 1969), and Harold Quinley, *The Prophetic Clergy* (New York: Wiley, 1974). A profile of contemporary clergy activism is found in James L. Guth, John C. Green, Corwin E. Smidt, and Margaret M. Poloma, "Pulpits and Politics: The Protestant Clergy in the 1988 Election," in *The Bible and the Ballot Box: Religion in the 1988 Election,* ed. James L. Guth and John C. Green (Boulder, Colo.: Westview Press), pp. 73–93.

34. Lyman A. Kellstedt and Mark A. Knoll, "Religion, Voting for President, and Party Identification, 1948–1984," in *Religion in American Politics,* ed. Mark A. Noll (New York: Oxford University Press, 1990), pp. 255–279.

35. For evidence on religious polarization of various party elites, see the following sources: national party convention delegates, Geoffrey C. Layman, "Parties and Culture Wars: The Politicization of Cultural Conflict in the United States" (paper presented at the annual meeting of the American Political Science Association, New York, September 1–4, 1994); major contributors, John C. Green, James L. Guth, and Cleveland R. Fraser, "Apostles and Apostates," in Guth and Green (ed.), *The Bible and the Ballot Box,* pp. 113–136; for state delegates, see the references in James M. Penning, "Pat Robertson and the GOP: 1988 and Beyond," *Sociology of Religion* 55 (fall 1994): 327–344; for religious professionals, Guth et al., "Pulpits and Politics," pp. 73ff; and for the mass public, Kellstedt et al., "Religious Voting Blocs."

36. For development of this theme, see "The Bible and the Ballot Box: The Shape of Things to Come," in Guth and Green, (ed.) *Bible and the Ballot Box,* pp. 207–227.

Index